D1610515

THE PURITAN PLEASURES OF THE DETECTIVE STORY

THE PURITAN PLEASURES OF THE DETECTIVE STORY

A personal monograph

ERIK ROUTLEY

LONDON
VICTOR GOLLANCZ LTD
1972

ISBN 0 575 01384 2

Printed in Great Britain by
The Camelot Press Ltd, London and Southampton

TO PATRICK
who said
'Why don't you send it to
Gollancz?'

Novelists are unpaid sociologists who make up for their lack of statistical evidence with inspired guesses.

—Ian Rodger
in *The Guardian*, 20 December 1967

ACKNOWLEDGEMENTS

The author expresses his thanks to the following publishers, agents and trustees for permission to make extended quotations from the sources named:

to Messrs John Murray Ltd and the Trustees and Estate of the late Sir Arthur Conan Doyle for extracts from the *Sherlock Holmes Short Stories* published by John Murray

to Messrs Hodder & Stoughton Ltd for extracts from *Dr Thorndyke, His Famous Cases*, by R. Austin Freeman, published by Hodder & Stoughton

to Messrs A. P. Watt and Lythway Ltd, Publishers, for extracts from *The Eyes of Max Carrados*, by Ernest Bramah, published by Lythway

to Messrs Hughes Massie Limited and Messrs William Collins, for an extract from *The Pale Horse*, by Agatha Christie, published by Collins

to Miss D. Collins, owner of the Chesterton copyrights, and to Cassell & Co. for extracts from *The Father Brown Stories*, published by Cassell

to David Higham Associated Ltd and Messrs William Collins for an extract from *Scandal at School*, by G. D. H. and M. Cole, published by Collins

to Hamish Hamilton, Ltd, for an extract from *The Novelist's Responsibility*, © 1967, by L. P. Hartley, published by Hamish Hamilton

to Hogarth Press, Ltd, for an extract from *Imagination and Reality*, by Charles Rycroft, published by Hogarth Press

to P. and M. Youngman Carter Ltd, for an extract from *More Work for the Undertaker*, by the late Margery Allingham, published by William Heinemann Ltd

Finally, the author offers his best thanks to the publisher and the editor for the great patience they have shown in preparing this book, for whose imperfections the author alone is responsible.

CONTENTS

Preface 13

1. Prologue: What Fun It All Was 17

I. THE MASTER

2. The Master — *Sherlock Holmes* 27
3. The Master's World — *Sherlock Holmes* 34
4. Romance — *Sherlock Holmes* 42
5. A Whisper of 'Norbury' — *Sherlock Holmes* 53

II. THE CLASSICS

6. Severe Science — *John Thorndyke* 63
7. In the Dark — *Max Carrados* 73
8. The Art of Making Objections — *Reginald Fortune* 81
9. The Mystery of Iniquity — *Father Brown* 89
10. The Fairy Tale and the Secret — *Father Brown* 104

III. PURITANS AND ROMANTICS

11. Coming of Age *E. C. Bentley: Freeman Wills Crofts: John Rhode* 119
12. Quartet of Muses: First Pair *Agatha Christie: Dorothy Sayers* 129
13. Quartet of Muses: Second Pair *Ngaio Marsh: Margery Allingham* 146
14. Politeness and Protest *Michael Innes: Edmund Crispin: Joanna Cannan: John Bingham* 157
15. And a Large Supporting Cast *Anthony Berkeley: John Dickson Carr: Josephine Bell: Gladys Mitchell: Christianna Brand: Glyn Carr: Thurman Warriner: Anthony Gilbert: Andrew Garve: Cyril Hare: Nicholas Blake:*

Josephine Tey: Georgette Heyer: Mary Fitt: Mary Kelly: Winston Graham: Macdonald Hastings: Stanley Hyland: John Trench: Georges Simenon: Nicolas Freeling, and others 170

16. Certain Americans *E. A. Poe: Ellery Queen: Erle Stanley Gardner: Patrick Quentin: Francis Kemelman: Lesley Egan, and others* 187

IV. EXCELLENCES AND LIMITATIONS

17. The Case against the Detective Story 201

18. On Being Serious-minded 212

Appendices: I For the Tidy-minded 233

II For the Faithful 243

Index 245

PREFACE

THIS STORY IS told of the late Henry Wheeler Robinson, Doctor of Divinity, Theological College Principal, and among the half-dozen most famous Old Testament scholars who wrote in English. Waiting for a train on Oxford station, he went to the bookstall and scanned the detective literature on display. Turning to the storekeeper he said, with laconic courtesy, 'Have you any more? I've read all those.' The storekeeper directed him to a further selection at the other end of the counter. 'Read 'em all,' said Dr Robinson, looking a little sterner. The man behind the counter then reached for a pile of detective books from a shelf under the counter. After a glance over them, Dr Robinson said again, 'Read 'em all.' Upon which the storekeeper leant across the counter and said, 'Well, sir, all I can suggest is that perhaps you might try some serious literature for a change.'

It is the memory of that formidable old saint that decides me not to publish this under an assumed name. Wheeler Robinson was known to his intimates—and that knowledge was shared with his awestruck pupils—as a profoundly learned and experienced connoisseur of detective stories. He had a most enviable library of them, collected over a long period. He knew the literature as intimately as he knew the Pentateuch. But he would not have written this book.

It is proper that this book should be written by one who has habitually attended, in writing, to subjects less austere than those which occupied Dr Robinson's well-filled professional life. Having far less to lose than he in the matter of reputation for zeal and high seriousness, I am now allowing myself an indulgence which I have long promised myself—a record of what I read in bed.

Some friends will be ashamed to acknowledge me after this: for what will often have appeared to them as a slightly frivolous mind will now manifest itself as an irretrievably trivial one. Others, I know, don't read *this* in bed: for them it will be poetry, or devotion, or the latest sociological Penguin. I respect that, but mine is not a mind that functions at all well after midnight. So there it is. The canon of Holmes remains on the table next to the alarm clock.

But a few years ago it occurred to me to say, 'Why be furtive? People know many worse things about you than this. You can't hope to fool them much longer.' And anyhow, I reasoned, what's *wrong* with it? It might even be interesting to find out what's wrong with it—and what's right about it. And more recently it suddenly struck me that there is a perfectly intelligible and serious reason why certain sorts of people like this sort of literature. So I set out on a new investigation of my own, and I found that there was something in it. Yes, by all the archons of Athens and by the beard of Dr Wheeler Robinson! There *is* something in it.

So I thought I would put down what this seemed to me to be; and the result has the great advantage that, if it is read by somebody who likes detective stories, we can have a quiet wink at each other over such palatable delicacies as the use of vowels in surnames by Doyle, while he who despises them will be enormously grateful to me for explaining to him why he does so.

No: this is not an encyclopaedia. Now that Dr Robinson has gone, who could write that? Your favourite detective author may go unmentioned. Or, which is much worse, he may get only a few lines where somebody you have no use for gets several pages. That will be exasperating for you. But to compensate for that, consider the pleasure that you, a moralist in spite of all that horrid permissiveness which has denied you the pleasures of detective reading, in spite of all that splendid and lofty disdain which a compulsive reader of Samuel Beckett must feel for the groundling who is capable of re-reading Allingham, will take in contemplating these acknowledgements of a misspent middle age. I simply do not see how anybody can fail to get some sort of perverse pleasure out of this book.

Having thus written my own review and to my present satisfaction anticipated the critics, I invite the reader, hawk or dove, to join me in nibbling these nuts and sherbets. In the immortal words of the most irresistible invitation since the days of Cromwell: 'The game is afoot, Watson. Into your clothes, and come!'

THE PURITAN PLEASURES OF THE DETECTIVE STORY

I

Prologue: What Fun It All Was

The coat-sleeves, the trouser-knee, the callosities of the forefinger and thumb, the boot—any of these might tell us, but that all united should fail to enlighten the trained observation is incredible.

Sherlock Holmes? No. Not yet.

Conan Doyle—he wrote it in a notebook after reading some detection of the primitive French school, and his biographer, John Dickson Carr, after reporting this, adds, 'Why not a novel about a detective?'[1]

Why not? Doyle had his own answer.

'I am sure that you inquired your way merely in order that you might see him.'
'Not him.'
'What then?'
'The knees of his trousers.'
'And what did you see?'
'What I expected to see.'[2]

'So ardent a bicyclist must be full of energy.'

She glanced down in surprise at her own feet, and I observed the slight roughening of the side of the sole caused by friction of the edge of the pedal.[3]

[1] John Dickson Carr, *The Life of Sir Arthur Conan Doyle* (paperback edition, Pan Books, 1953, p. 51).

[2] 'The Red Headed League', S. 44 [Note: the references in this form refer to (S) the Short Stories and (L) the Long Stories in the two volumes of John Murray's Collected Edition.]

[3] 'The Solitary Cyclist', S. 640.

> 'Do you not find,' he said, 'that with your short sight it is a little trying to do so much typewriting?' . . .
>
> 'You have heard about me, Mr Holmes,' she cried, 'else how could you know all that?' . . .
>
> 'You appeared to read a good deal upon her which was quite invisible to me,' I remarked.
>
> 'Not invisible, but unnoticed, Watson. You did not know where to look, and so you missed all that was important. I can never bring you to realise the importance of sleeves, the suggestiveness of thumb-nails, or the great issues that may hang from a bootlace. . . . My first glance is always at a woman's sleeve. In a man it is perhaps better first to take the knee of the trouser. As you observe, this woman has plush upon her sleeves, which is a most useful material for showing traces. The double line a little above the wrist, where the typewritist presses against the table, was beautifully defined. The sewing machine, of the hand type, leaves a similar mark, but only upon the left arm, and on the side of it furtherest from the thumb.'[4]

The great issues that may hang from a bootlace, and the strange behaviour of the typist who pressed against the table: it's all there—the pleasure, the skill, the amiable spoof and humbug, of the detective story.

People born in 1887 are now in their eighties: so is the English detective story. Its expectation of life may well be about the same as that of the human generation which was born in the year of the publication of *A Study in Scarlet*. Whatever is beyond fourscore years, said the Psalmist, is labour and sorrow. In the case of the detective story—quite possibly. Did it, during the threescore and ten, so number its days as to apply its heart unto wisdom?

The Sherlock Holmes stories are the Bach of detective fiction: anyhow, the short stories are to detective fiction what the Forty-Eight Preludes and Fugues of Bach are to music. There's nothing in the development of classical and romantic music up to 1900 that is not foreshadowed in J. S. Bach: nor anything in the development of the classical and romantic detective story that is not foreshadowed in Holmes.

By the same token, detective fiction had its Palestrinas and even its plainsong, as it has its Stravinskys and may well

[4] 'A Case of Identity', S. 66.

develop its Schoenbergs and John Cages. Detective addicts and practitioners have shown that earlier ages did produce the occasional example. Dorothy Sayers pointed out that there is one in the Old Testament Apocrypha, the 'Story of Susanna', one in ancient Greek literature, 'The Tomb of Rhampsinitus', and one in the Aeneid.[5] The story in I Kings 10 which seems to be the best biblical evidence for Solomon's fabled wisdom (there's plenty against it) could be called a detective tale, and so could the story of David and the straying animals in I Samuel 9. In English literature there is *The Moonstone* (1868), which T. S. Eliot called 'the first, the longest and the best detective story in the English language'. Mrs Henry Wood and Anthony Trollope have detective episodes and stories to their name. But in one way or another all these (*The Moonstone* included) are called 'detective' only by those who have perceived the true nature of the detective story by reading the work of the 'orthodox' school founded by Doyle.

For a detective story, properly so-called, is a story involving crime, a police force, a detective (who may or may not be a member of that force) and a solution. It must evoke a major interest in the finding of that solution. Without these properties any story that appears to be 'detection' is so called only by analogy.

Behind Holmes stands Aristide Dupin. Edgar Allan Poe published *The Murders in the Rue Morgue* in 1841, and that began it all. He was quickly followed by the primitive French school of detection writers, Gaboriau, Leroux and the rest, whose works, laborious as they now appear, captured the imagination of their time. Any Englishman who knows the literature to any extent is content to see in these the heralds of Doyle—the anabaptists who stand behind the true puritans. There is nothing in them that Doyle did not do better. When Holmes remarks that Poe's Dupin is a bungler, he may be exaggerating in his characteristically impatient fashion; what he may have meant was that Doyle was a better artist than Poe. When it came to capturing the affection and imagination of the English bourgeois, Dupin was not so much a bungler as a non-starter when put in the same race with Holmes.

[5] See the first four stories in the first series of *Great Short Stories of Detection, Mystery and Horror* (ed. Sayers, Gollancz, 1928).

There are, I think, three conditions that must co-exist in order to form a climate in which the detective story can flourish: and as soon as we mention them we shall see that they did co-exist very felicitously in a certain class of English society about the time the detective story was, on my hypothesis, invented. These conditions are, first, a tradition of integrity in the police force; second, a readiness in the reader to accept a 'hero' played perfectly straight, a detective who never fails; and, third, an eagerness in the reader to take pleasure in the special activity of observation.

In respect of the first of these, we can recall that the first uniformed police walked the streets of London on Michaelmas Day, 1829 (so the police force was two generations old when Inspector Lestrade made his bow). The organisation of the police force was the creation of Sir Robert Peel, who was born ninety-nine years before *A Study in Scarlet* and died in 1850. As the persistence of such titles as 'sergeant' in the English forces and 'captain' and 'lieutenant' in the American implies, it was a development from the army. In older times the keeping of civil peace was the army's business, shared, since times of considerable antiquity, with those known as 'the watch'.

'Policeman' is a comfortably modern term, but 'watchman' has an ancient ring: indeed, it has a biblical ring. 'Watchman, what of the night?'—'Except the Lord keep the city, the watchman waketh but in vain'—you might roughly say that both those phrases refer to the police of their time, the guardians of civil peace. Quite often in those days the watchman was a member of the armed forces watching from a tower to give warning of an approaching enemy—a soldier, or, to bring him right up to date, a radar-scanner, rather than a policeman. It all depended on the conditions and the necessities of any given time whether he was more like a soldier or more like a policeman. There are those who say that the 'soldiers' to whom John the Baptist said 'Do violence to no man' (St Luke 3. 14) may properly be thought of as police officers.

'The watch', anyhow, became part of English life at an early date, and is mentioned in the Statute of Winchester (1285). But the watchman was then, and for many centuries afterwards, a night watchman. The remarkable thing about Peel's police force was that it was from the first a twenty-four-hour force, working by day as well as by night. The extraordinary prescience of this is indicated by a comment in John Moylan's very handy pamphlet, *The Police of Britain*:[6] 'It is the afternoon and evening hours that normally make the greatest call on police, because it is then that housebreaking and other forms of thieving are most prevalent, and traffic is heaviest.' Peel saw what was coming. But even more remarkable than this was his invention of a force which managed to keep the image of army discipline and integrity while becoming entirely divorced from the army's tradition of violence and war. In other cultures the keeping of peace was quite naturally associated with a display of naked power. The Roman police force was part of an Imperial civil service which lost no opportunity of planting in the public mind an image of power and force. There are many contemporary witnesses to the corruption of police forces by the re-introduction of traditions of violence. But the police-image in the classical and romantic detective story is never an image of naked power. More often (and this is the most revealing thing of all) it is an image of somewhat thick-headed rectitude. It is some time before we get the brilliant policeman in best-selling detective literature. It is thoroughly characteristic of the culture we are here investigating that the police force should be intellectually vulnerable but morally impregnable.

If the police are like that—and it is important to the culture that they should be—it is natural not to expect policemen themselves to be heroic supermen. If they are they'll get too like the army—I think that is why it does not occur to Doyle and his kind to make them too splendid. The very essence of the thing is that they should, however grudgingly, accept correction by the superior intelligence from which such correction comes. The police themselves are subject to law, and among other laws to that of truth: an army when it is doing the most characteristically army things (anyhow in 1887) is a law to itself. So we have our classical gallery of intellectual supermen who know that they can trust the police to admit when they are wrong. Given the superman, he can be as super as his creator chooses to make him. The classical style goes for superiority of intellect, the romantic style in its primitive forms for superiority of character. That is a development we shall

[6] British Council, 1946.

observe as we pursue the tale. But behind it all is an assumption that the reader accepts, admires and puts his faith in superiority of some kind—fundamentally, superiority of a law which keeps the peace and sees justice done, and, in the foreground, superiority of intellect or of character.

All that is very obvious. I think that the third point is less often given its due importance. You may well say that the whole point of a police force was to make the world safe for the kind of society that England was nourishing—a bourgeois society. In the upper strata of society there were people whom on the whole the police didn't need to help, or who when they got themselves into difficulties were beyond that kind of help: and in the lowest strata there were people to whom traditionally the police remained hostile. It was the people in the middle who most needed their property guarded and their rights kept safe—simply because there wasn't all that much in the way of property or rights to guard, and the loss of it was their greatest fear. Very well, then: when the detective writer brought to the foreground of his story this quite new insistence on observation he was not only doing what novelists either did not do or did in a different way or for a different purpose; he was also doing what the bourgeois welcomed and needed. I think it could be shown—this is not the place to try to prove it—that the late Victorian bourgeois was cramped by a convention that a very large number of things were beneath his notice, generated by the romantic emphasis on great thoughts, great destinies, and great issues, together with the necessity of avoiding in his personal demeanour (for the sake of keeping his precarious position *vis-à-vis* his neighbours) anything that anybody could call trivial. The introduction into the foreground of a story of the minute particulars of life—such as trouser-knees and thumbs—and the invitation to admire a superman whose superiority lay partly in observing and remembering such minute particulars, was a sudden and unexpected refreshment to people who were living in this convention of abstraction and high-mindedness.

And then, of course, there wasn't any sex: but that is something else again. The elimination (you can't entirely eliminate it, but they nearly did) of 'love-interest' from the classical detective story completed the design. Love-interest is the area of 'minute particulars' into which the ordinary novelist was permitted to go. Observation, in detective fiction, replaced it as the surface-adhesive that held the reader's attention from page to page. The result is an intellectualism which is not abstract: reasoning from physical data (from psychological data in the romantics). And if you have a form of fiction which is intellectual, then that form of fiction is fit for a Victorian man to read; he need not be ashamed of reading it as he might be of reading Mrs Henry Wood, who was strictly, according to his code, for the wife. This was manly stuff. It accepted the physical world but kept clear of that part of the physical world which was embarrassing. So this good man, prince or priest or thrall, bought his *Strand Magazine* in 1887 and felt liberated. Changes in the conventions which nourished him and cramped him have generated the changes observable in the detective story during the next seventy years: removals of some of the conditions altogether have perhaps made detective stories unnecessary—that is a question we shall leave open for the present.

[illegible]

intense paragraphs and which the ordinary novelist may [illegible]
[illegible]
[illegible] that hold the reader's attention from page to
page [illegible] mathematics which is not abstract:
[illegible]
[illegible]
[illegible]
[illegible]
[illegible]
[illegible] world [illegible]
[illegible]
[illegible]
[illegible]
[illegible]
[illegible]
[illegible]
[illegible]
[illegible] we shall leave [illegible] to the [illegible]

I

THE MASTER

2

The Master

THIS IS NOT a contribution to Sherlockiana, but the existence of the cult of Sherlock Holmes is itself very much in the field of our enquiry. How Doyle wrote these tales, how people devoured them and howled for more, how they provoked a considerable sub-literature devoted entirely to them and to their hero, how a Sherlock Holmes Society formed itself, and how Holmes was commemorated in 1954 on the centenary of his supposed birth —this is all a matter of history. I do not propose to debate the minutiae of textual criticism or biographical hypothesis in connection with these stories; I shall not decide whether or not Mr Baring Gould was right in his conjecture that Holmes died in 1957 aged 103, and, like Shakespeare, on his birthday, though if he did, then it was indeed a symbolic demise, giving us with nice exactness our threescore years and ten from 1887. All this I leave to others, and when they do it, I enjoy their work.

But, being among those upon whom this character cast his spell in our youth, I am now as much interested in the spell as in the character. Let us first observe the character.

He was, according to the principles mentioned above, a superman of the intellect who had a squirrel-like faculty for hoarding miscellaneous information. It would have been quite improper in that virile age to represent him as anything but physically tough, able to defend himself in combat, and in first-class physical condition. Yet he is the obvious reverse of the muscular English animal who peoples the novelettes of that and later ages.

> Sherlock Holmes was a man who seldom took exercise for exercise's sake. Few men were capable of greater effort, and he

> was undoubtedly one of the finest boxers of his weight that I have ever seen; but he looked upon aimless bodily exertion as a waste of energy, and he seldom bestirred himself save when there was some professional object to be served. Then he was absolutely untiring and indefatigable. That he should have kept himself in training under such circumstances is remarkable, but his diet was usually of the sparest and his habits were simple to the verge of austerity.[1]

This, then, is no public-school athlete. 'You live in a different world to me,' he said to Overton, 'a sweeter and a healthier one.' Thus ruefully he excuses his ignorance of the name of the Cambridge University rugger captain.[2]

And then there is that confounded cocaine-bottle. It looks as if the good Watson managed to cure him of that addiction, for it is only in the earlier tales that we hear of it. This is a barbarous detail which contributes to the atmosphere of mystery that surrounds him—a Gothic nod to Wilkie Collins's preoccupation with the spooky and unnatural. Many years ago the eminent principal of a theological college in Oxford[3] said that he never believed in that bottle because a drug-taker would have smoked cigarettes, never a pipe. Holmes was clearly one of those who preferred a pipe except when 'there was some professional object to be served': we hear of his chain-smoking cigarettes only in 'The Golden Pince-Nez'—and there was indeed a professional purpose there.

So his worst enemy would be unable to call Holmes a gorgeous hunk of man. But he was physically efficient in such a sort as would serve his astounding mental energy. Watson's summary of his attributes and limitations, drawn up early in their association, began like this:

> Knowledge of Literature—Nil
> Knowledge of Philosophy—Nil
> Knowledge of Astronomy—Nil
> Knowledge of Politics—Feeble.

Subsequent information shows Watson to have been badly astray in items 1, 2 and 4, and as for no. 3, his inclusion of it was

[1] 'The Yellow Face', S. 334. [2] 'The Missing Three-Quarter', S. 811.
[3] Not the one mentioned in the Preface.

provoked by Holmes's tart rejoinder to his observations about outer space:

> 'But the Solar System!' I protested.
> 'What the deuce is that to me?'[4]

Quite so. Holmes was an applied-scientist, not a theoretical scientist, and certainly not the sentimental son of a scientific age. He wanted to know whether a piece of information, true or false, was relevant; if it wasn't, it was discarded.

His creator says he was an accomplished musician, but this is not a field where the creator can follow the creature very far. You might agree that anybody who can make a tolerable sound on a violin by laying it across his knee may be a musician of some talent. One hopes that the author of the definitive monograph on the motets of Lassus is misrepresented by his chronicler, who, listening to Sarasate playing in St James's Hall, says that he

> sat in the stalls, wrapped in perfect happiness, gently waving his long thin fingers in time to the music.[5]

Perhaps the best judgement is that Watson was as sentimental in his approach to music as he was in his approach to science. If Watson, then presumably Doyle also; the music-*motif* is brought in to contradict the suggestion that Holmes is a mere walking intellect: so music isn't, for him, a function of the intellect. On the contrary, it is a generator of mystique. Holmes could not have been a pianist—amateur piano playing was for gently nurtured young ladies and professional piano playing was for Paderewski and Pachmann, whom Holmes didn't go to hear. No, it was the violin—to those blessed with unmusical ears the most romantic of all instruments.

Music, on which the chronicler shows so unsure a touch, is Holmes's only outside interest. The emphasis otherwise is entirely on intellectual concentration, and this conveniently disposes of the sex interest. It is dismissed on the first page of the

[4] *A Study in Scarlet*, ch. 2. L. 17.
[5] 'The Red Headed League', S. 45. Do not miss Guy Warrack's far from trifling monograph, *Sherlock Holmes and Music* (Faber, 1947).

first of the short stories, never to reappear, and it is all done very tidily.

> It was not that he felt any emotion akin to love for Irene Adler. All emotions, and that one particularly, were abhorrent to his cold, precise and admirably balanced mind. He was, I take it, the most perfect reasoning and observing machine that the world has ever seen: but, as a lover, he would have placed himself in a false position. He never spoke of the softer passions, save with a gibe and a sneer.[6]

Well might Watson say so. His announcement of his own engagement, on the penultimate page of *The Sign of Four*, was not received with enthusiasm by Holmes:

> 'Miss Morstan has done me the honour to accept me as a husband in prospective.'
>
> He gave a most dismal groan.
>
> 'I feared as much,' said he. 'I really cannot congratulate you. . . . Love is an emotional thing, and whatever is emotional is opposed to that true, cold reason which I place above all things.'[7]

That, then, is the build-up. Remote and lonely genius with only one outside interest and only one non-professional friend: that is Holmes. This makes it all the more impressive when his creator permits his superhuman competence and ability to be modified by two strong humanising factors. One of these is the capacity for failure which his creator is prepared to admit in him almost from the outset: the other, his capacity for personal friendship with Watson himself, which in later years found expression in quite surprising terms.

In the first *Strand Magazine* year, 1891, Doyle produced 'The Five Orange Pips', and during the next year 'The Engineer's Thumb' and that extraordinary tale, 'The Yellow Face'. This last story, standing second in the *Memoirs*, is, from the point of view of the emotionless reasoning-machine, as unsatisfactory as any in the whole saga: yet it contains more than one point of peripheral interest, of which one is its superb exit-line:

[6] 'A Scandal in Bohemia', S. 3.

[7] *The Sign of Four*, ch. 12. L. 270.

> 'Watson,' said he, 'if it should ever strike you that I am getting a little over-confident in my powers, or giving less pains to a case than it deserves, kindly whisper "Norbury" in my ear, and I shall be infinitely obliged to you.'[8]

The 'Orange Pips' and the 'Thumb' show Holmes following a trail but arriving at its end too late to prevent tragedy in one case or to apprehend criminals in the other: and the whole issue with Moriarty, and the end which Doyle originally designed for it (the closing scene in 'The Final Problem') introduces a deeper contrapuntal note altogether. It was a touch of Irish pessimism and realism that made Doyle the artist want to dispose of Holmes, just as much as a touch of impatience that drove the busy doctor to get him out of the way. *The Valley of Fear*, published twenty years after the appearance of 'The Final Problem', harks back to the Moriarty era in dramatic date and leaves Holmes staring into the future and swearing to get even with the sinister professor. Doyle needed to modify his superman.

And to some extent, when he came to terms with the public's demand for a resurrection, his superman is modified after his reappearance. He is less intense, more open to the movements of the affections, as many Sherlock commentators have noticed. There are three places in particular, much prized by the devotee because of their rarity and their incongruousness with the rugged archetype of the Holmes character, where pure emotion breaks through. Observe how late they all come.

> 'Thank you!' said Holmes. 'Thank you!' And as he moved away it seemed to me that he was more nearly moved by the softer human emotions than I had ever seen him.[9]

That is at the climax of 'The Six Napoleons'. Following the gruesome experiment in 'The Devil's Foot', we have this:

> 'Upon my word, Watson!' said Holmes at last, with an unsteady voice; 'I owe you both my thanks and an apology. It was an unjustifiable experiment even for oneself, and doubly so for a friend. I am really very sorry.'

[8] 'The Yellow Face', S. 354. [9] S. 763.

'You know,' I answered, with some emotion, for I had never seen so much of Holmes's heart before, 'that it is my greatest joy and privilege to help you.'[10]

And at the end of 'The Three Garridebs' it happens again:

'You're not hurt, Watson? For God's sake, say that you're not hurt!'

It was worth a wound—it was worth many wounds—to know the depth of loyalty and love which lay behind that cold mask.[11]

This last is Holmes at forty-eight (1902); what may be more to the point, it is Doyle at sixty-five (1924). The earlier Holmes is more like this:

'Today must be a day of inquiries.'

'My practice——,' I began.

'Oh, if you find your own cases more interesting than mine,' said Holmes with some asperity.

'I was going to say that my practice could get along very well for a day or two, since it is the slackest time in the year.'

'Excellent,' said he, recovering his good humour.[12]

or this:

'You have erred, perhaps,' he observed, taking up a glowing cinder with the tongs, and lighting with it the long cherry-wood pipe which was wont to replace his clay when he was in a disputatious rather than a meditative mood,—'you have erred, perhaps, in attempting to put colour and life into each of your statements, instead of confining yourself to the task of placing upon record that severe reasoning from cause to effect which is really the only notable feature about the thing.'[13]

Brusque, impatient, resourceful, magisterial—such epithets come to mind sooner than tender or sympathetic in the early Holmes. But things alter with the passing of years, as these four passages in which he is dealing with women clients indicate:

[10] S. 1060. [11] S. 1213. [12] 'The Naval Treaty', S. 515–16.
[13] 'The Copper Beeches', S. 275.

> [Miss Mary Sutherland] He looked over her in the minute and yet abstracted fashion which was peculiar to him.[14]
>
> [Miss Violet Hunter] He looked her over in his searching fashion, then composed himself with his lids drooping and his finger-tips together to listen to her story.[15]
>
> [Miss Violet Smith] My friend, who loved above all things precision and concentration of thought, resented anything which distracted his attention from the matter in hand. And yet without harshness which was foreign to his nature, it was impossible to refuse to listen to the story of this young and beautiful woman . . . who . . . implored his assistance and advice.[16]
>
> [Mrs Warren] Holmes leaned forward and laid his long thin fingers upon the woman's shoulder. He had an almost hypnotic power of soothing when he wished.[17]

Nonetheless, for all this it is the character of the archetypal Holmes that matters—the Holmes who captured the *Strand* readers of the first years. Doyle's success in creating him depended on a concentration on his own part devoted to the fashioning of an image that was ruthless, virile, but with no trace of violence. This concentration was as great as that which he attributed to Holmes himself. It is all summed up in the Holmes creed, set out in the second chapter of *A Study in Scarlet*, and this creed contains almost word for word the quotation from Doyle's notebook with which chapter I began:

> By a man's finger-nails, by his coat-sleeves, by his boot, by his trouser-knees, by the callosities of his forefinger and thumb, by his expression, by his shirt-cuffs—by each of these things a man's calling is plainly revealed. That all united should fail to enlighten the competent inquirer in any case is almost inconceivable.[18]

'What ineffable twaddle!' said Watson. 'I never read such rubbish in my life.' Not so the readers of the *Strand*, who insisted that Watson's creator should give him leisure to repent.

[14] 'A Case of Identity', S. 58.
[15] 'The Copper Beeches', S. 278.
[16] 'The Solitary Cyclist', S. 639–40.
[17] 'The Red Circle', S. 948.
[18] L. 20.

3

The Master's World

IT IS HARDLY likely that Doyle's calculations in the matter of building up a surrounding history of the Holmes saga were precise or fully conscious; but what he produced in the end was not only a character but also enough intimation of a surrounding and on-going history to attract and then to tantalise the imagination of his readers. Hence the Sherlock Holmes societies and commentators.

Different writers in this field have had different views about the handling of the background history of their characters. At one extreme, Chesterton's Father Brown is entirely mythical. We do not even know his Christian name. There is no indication that he was a month older at the end of *The Scandal of Father Brown* than he was at the opening of *The Innocence*. At the other extreme, Dorothy Sayers not only showed her Lord Peter Wimsey passing through a personal history and reacting to the known history of his time: she produces in the later books a three-page biography of Wimsey telling us in what year he was born and where he went to school.[1] Between these two poles all the techniques of detective and other serial novelists find a place. A Father Brown Society, dedicated to research into Father Brown's personal history, would complete its business in half-an-hour and close down; so would a John Thorndyke Society or a Reginald Fortune Society. On the other hand, you cannot even suppose the existence of a Peter Wimsey Society,

[1] Wearing one of her other hats, Dorothy Sayers used the fact that her hero had developed an 'unwritten past' to illustrate a very interesting, if somewhat perverse, philosophical point about Creation and History in an essay entitled 'Creative Mind'. See her *Unpopular Opinions* (Gollancz, 1946, pp. 54–6).

because nothing remains to be found out, all the details having been already provided by his creator.

Conan Doyle lies exactly half-way between the two ends of this axis. He often, but not always, gives the date of a case (in one case the date is manifestly implausible even to the casual reader);[2] but he never tells us how old Holmes and Watson are—the 'sixty' in 'His Last Bow'[3] would be dismissed as an approximation were it not the only clue of its kind in the whole series. Apart from those later stories the personality of Holmes suffers only subtle changes (and this, we have agreed, not by his creator's conscious design)—changes which are no more than the consequence of advancing from (we will suppose) the age of thirty-two to that of forty-eight. And if you compare the highly circumstantial account of Holmes's supposed death (1891) in 'The Final Problem' with the equally delusive 'death' of Wimsey in 'The Cave of Ali Baba' (1927)[4]—you find that, although both happen to be thirty-seven at the time of their supposed deaths, Doyle leaves his readers to deduce that, while Sayers provides Wimsey with a full-length obituary and the amount of his will.

As for the actual movement of history, we wait until the very end of the short stories for a mention of a telephone,[5] and until 'His Last Bow' for a car.[6] For the rest, it is the gaslight and the hansom that set the pace, together with the telegraph for swift communications and the railway for long journeys. And as for personal histories, Doyle leaves us in such confusion about Watson that two of the favourite critical points for commentators have been—what was his Christian name and how many times was he married? Yet we seem to know much more about him than we do about Flambeau.

The way in which Doyle steered down the middle channel between extremes which the other writers preferred, this way or that, is something you notice at other levels once you have noticed it at this one. Take, for instance, the literary form of the

[2] 'Wistaria Lodge', S. 891. The impossibility of '1892' needs no comment here.

[3] S. 1076.

[4] *Lord Peter Views the Body* (1928), no. 12.

[5] 'The Retired Colourman', S. 1352.

[6] A Benz for the Baron, a Ford for Altamont, S. 1069, 1073.

story-sequence, which we may call the loose-coupled serial. These stories are half-way between what we call in the modern sense the saga, and the popular serial of juvenile adventures.

At one end you have *The Forsyte Saga*, and other massive exercises in continuous narrative such as those of Louis Golding, Compton Mackenzie, Hugh Walpole and Henry Williamson. Here an author builds up a dynasty of characters who react continuously and progressively to surrounding history, and thereby constructs a weighty comment on the history as well as a family of well rounded characters. At the other end you have Richmal Crompton's ageless eleven-year-old William, who is simply there as a peg to hang adventures on. In the episodic serial of this sort, so popular with radio and television audiences, development of character is virtually impossible: the central character has to remain stable so that the adventures can vary but still form a series. But it is interesting that detective literature is the one form in which it is taken for granted that loose serial will be employed, whether in long or in short stories. It is when detective narrative becomes detective novel that you move nearer the 'saga' form: but the unnatural adventure-content in such stories almost always ensures that in fact the movement in that direction is slight.

Doyle's achievement here was to create a loose-coupled serial whose central character really did inspire people to suggest erecting a statue to him. Holmes does stand in public esteem along with Peter Pan, the Proudies and the great creations of Dickens—but Holmes was an adventurer around whom thrillers gathered, and you can't say that of the others.

The reason why detection goes so closely with this form is that the form permits the author to keep adventure within a circle of security, represented by the outlines of the hero's character. Holmes is friendly and has moral status, and that makes one feel safer when one sets out with him into another London fog.

The reader—we have described his limitations already, so this fits—wanted not only adventure but the strict circumscribing of adventure. He was not yet ready for bizarre anti-adventures of the kind he now asks for. He was reading for relaxation, and for the relaxation of a not too enterprising mind which set strict limits to the demands it would tolerate. He was satisfied when he got a strict counterpoint between adventure and security. He did not want to see the criminal normally getting away with his crime, or the hero normally failing to find a solution: still less did he want to have his moral assumptions outraged or even questioned. In meeting this demand Doyle succeeded so resoundingly because he knew how to steer down the centre, to maintain the required balance.

Collateral evidence is provided if one looks for social comment in his stories. Heaven knows one should not expect much: but it does just happen that Doyle not infrequently gets involved, in one way or another, with foreign races, and that, in an age of great sensitiveness concerning racial matters, is very convenient for the investigator of his material.

He is no Dickens (detection does have its Dickenses, and Dickens did not altogether disdain detection) so we shall find nothing in his work of such choice satire as Mr Podsnap talking to a Frenchman as though the Frenchman was slightly deaf. But a brief investigation in this field gives a certain touch of satisfaction. Taking the farthest throw first, there is the 'huge and hideous mulatto' in the newspaper report that forms part of 'Wistaria Lodge',[7] and there is the remarkable visitor whose irruption into the Baker Street lodgings opens 'The Three Gables':

> The door had flown open and a huge negro had burst into the room. He would have been a comic figure if he had not been terrific, for he was dressed in a very loud grey check suit with a flowing salmon-coloured tie. His broad face and flattened nose were thrust forward, as his sullen dark eyes, with a smouldering gleam of malice in them, turned from one of us to the other.[8]

That is broadly what one expects Englishmen to write about negroes at the turn of the century, and a conservative Englishman to write as late as 1926 (when 'The Three Gables' appeared). But the negro, it turns out, was acting on instructions from Barney Stockdale, and soon changed his tune when Holmes got on his wavelength. 'The Yellow Face' (1892) contains both an illustration of the colour-bar mentality and a criticism of it. The little black girl is received into the English family, and her American mother's fears that her second

[7] S. 910. [8] S. 1159.

husband will reject the girl are, as it turns out, unfounded. Once again—Doyle steers down the middle.

He has a special sympathy with the Indians. There is a considerable Indian undertone to much of the accompaniment to his tales: Pondicherry gives a romantic and sinister flavour to *The Sign of Four* and 'The Five Orange Pips'. The reptile in 'The Speckled Band' comes from India, along with the cheetah, as reminders of Dr Roylott's residence there. So, of course, does Watson's jezail bullet. The Mutiny is in the background of 'The Crooked Man'. All this is characteristic of the Empire-building Englishman. But once again, in 'The Three Students', Doyle criticises Watson's judgement of the Indian student as a 'sly fellow' by acquitting him of the misdemeanour of taking notes from the proof of an examination paper.[9] Down the middle again.

Indeed, the stories reflect fairly faithfully the thought of the ordinary, not too enlightened, middle-class Englishman about the subject races: the ethos is conservative with a very light touch of criticism. India is the foreign country the English most often hear about at that date. Nearly all the other countries are entirely mysterious. People did not travel as they do now. The best most of them can do is to accept the stereotyped legend about whatever country is being mentioned.

It is very much so with America. There is only one American reference in the pre-Reichenbach short stories, apart from the origin of Mrs Grant Munro in 'The Yellow Face', and that is the introduction of Miss Hatty Doran, who turns out to be Mrs Francis Hay Moulton, in the story of 'The Noble Bachelor'. What we there learn of Americans is that they tend to be very wealthy ('Her father is very rich', 'He is said to be the richest man on the Pacific Slope'), impulsive ('I just made up my mind to run away, and explain afterwards'), and, at the best, frank and honest ('For my part I should like all Europe and America to hear the rights of it'). Holmes's judgement about America at this date concludes the story:

> 'It is always a joy to me to meet an American, Mr Moulton, for I am one of those who believe that the folly of a monarch and the blundering of a Minister in far gone years will not prevent

[9] S. 775.

> our children from being some day citizens of the same world-wide country under a flag which shall be a quartering of the Union Jack with the Stars and Stripes.'[10]

Amiably high-minded, that, in the manner calculated to please a reader who is not fastidious about heraldry. Apart from one 'I guess' from the lady, no attempt is made to reproduce American speech. Doyle has not yet travelled on the American mainland.

The America of *A Study in Scarlet* is less the land of Abraham Lincoln than that of Brigham Young and his strange, self-sufficient Mormon community that made its own laws and enforced them with terrible ruthlessness. Mormonism is here a secret society on all fours with the Scowrers in *The Valley of Fear* (written in 1915 but depicting the society of thirty years earlier) and the Ku Klux Klan of 'The Five Orange Pips'. Despite Holmes's diplomatic speech recorded above, America is a place where wild and primitive things happen, with strange consequences in rural England.

This brings us to Mr Abe Slaney of Chicago. Chicago is still a hick town, an agricultural centre, and the headquarters of gangsterism. It has hardly yet lost that last distinction, but it was in those days the typical home of the Irish-American rancher rather than that of central European engineers and theologians as it is now. Mr Slaney's early love for the daughter of a gangster-boss lay behind the dark business of 'The Dancing Men'.

Americans as citizens of the United States rather than as emigrant Irishmen and Scots appear only in the latest stories. There is 'Killer Evans', naturally of Chicago, in 'The Three Garridebs'—an ingenious and ruthless character indeed—and there is the naïve, power-haunted Gibson in 'Thor Bridge', whom Holmes talks into sense. That is what several journeys to America in the later part of his life did for Doyle (those two stories were written respectively in 1924 and 1922). But on the whole there is not much to choose between the Americans of the late Doyle and those of the early Wodehouse.

It is much the same with Australians. Australia comes through as a land of anarchy and enterprise containing secrets

[10] S. 246.

which explain crimes that come under Holmes's notice. Doyle knew Australia; there is one piece of evidence that Watson knew it, in *The Sign of Four* (L. 178). The respectable Mr McCarthy of Boscombe Valley, Herefordshire, turns out to be 'Black Jack of Ballarat',[11] and Holmes's first recorded deductive demonstration is to say to the senior Trevor, in 'Gloria Scott', 'You have been in New Zealand'.[12] Lady Brackenstall, in 'The Abbey Grange', began life as Miss Mary Fraser of Adelaide, and 'Holy Peters', the ruffian in 'Lady Frances Carfax' who poses as a clergyman, was 'one of the most unscrupulous rascals that Australia has ever produced'.[13] Australia is, acceptably to author and reader, the origin of lawlessness and licence.

By the same token Latin American women are deeply passionate and surrounded with mystery:

> 'A South American household. My instinct felt the presence of those weapons on the wall before my eyes ever saw them . . . one of those arrows dipped in curare or some other devilish drug.'[14]

Quite so. The South American poison unknown (or just about known) to science. There is some sultry passion, too, on the distaff side in 'Thor Bridge'; and South America provides an origin for abominable pagan rites in 'Wistaria Lodge'. The poison really unknown to science comes, in the Holmes canon, not from South America but from the 'Ubangi district of Africa', and the context of its appearance includes these very typical words from the formidable Dr Leon Sterndale—

> 'I have lived so long among savages and beyond the law . . . that I have got into the way of being a law to myself.'[15]

The underlying assumption is that foreign countries are more lawless than Britain. It is a long journey from there to Laurens van der Post.

By contrast with the remoter countries, those of Europe play only a small part in the stories. Doyle has travelled rough and wild in his youth; only later did he become a more 'civilised'

[11] S. 100. [12] S. 376. [13] S. 1028.
[14] 'The Sussex Vampire', S. 1194. [15] 'The Devil's Foot', S. 1062.

traveller. In consequence we hear of only one important reference to a European country in the pre-Reichenbach tales, and that is to, of all places, Greece. The great thing about 'The Greek Interpreter' is not that it introduced Holmes at his best, for it hardly does that, but that it is our first meeting with his brother Mycroft ('You would be right in a sense if you said that occasionally he *is* the British Government'),[16] and that it gives us the only reference Holmes ever makes to his ancestors.[17]

Latin Europe provides secret societies and underworld activities in Doyle's unforgettable picture of London's dockland in 'The Man With the Twisted Lip', and more explicitly in 'The Six Napoleons', 'The Red Circle', and 'The Three Gables'. There is a German schoolmaster in 'The Priory School' who is wrongly (with characteristic insular haste) accused of being a murderer, and the eerie self-experiments of Professor Prestbury have their origins in a Himalayan monkey-gland distributed by a sinister Slav. There are a couple of Russians of dubious antecedents in 'The Golden Pince-Nez', and there is a wild whaling journey to Norway in the final narrative in 'Black Peter' (Doyle had been on a whaling expedition in 1880).[18] And of course there are all the unrecorded cases in foreign countries, the continental episode (one of Doyle's rare passages of pure fun) in 'Lady Frances Carfax', and the immortal Reichenbach scene itself in Switzerland.

Doyle's use of references to foreign countries is purely romantic: the effect he gets by these references is achieved by appealing to the reader's ignorance, not by appealing to his knowledge. It is the colour and smell and legend of the foreign country that Doyle wants, not its history or culture. His reader was quite content with that.

[16] 'The Bruce-Partington Plans', S. 970.
[17] 'The Greek Interpreter', S. 478.
[18] J. Dickson Carr, op. cit., p. 35.

4

Romance

ALL THIS SUPPORTS the conclusion that the Holmes stories are in a way the distillation of romantic literature: romantic literature brought to a special eminence by the injection of a non-romantic element. Holmes is what he is because of the counterpoint between the character of the cold logical reasoner and the romantic remoteness of this character from the ordinary run of fictional heroes. This produces a transformed or revived romance which, after the exaggerations of popular Victorian melodrama, proved to be a much needed refreshment for the devotee of light reading. It has no pretension to compete with great novel-writing, but it is exactly what the undemanding reader wanted after all the syrup that he had before been obliged to ingest.

Doyle was a born romancer. His non-Holmes stories range over the world and over the known territory of strange human experience. It is important to remember that, because it puts the restraint and austerity of the Holmes stories in its proper proportion. A reading of his collected non-Holmes stories shows how heavily he leaned on the stock romantic 'thriller' props: the adventures of a penniless man, the mysteries of the mind—sometimes the deranged mind—the ghostly, the parapsychological. To be fair, he was a responsible historian: he was prepared to do a great deal of honest research in preparation for *The White Company*. But he had, like Poe, an eye for the grotesque and bizarre and a gift for communicating them. He does not come up to Poe in communicating ultimate irrational horror, but this will be because he is a man of science (and indeed a respectable doctor). Neither—and this is profoundly important—was he in the least vulnerable to superstition. On the contrary, he had been brought early to scepticism by his consciousness of the conflict between the primitive Irish Catholicism of his upbringing and the requirements of the science of medicine.[1] He had found himself in the early eighties as a romantic writer; but the discovery of the possibilities of detection was a liberation for him, because in working out this form he could organise an encounter between romance and scientific precision such as his soul was crying out for. After all—who before him had consciously admitted the new science to his literary consciousness? Was not every major novelist before him a person absolutely rooted in what Lord Snow has taught us to call the First Culture? This is not to say that Jane Austen and George Eliot, Trollope and Thackeray and Dickens were scholars in Greek and Latin; but it is certainly confirmed by the number of nineteenth-century novelists (Dickens apart) who relied on the countryside rather than the town for their background, or on high society for their social milieu. The rustic and the aristocrat were alike insulated from the grosser incursions, and largely without need of the benefits, of the new science. It was your town dweller who knew what industrial squalor meant, your bourgeois who knew what money machines would bring him: and these are celebrated well enough in Dickens, but not much elsewhere.

H. G. Wells, you may say, is the high priest of scientific romance—now classified as science-fiction. Doyle is not a science-fiction writer in the Holmes stories. If Doyle's stories are scientific romances in any sense, we are bound to mean by so calling them that, whereas the science in H. G. Wells is physics, in Doyle it is basically logic. (Chemistry for Holmes is logic made physical: so it is naturally his hobby.) It is knowledge organised by logic that gives you the detective story, and since the science of logic is basically deductive, it must follow that what social comment you get from a detective story comes from within a known human situation, whereas what you get from a science-fiction story comes from an artificially imagined position outside the known human situation. Wells puts a man on the moon, or into the twenty-first century, or in possession of supernatural faculties, and lets him comment from there on what 1910 is thinking. Doyle puts him in Baker Street a few

[1] J. Dickson Carr, op. cit., p. 37.

hundred yards from the underground station and lets him wait for clients.

The point about detection as limited and restrained romance is supported by observing how very little actual travelling there is in the Holmes stories when they are compared with the total Doyle output. Spatial travel is not a major factor in the structure of these tales. No lost continents here; if any continents are mentioned (like the three separate ones in which Watson gained his experience of women)[2] they are merely background material.

All the Holmes cases begin in London, with the exception of one or two which come to him when he is taking an unusual and enforced holiday ('The Reigate Squires' and 'The Devil's Foot'). The conurbation of London was far less extensive then, of course, than it is now. The London County Council was constituted under the Local Government Act of 1888, but its further edges were still virtually 'in the country'. This, for example, is a description of a place somewhere in the neighbourhood of Brixton:

> Then came rows of two-storied villas, each with a fronting of miniature garden, and then again interminable lines of new, staring brick buildings—the monster tentacles which the giant city was throwing out into the country.[3]

For our present purposes, taking into account the emphasis with which the narrator mentions any journey south of the river, we will imagine a circle drawn with the centre at 221B Baker Street and extending for a radius of five miles but cut off at the south by the Thames. If we divide the cases between those which fall within this area and those which take us outside it, we find that twenty of the sixty cases are conducted entirely within it. In the others, Holmes travels more than two-hundred miles only three times (Devon and Cornwall, and in one case he is there already when the story opens), over a hundred miles five times (Hereford, Birmingham, the Peak District and twice to Norfolk), and over fifty miles six times (Oxford, Cambridge, the south coast twice and Winchester twice: but he is already in Oxford when that particular case

[2] Impossible to resist this classic from *The Sign of Four*, L. 152.
[3] *The Sign of Four*, L. 163.

opens, and he is living in retirement on the south coast when 'The Lion's Mane' comes under his notice).

It is not in spatial travel that romance is really situated—although many of the journeys are made exciting enough in their own right. It is perfectly possible, as Doyle shows in two late cases, 'The Dying Detective' and 'The Marazin Stone', to construct a story which does not require Holmes to leave Baker Street at all. But elsewhere the romantic technique shows itself very plainly. I am thinking especially of the names he chooses for his characters. Doyle seems to have needed to find names for just under five hundred characters, so we can forgive him for four Hudsons and a Hudson Street, four Violets, four Saunderses, four Wilsons and four Mortimers, twenty-six Johns and eighteen Jameses, when we meet such memorable names as Thaddaeus and Bartholomew Sholto, the two McMurdos, Boss McGinty, Enoch J. Drebber and Mordecai Smith. Some of this was probably unconscious: it was not surprising that Doyle should have had a leaning towards the rich Irish vowels and diphthongs which we hear in his own name, nor that that sojourn in the city of Edinburgh which gave him Holmes's archetype in Professor Bell should leave him with a predilection for Scottish names. It is remarkable that he never took Holmes to Scotland (he hardly ever refers to Scotland except on two occasions when he gives Dundee as the port of origin of a ship—'The Five Orange Pips' and 'Black Peter'). Neither does he take Holmes to his own native Ireland. But Scots and Irishmen are all over the scenery—Douglas, Scott, Rae, McMurdo, Knox and Menzies in *The Valley of Fear*, and in the short stories, among many others, more than one Munro, a Sutherland, a St Clair, a Miller, a Hunter, a Lauder, a McFarlane, a McLaren, a Dunbar, a Sutro, a Macpherson and a Murdoch. There are at least thirty-five unquestionable Scots names in the Holmes stories. Wales provides (from its admittedly smaller store) only five undeniable patronymics—Howells, Evans, James, Jones and Williams, with a doubtful sixth in 'Birdy Edwards'.

While the subject matter is faultlessly cerebral, the décor is faultlessly stirring. The occasional references to the weather in the openings of the short stories contain some of the most famous passages:

> It was in the latter days of September, and the equinoctial gales had set in with exceptional force. All day the wind had screamed and the rain had beat against the windows, so that even here, in the heart of great, hand-made London, we were forced to raise our minds for the instant from the routine of life, and to recognise the presence of those great elemental forces which shriek at mankind through the bars of his civilisation, like untamed beasts in a cage. As the evening drew in, the storm grew louder and louder, and the wind cried and sobbed like a child in the chimney.[4]

> It was a wild, tempestuous night towards the close of November . . . Outside the wind howled down Baker Street, while the rain beat fiercely against the windows. It was strange there in the very depths of the town, with ten miles of man's handiwork on every side of us, to feel the iron grip of nature, and to be conscious that to those huge elemental forces all London was no more than the molehills that dot the fields.[5]

There are excellent evocations of Baker Street in the snow of winter, or in the height of August heat ('The Beryl Coronet' and 'The Cardboard Box'), and the pelting rain of 'The Naval Treaty' is as inseparable from the story as the dense fog of 'The Bruce-Partington Plans'; but it is the wind that makes Watson talk like a local preacher. I suppose that the most extraordinary passage exemplifying the romantic treatment of nature is this strange soliloquy in 'The Naval Treaty'—on the whole the oddest passage in the Holmes collection:

> 'There is nothing in which deduction is so necessary as in religion,' said he, leaning with his back against the shutters. 'It can be built up as an exact science by the reasoner. Our highest assurance of the goodness of Providence seems to me to rest in the flowers. All other things, our powers, our desires, our food, are really necessary for our existence in the first instance. But this rose is an extra. Its smell and its colour are an embellishment of life, not a condition of it. It is only goodness that gives extras, and so I say again that we have much to learn from the flowers.'[6]

[4] 'The Five Orange Pips', S. 103–4.
[5] 'The Golden Pince-Nez', S. 783.
[6] 'The Naval Treaty', S. 513.

The surprise which Phelps and his sister show at this speech is no greater than that which the reader might feel. He can sympathise with Mrs Harrison's next comment:

> 'Do you see any prospect of solving *this* mystery, Mr Holmes?'[7]

The one other place where Holmes traverses metaphysics to the frontier of religion is in 'The Cardboard Box', where we get similar sentiments in the negative sense:

> 'What is the meaning of it, Watson?' said Holmes, solemnly, as he laid down the paper. 'What object is served by this circle of misery and violence and fear? It must tend to some end, or else our universe is ruled by chance, which is unthinkable. But what end? There is the great standing perennial problem to which human reason is as far from the answer as ever.'[8]

Whatever else this is, it is a good example of deism, or natural religion: and as such it is perhaps classical rather than romantic. But it transcends classicism in being part of the Holmes ethos, which is so profoundly and almost religiously naturalistic. Reason is all for him, and reason is translated through natural processes and natural phenomena. To the reader, though, passages like this look like an admission that there is something beyond reason. And if this is not Christian doctrine (and it isn't), then it is romantic.

In order to get this clear, it is worth while to assess the romantic content of Holmes against the seven categories which C. S. Lewis provided in the Preface to his *Pilgrim's Regress* (3rd edition, 1948). He said that there were in the romantic consciousness these constituents: (1) Dangerous adventure, (2) the marvellous and mysterious, (3) the cult of titanic and more-than-life-size character, (4) indulgence in anti-natural and abnormal moods, (5) egoism and subjectivity, (6) a revolt against convention and any given 'civilisation', and (7) sensibility to natural objects, of a solemn and enthusiastic kind.

Why, he might have been writing about Holmes.

(1) Dangerous adventure?

[7] Ib. My italics, which I suspect give the necessary emphasis.
[8] S. 946–7.

> It was a bitterly cold and frosty morning during the winter of '97 that I was wakened by a tugging at my shoulder. It was Holmes. The candle in his hand shone upon his eager, stooping face, and told me at once that something was amiss.
> 'Come, Watson, come!' he cried. 'The game is afoot. Not a word! Into your clothes and come!'[9]

(2) The marvellous and mysterious? Why, yes: the Irish names, the violin, the gaslight, the grandiloquent language, and above all the withholding of explanations until the climactic moment. 'You know my methods, Watson. Apply them.'

(3) The titanic and superhuman? Applied with a light touch, but thereby the more impressive:

> 'I understand you have already managed several delicate cases of this sort, sir, although I presume they were hardly from the same class of society.'
> 'No, I am descending.'
> 'I beg your pardon?'
> 'My last client of the kind was a king.'[10]

Thus cutting a peer down to size, or pulling Lord Cantlemere's leg, or telling home truths to the Duke of Holdernesse, or straightening the poker that Dr Grimesby Roylott had twisted, Holmes shows himself more than equal to demanding situations. In a description of himself Holmes takes this as far as the disciplines of the form permit:

> To carry the art, however, to its highest pitch, it is necessary that the reasoner should be able to utilise all the facts which have come to his knowledge, and this in itself implies, as you will readily see, a possession of all knowledge, which even in these days of free education and encylopaedias, is a somewhat rare accomplishment. It is not so impossible, however, that a man should possess all knowledge which is likely to be useful to him in his work, and this I have endeavoured in my case to do.[11]

[9] 'The Abbey Grange', S. 833. [10] 'The Noble Bachelor', S. 231.
[11] 'The Five Orange Pips', S. 116.

This shows well the limitations on superhumanity which Doyle laid on his hero; but now and again he is allowed a little licence. There are those deductive demonstrations at all seasons, and there are the two famous essays in thought-reading, and occasionally he produces recondite knowledge that staggers his hearers; once, brutally, he does this in what is a pure bluff in Watson's own field:

> Shall I demonstrate your own ignorance? What do you know, pray, of Tapanuli fever? What do you know of the black Formosa corruption?[12]

But nearly always the titanic is subtly rather than weightily emphasised, and it is this which gives rise to the greatest stylistic distinction in the stories: this formula—

> 'I followed you.'
> 'I saw no one.'
> 'That is what you may expect to see when I follow you.'[13]

which reached its apotheosis in what has become almost a household quotation, the epigram about the dog in the night time.[14]

(4) Indulgence in anti-natural and abnormal moods? Well, there is the cocaine bottle, and there are his generally anti-social hobbies and untidy habits, as his biographer mentions more than once, but never without affection:

> His incredible untidiness, his addiction to music at strange hours, his occasional revolver practice within doors, his weird and often malodorous scientific experiments, and the atmosphere of violence and danger which hung around him made him the very worst tenant in London.[15]

There is all that, of course: but there is also Holmes's dissenting attitude to popular values and resistance to social pressures which appears in those encounters with the more arrogant nobility that we have mentioned, and in all those traits which Watson calls 'Bohemian'.

[12] 'The Dying Detective', S. 1004. [13] 'The Devil's Foot', S. 1063.
[14] S. 326–7. [15] 'The Dying Detective', S. 1000–1.

> 'And from a noble client?'
> 'One of the highest in England.'
> 'My dear fellow, I congratulate you.'
> 'I assure you, Watson, without affectation, that the status of my client is a matter of less moment to me than the interest of his case.'[16]

This, of which plenty more examples will occur to the reader, takes care of categories (4) and (6), and to some extent of the fifth, which mentioned 'egoism and subjectivity'. I fancy that we find a response to this in those places where Holmes stands apart from accepted conventions of police procedure and even very occasionally from the law.

> 'After all, Watson . . . I am not retained by the police to supply their deficiencies. If Horner were in danger it would be another thing, but this fellow will not appear against him, and the case must collapse. I suppose that I am committing a felony, but it is just possible that I am saving a soul. The fellow will not go wrong again.'[17]

In 'The Abbey Grange' he satisfies himself that the gallant Captain Croker has killed only in self-defence and dismisses him with a handshake. In one special and very unusual case he behaves like a Robin Hood, or a Raffles, and breaks into and enters the house of Charles Augustus Milverton. In 'A Case of Identity' he dismisses the criminal with a stern warning. All this is very much in keeping with the 'lonely genius' build-up; but once again, what is most notable is the way in which Doyle insists that Holmes shall keep within tolerable bounds the tendency of the one-man intellect to become a one-man judge and jury. Too much licence there will lead to anarchy—and anarchy is the enemy of detective literature.

When we get to Lewis's seventh category, there is no more to be said than what was illustrated in quotations [4] and [5] above in this chapter, together with quotation [6] about the religious significance of roses. No: there is no question that the Holmes creation fits without the least necessity of forcing at any

[16] 'The Noble Bachelor', S. 225. [17] 'The Blue Carbuncle', S. 172.

point into the definition of romanticism that Professor Lewis provided.

But it is romanticism lightly handled. No doubt there is much stylised stuff here; the women tend to be tall and distinguished (but so are John Buchan's, and Buchan never created a Violet Hunter or indeed a Mary Morstan); the police are either, in the early stages, contemptuous, or, in the later stages, respectful (but never forget Lestrade's two great moments of generosity).[18]

Holmes may himself be solemn, remote and magisterial, but from whom else in the business would you hear this?

> 'Don't drop the instruments, I beg. Your arrest as a suspicious character would be a most unfortunate complication.[19]

There are touches of lightness which let the fresh air in on the sultry romantic scene; and there are, wherever you touch them, constant indications in the stories that their author is always alert to the danger of over-ripe romanticism. The Sussex Vampire may look like a vampire, but it turns out to be something much more familiar and dangerous.

> The idea of a vampire was to me absurd. Such things do not happen in criminal practice.[20]

It is, I think, this constant tension between the far-flung remoteness of romanticism and the restrictions of reason tied down to physical particulars that form the dynamic of the detective story as Doyle understood it. And a glance back at Poe shows how skilful he was—as will the glances we shall take at some of his immediate successors. Poe's detection was strange literature! 'The Gold Bug' is a thriller based on the decoding of a cipher—and the decoding of the 'Dancing Men' cipher was conducted on exactly the same principles that Poe expounded. That is a tolerable yarn: but 'The Murders in the Rue Morgue' and 'The Mystery of Marie Roget' are far from tolerable yarns. Even 'The Purloined Letter' only just gets by with its

[18] At the end of 'The Norwood Builder', S. 606–7, and 'The Six Napoleons', S. 762.

[19] 'The Bruce-Partington Plans', S. 992.

[20] S. 1194.

surprise ending. Dupin is, compared with Holmes, a stick. As for the other characters, they don't exist at all: some are even without names, referred to as 'Monsieur D——' or what not. You really cannot pretend that this is literature, with all its pedagogic verbosity and creaking rhetoric. Gaboriau is hardly better: Leroux is certainly much better.

With Doyle there is inevitably a touch of double-talk. Holmes sets himself up as a thinking machine and reproves Watson for romanticising his stories, but Holmes is a born actor who can't resist 'the touch of drama'. Holmes and his creator may try to tell us all that the interest of a detective story is purely cerebral, that it need be little more than a diagram of intellectual encounters. That, though some people have believed it and echoed it, is rubbish. The interest of a detective story is in the people who walk and talk in it—it is as much so with Holmes as with anyone else.

But now that we have said it, we have let a cat out of the bag—a cat which has been impatiently calling from within for some time. There is a certain amount of gentle humbug about all this. Those who defend the detective tale and those who attack it go equally astray if they do not correctly assess the humbug-content of this kind of literature: and the best and most painless way of doing this is to assess the humbug-content in Holmes himself.

5

A Whisper of 'Norbury'

IT WAS RONALD KNOX who first drew attention to Holmes's now famous 'howler'. In deducing the direction of a bicycle's travel from the superimposition of its tyre-treads (in 'The Priory School'), Holmes was guilty of false reasoning. It simply can't be done, and once Ronald Knox observed that this particular emperor had no clothes on we had to accept it as a momentary deviation on the Master's part.

But there are other cats waiting in the bag: quite a queue of cats. There was that business about Miss Violet Smith—who really seems to have had an unadmitted effect on Holmes, let alone Watson—when Holmes deduced 'from a certain spirituality about the face' that the lady was a musician.[1] Well, that's more than most musicians would hazard. She might as well have been a confidence-trickster or a cook. And what about that marvellous piece of bluff where Holmes claimed to read Watson's thoughts?[2] That deserves a little closer scrutiny. There is no reason in the world why a single one of Holmes's deductions should be safe. It is borrowed from Poe: he says as much—and none the better for that. It's probably the most discreditable piece of 'titanism' that Holmes descends to.

And the mud-splashes on Watson's greatcoat? Holmes deduces that he was not alone in the cab, since a solitary passenger never sits in the corner of a cab.[3] Observation shows that this is never true of a modern taxi, and Watson's reply might have been, 'On the contrary, Holmes; I had no companion. I sat in the corner until a large splash of mud from the gutter warned me to sit in the centre.'

[1] 'The Solitary Cyclist', S. 640. [2] 'The Cardboard Box', S. 924–6.
[3] 'The Disappearance of Lady Frances Carfax', S. 1019.

Some of the recorded deductions are as solid as rock: others are nothing but examples of a quite distinguished allowance of good luck. Dear old Henry Baker's hat, now—how about that?[4] Holmes deduces that the owner of the hat must be an intellectual because the hat is a large one. 'For answer Holmes clapped the hat on his head. It came right over his forehead and settled on the bridge of his nose.' Upon which Holmes said, 'A man with so large a brain must have something in it.' It follows, then, that the owner of the hat had a larger brain than Holmes. With more in it?

How much this kind of spoof indicates positive guilt in the author we cannot really judge. That judgement is made especially difficult by two pieces of evidence that Conan Doyle was certainly capable of cutting his hero down to size. They appear in two non-Holmes mystery stories and I think they are conclusive. One of these is 'The Lost Special', where the mystery is the complete disappearance of a train somewhere in Lancashire. Among those who offer solutions to the mystery is 'an amateur reasoner of some celebrity' who writes to *The Times* a letter containing what turns out to be a quite wrong solution, but containing also this opening sentence:

> It is one of the elementary principles of practical reasoning that when the impossible has been eliminated the residuum, *however improbable*, must contain the truth.[5]

Who can the writer be but Holmes? The dramatic date of the letter, 3 July 1890, is right in the middle of the 'vintage' Holmes period.

But that is not all. Two stories later in the same book we find 'The Man with the Watches': and here we have a letter in the *Daily Gazette* from 'a well-known criminal investigator', whose transcription runs just beyond two pages, and which again proves to be entirely erroneous in its offered solution. Holmes again? What other 'well-known criminal investigator' was in business at the time? The date? 1892. Ah well: all Doyle has forborne to record is that the envelope bore a foreign stamp.[6]

[4] 'The Blue Carbuncle', S. 154.

[5] *The Conan Doyle Stories.* (John Murray, one-volume edition, 1929), pp. 559–60.

[6] Ib., pp. 596–9.

Anyhow, this element of harmless humbug was all part of the appeal which the Holmes stories made to their readers. Doyle's prodigious success is not primarily due to any calculated effect, but to the kind of coincidence which really shapes nine-tenths of all outstanding successes. We have already referred to the various aids to the success of the Holmes saga—the establishment of a police force in which the country had shown confidence, and the general climate of security and superiority which in the year of Queen Victoria's Golden Jubilee was at its sunniest. This helped, but it was not all that Doyle needed, nor all that he got.

What he may have been only half-conscious of was the hospitality that the English bourgeois, because of its puritan background, was waiting to give to his offerings. Holmes satisfied a craving which had emerged from the puritan background—there is no doubt of that.

I mean in this context what ought to be called secular puritanism. The positive principle in the English puritan tradition (which is, as I believe, not wholly or even primarily a religious movement) has three basic constituents: intellectualism, moralism, and the acceptance of the values of the city. The weighty religious associations of puritanism are the result of its having manifested itself at a time when religion was in any case the chief talking-point of every articulate Englishman—the sixteenth century. But you can be, and by Holmes's time people of several generations had been, committed to the values of secular puritanism without holding dissenting religious views, or indeed any religious views at all. Most puritans today are humanists.

Puritanism has gathered to itself various opprobrious connotations which for the present must be set aside. It is obvious that intellectualism can mean a prosy, unimaginative outlook coupled with a contempt for anybody who works with his hands and a fear of the body. Moralism can be stuffy, bigoted and pharisaical. Acceptance of the city can mean connivance at rent-profiteering and a leathery conscience about slums and prostitution; and puritans have often been thus describable. But, equally, the puritan values can be expressed as a love of just and rational conversation, a passion for social justice which leaves room for individual development and distinction, and a denial that in order to live the good life you must live in the English countryside. Puritans have also been describable in those terms. Since puritanism is not landed but commercial: since it exalts the astute merchant as he is in competition with the economically illiterate squire: since it is of the Galsworthy rather than of the Wodehouse world, it is easy to find it exasperatingly philistine and strenuous. But you don't understand it until you have seen that one of the most authentic manifestations of the puritan ideal is the conversation of the old-fashioned, all-male, Oxford or Cambridge Senior Common Room. Puritanism is rational, wary against hypocrisy and self-deception, often of limited imagination, but always of unlimited optimism about the possibilities of achievement by the human mind.

Those were the values which made Victorian life, pre-eminently in London, what it was. They were responsible for the best and the worst in that life. And upon the whole the novelists were, by habit if not by conviction, anti-puritan. Consider the sociological implications of this passage from the first chapter of Trollope's *Doctor Thorne*, written in 1858:

> England is not yet a commercial country in the sense in which that epithet is used for her; and let us hope that she will not soon become so. . . . If in western civilised Europe there does exist a nation among whom there are high signors, and with whom the owners of the land are the true aristocracy, the aristocracy that is trusted as being best and fittest to rule, that nation is the English. Choose out the ten leading men of each great European people. Choose them in France, Austria, Sardinia, Prussia, Russia, Sweden, Denmark, Spain (?), and then select the ten in England whose names are best known as those of leading statesmen; the result will show in which country there still exists the closest attachment to, the sincerest trust in, the old feudal and now so-called landed interests.

That is how Trollope saw it. He was the best Victorian novelist of high rustic life, and his faith was firmly attached to the land. But who was writing for the other England—the nasty commercial money-making England that had to live through London fog when the country grandees had long since gone back to Framley and Courcy? Dickens, obviously: but

Dickens is *sui generis*—uniquely entertaining, but also uniquely indignant. Dickens is in some sort a novelist of the puritan social conscience attacking the consequences of puritan enterprise. Where others wrote about country peasants, or the aristocracy, or the army, or religion, Dickens wrote about London and Manchester and wrote about them with anger.

Dickens in his puritan phases was a puritan preacher. It becomes easy to see how much more difficult it would be to become a puritan entertainer. If the man in the bank or the Stock Exchange, the shopkeeper or hotelier in Victorian London wanted social criticism and conscience-stirring evangelism, there it was for him in Dickens. But what was there which could, by evoking an acceptance of the puritan values, offer him relaxation?

Does a puritan ever relax? That is the deep and religious question to which the answer is yes when you have fully explored the meaning of the question. (I hope to do so: but not in this book.) The superficial answer with which we have here to be content is that a puritan does relax but doesn't want to stop being a puritan when he does so. Many forms of relaxation give him a bad conscience. In particular, in the literary field, he is not happy about relaxing with fiction, because fiction is 'make-believe', and 'make-believe' is, in any sense, anathema to a puritan. Secular puritanism insists that make-believe is for women and children: for men, the world of reality is their field of conquest and their faculties must not be blunted by fantasy. (There's another enormous and fascinating question for exploration some other time: what precisely was a puritan *woman*?) Preaching he could understand, whether religious or social. That which addressed his conscience he could not reject. But this was something which even he could not put up with all the time. What he needed was a literature which accepted what he accepted, that met him where he was and for a few relaxed moments confirmed him instead of challenging him. So if somebody will do that, he will collect heavily from the queue of readers.

What this amounts to is to say that it was hardly Doyle himself but his readers who were the architect of his success. Doyle was a (not eminently faithful) Catholic from Ireland, moved to write the Holmes stories by a clinical interest in criminology that was really aroused by the detective work of the new medicine which he studied in Calvinist Edinburgh. But he gave his reader a man who lived in London at an identifiable address, who was himself as nearly classless as any fictional character has ever been, who walked the streets and travelled in trains and went to identifiable places like Birmingham and Winchester, whose biographer wrote '1887', not '18—'; and this character held the reader's interest by the manly exercise of intellect in the cause of exposing the truth about perfectly possible and familiar situations. A generation brought up to believe that reading fiction was women's work but in men a sign of degeneracy was presented with a literature of which it need not be ashamed.

When you see it that way, the 'humbug' content of the stories is capable of a perfectly innocent explanation. It is the earthy probability of all the situations that causes the humbug to stand out: indeed, it looks pedantic to refer to it at all, and most readers hardly notice it. Moreover, the humbug is entirely confined to those passages where Holmes is demonstrating deductive talent. It is never to be found where it would do infinitely more damage, in the psychological structure of characters. Never for one moment does Holmes act 'out of character': nor does Watson. He surprises you, but you never reject a word he says as being an impossible speech for the character you have been given by the author. It may not have been particularly difficult to create him and to keep him in order; but his creator never misses a trick in his dealings with him as he develops. The humbug is all on the surface; it is a transgression of the rules of logic in the cause of putting logic in the foreground of the reader's mind. That was Doyle's chief purpose—to build up a fictional world in which, given the puritan values, things came out right, in which the machinery always in the end clicked home, in which what the puritan looked for was freed of frustration and vexation. For this purpose he sometimes exaggerated Holmes's powers: but then for the same purpose he sometimes deliberately played them down and left Holmes with a case whose solution he was not himself responsible for finding. Those bicycle tracks are compensated by 'Norbury'.

It is along these lines that I think the success of the detective story can be explained. What Doyle did was to establish firmly what others had stumbled on by accident or had imperfectly contrived. Detection, from being an incident or an eccentricity, now became a literary form. He provided the 'Well-Tempered Klavier' of detection: his successors did nothing important that he had not at some time thought of.

II

THE CLASSICS

6

Severe Science

> The man . . . who would successfully practise the scientific detection of crime must take all knowledge for his province. There is no single fact which may not, in particular circumstances, acquire a high degree of evidential value; and in such circumstances success or failure is determined by the possession or non-possession of the knowledge wherewith to interpret the significance of that fact. [33–995][1]

A CHARACTER AS powerful as Sherlock Holmes, chronicled in a style as idiosyncratic as Watson's, was bound to attract imitators. Such imitators have been of three kinds: the parodists, with whom we need not be concerned at all, the apocryphists, who have almost to a man demonstrated that it is not half so easy as it appears to re-create either the man or the style convincingly, and the disciples. Having observed in passing that the one person who showed himself capable of writing a persuasive apocryphal story of Holmes is John Dickson Carr,[2] who is in any case a master of English styles in imitation of many periods, our business is with the disciples. In the first instance it will suffice to look at three: the three including one manifest rebel.

[1] *Dr Thorndyke, His Famous Cases as Described by R. Austin Freeman*, a representative but not exhaustive collection of short stories published in 1929 by Hodder and Stoughton. References in the following pages are to the number of the story and the number of the page in this edition.

[2] 'The Highgate Miracle', the fourth story in *The Exploits of Sherlock Holmes* (ed. John Dickson Carr and Adrian Conan Doyle, John Murray, 1954). Readers will recall Carr's excellence as a 'period' writer in *Bride of Newgate* (Cape, 1952) and other detective stories set in historical milieux.

First, Austin Freeman: and of him it is difficult to say anything kind concerning his style and literary deportment. It really is a question what pleasure anybody can have taken, and what pleasure some still take, in reading the memoirs of Doctor Thorndyke. This Thorndyke has survived fifty years, to appear as a reprint in a very popular paperback series, so he must be counted one of the major figures in the literature. But what literature! Granted, it is a great deal better than the literature of the forgotten underworld of immediately post-Doyle detection; but it really can safely be said that there is no author now living and writing in this field who is capable of setting down such massive blocks of literary gobbledygook as Freeman habitually did. No writer whom we shall meet in these pages was so consistently given to cliché, or so regularly apt to take down his paragraphs in pre-cast units from well-labelled hooks in his workshop. Only one, anyhow, comes near him in this achievement.

Dubious literature in this field was accepted uncritically by serious readers: there can be no doubt of that. Nowadays there is bad writing in detective literature, if you set the boundaries of the field wide enough: but it goes with bad construction and plotting. The age of the detective story which was bad literature but good detection has given place to the thriller which at its best is very good writing but has virtually no detective interest. Doctor Thorndyke is a respectable pioneer in the field of the strictly utility detective.

He looks like an adaptation of Sherlock Holmes to the early age of electricity. All that is of 'gaslight' is stripped away; so are all the endearing and humanising eccentricities that bring Holmes to life and make him a sensational success in an age for which Thorndyke has very little appeal. Holmes could deviate from personal precision—the jack-knife doing duty as a letter-spike and the persian slipper as tobacco pouch. In Thorndyke's well-kept chambers at 5 King's Bench Walk such things would not have been tolerated for a moment.

The similarities between Thorndyke and Holmes are striking; the dissimilarities disconcerting. We are tempted to believe that Thorndyke met Holmes (I suppose he may have been fifteen years younger), and thought him a flamboyant and over-emotional adventurer who prostituted his scientific talents. He does not mention him, even in the terms in which Holmes mentions Dupin; but if he did his comment might well be somewhat tight-lipped.

Like Holmes, Thorndyke is a bachelor. Like Holmes he has a Watson, and in most of his cases this Watson is a doctor. Of the thirty-seven under review here, thirty-five are narrated by Christopher Jervis, M.D. (no untidy perplexities about his first name); one other is related by a Doctor Jardine [27] and the remaining one by a lawyer called Anstey [28], who also appears in another story as a minor character [9]. But Thorndyke cannot manage merely with a Watson. He needs also a Polton. Polton is vastly important. He is the mechanic, photographer and general factotum in the house. The stinking chemistry of 221B is relegated, as is only proper, to an upper room in those demure chambers. In this manner, Thorndyke is far more magisterial than Holmes: when they are out on a case it is Dr Jervis's business to hold the instruments, like a nurse in the operating theatre waiting on the surgeon. At home, Polton does the dirty work.

There is a technological advance here. Photography is no part of the Holmes set-up, nor does the chemistry do much to assist the detection; it is, for Holmes, a distraction from it. Thorndyke would be pained to be called an amateur, just as Holmes delighted in that epithet. He is a medical jurist, superbly competent in both law and medicine. He is a legitimate polymath, and comes up as a professional non-police detective. He shares with Holmes a sense of the dramatic and a capacity for springing surprises on both police and civilians who are following his reasoning only from a distance. He talks to Jervis on many occasions as one may suppose a distinguished silk to talk to his junior, although in fact Thorndyke is not an advocate [17–538], and his appearances in court are confined to those which it is proper for an attorney to make.

It was only the exceptional case which took Holmes far from Baker Street; but in comparison with Thorndyke, Holmes is a restless gadabout. One of these thirty-seven cases takes him as far as Buckinghamshire and two to Essex: the rest are in London or Kent, apart from a few whose locality is unidentifiable but presents no features inconsistent with the scenery of the home counties. Nearly all the people in the stories have good commonplace urban names—'Cadmus Bawley' sticks out as a rare exception. In fact, the romantic trappings are cut down to the barest minimum. No Thaddaeus Sholtos, no 'rascally Lascars of the vilest antecedents', only one secret society—from Sierra Leone [31]; a wicked negro in [31] is balanced by an innocent one in [20]. The only concession to romance is a tendency to lay emphasis on railways (a symbol of the puritan tussle with romance), such as we find in six of the first sixteen stories. That apart, the 'romance', the 'trajectory', of the stories is entirely in their use of what was still to the layman-reader the 'new science'.

We are told nothing about John Thorndyke himself apart from what we have to be told about his professional standing. There are only two references in the stories which give us any idea of their dramatic date. One is 'The Missing Mortgagee' [5], which places it in 1908 [5–199]; the other is in 'Gleanings from the Wreckage', which makes a reference to the 'old days' of 1915 and places it after the end of the First World War [21–608]. Where it is necessary to the story, month and day are given, but never, apart from those two accidental examples, the year. Even the titles of the stories are almost uniformly prosaic—'The Anthropologist at Large', 'The Pathologist to the Rescue', 'The Naturalist at Law'. Nothing here like 'The Second Stain'.

It is in his conversational methods and occasionally in his handling of situations that Thorndyke looks most like Holmes. Here and there the eye might be deceived for a moment:

> 'London is an inexhaustible place,' he mused. 'Its variety is infinite. A minute ago we walked in the glare of light, jostled by a multitude. And now look at this little street. It is as dim as a tunnel, and we have got it absolutely to ourselves. Anything might happen in a place like this.'[3]

Watson would have known what kind of silence to keep in such company. Or what of this?

> 'A detailed description is, of course, impossible. I can only sketch out the probabilities. But if you should happen to meet with a negro—a tall negro with a bandaged head of a contused

[3] 'The Magic Casket', 13–398.

wound of the scalp and a swollen leg—you had better keep your eye on him. The leg which is swollen is probably the left.' The inspector was thrilled, and so was I, for that matter.[4]

I have said that he never mentions Holmes; but just occasionally he seems to venture on what could be construed as a gentle and polite criticism of Holmes's dashing dogmatism:

'It suggests to me,' replied Thorndyke, laying down the lens through which he had been inspecting the hairbrushes, 'a middle-aged or elderly man with a shaven upper lip and a beard; a well-preserved, healthy man, neat, orderly, provident and careful as to his appearance; a man long habituated to travelling, and—though I don't insist on this, but the appearances suggest that he had been living for some time in a particular household, and at the time when he lost his bag, he was changing his residence.'

'He was that,' chuckled the inspector, 'if the constable's account of the way he went over that wall is to be trusted. But still I don't see how you arrived at all those facts.'

'Not facts, Badger,' Thorndyke corrected. 'I said suggestions. And those suggestions may be quite misleading.'[5]

If Thorndyke were ever pressed to a decision, he would be bound to say that the trained scientist's ability to distinguish fact from speculation was more valuable than the inspired guess of the amateur: he does indeed say so at the end of the first story, commending to his colleague and therefore to the reader 'the urgent need of a trained scientist to aid the police [1–53].

On the other hand, he is capable of throwing dust in the eyes of those who witness his deductive performances when this does not involve their being positively misled:

'Possibly a watery solution of strophanthus.'
'Why strophanthus?' I asked.
'Why not?'[6]

And he frequently assures his colleagues that all the evidence required for a solution of a problem is before him, even if he

[4] 'The Pathologist to the Rescue', 20–598.
[5] 'A Fisher of Men', 35–998.
[6] 'The Case of the White Footprints', 31–901.

cannot make use of it. We must add that he rarely uses the word 'elementary', but otherwise it is in the Holmes manner.

So is the climactic section of 'The Seal of Nebuchadnezzar' [24], one of the best of the stories. First we come across this—a very good conflation of Thorndyke-Holmes:

> 'There is a difference of nearly two millimetres . . .'
>
> 'Ah, Thorndyke,' said Broadribb, 'that keeper hadn't got your mathematically exact eye; and, in fact, the precise measurements don't seem to matter much.'
>
> 'On the other hand,' retorted Thorndyke, 'inexact measurements are of no use at all.'[7]

Yes—that is quite good. Doyle would have tautened it. I suspect it would have read something like this:

> '. . . and in fact the exact measurements don't seem to have much significance.'
>
> 'On the other hand, inexact measurements have no significance at all.'

Two pages later we have this, which again echoes the Master:

> 'I am sorry to be so evasive . . . but this case is so extremely speculative that I cannot come to any definite conclusion until I have more data.'[8]

From that moment this particular story concedes more and more to Holmes, until we find Thorndyke standing with a plaster bust in his hand which a police officer has observed to be slightly damp. Knowing that for twenty pages we have been looking for a small cylindrical seal, and like all educated men have read 'The Six Napoleons', we are in no doubt about what happens next, and where the seal will be. But the reader needs only to lay the page alongside the corresponding page in the archetype to decide which author can write. It is not that Thorndyke's plot fails of a dramatic climax; it is merely that its author's verbosity prevents his communicating it.

[7] 'The Seal of Nebuchadnezzar', 24–700. [8] 24–702.

> Drop it he did; and in a perfectly deliberate, purposeful manner, so that the bust fell on its back on the marble floor and was instantly shattered into a hundred fragments. It was an amazing affair. But what followed was still more amazing.[9]

There aren't many pages in Thorndyke's memoirs which don't give jabs of pain to the sensitive reader. Thorndyke is always saying 'very singular' (where Holmes would have said 'singular'), meaning 'remarkable'. Our leading quotation is a tolerable example of Dr Freeman's stylistic club-footedness.

The strength of the stories is in their specialism. So much in the Poe-Doyle romantic tradition has been pared away, and so much more is lost by the absence of any literary grace or sting, that it becomes the more remarkable that the stories retain any interest at all. They do retain it because of their author's single-minded devotion to the task of showing 'science' as relevant to that everyday life which detective stories deal with.

This single-mindedness, already exemplified in so many ways, can be seen most impressively in the way in which the reader is called upon to take only a small interest in the crime as such. The first six stories are 'inverted' in form—that is, they describe the devices of the criminal and then describe the means by which what he has hidden is uncovered (in the fourth it turns out that there was no crime at all). Detection is strictly the point, not criminal psychology. Fifteen of these thirty-seven cases involve murder (though in no fewer than nine others murder is suspected and later found not to have taken place). There are six thefts, four frauds (of which three look at first like murders), one abduction, one arson, one attempted murder, and one case of conspiracy to procure suicide. In four of the proved murders the criminal commits suicide, in one he accidentally dies, and in three he escapes altogether. In the conspiracy case Thorndyke says that the case could never have been proved although he is morally and logically certain of its rightness. Three apparent murders turn out to be accidents, and in two stories there is no crime. The murderers actually arrested (and presumably, though only in a minority of cases is it actually stated, convicted) number only seven. All the stories end

[9] 24–706.

abruptly and almost always without a Holmes-like *coda*; as soon as the detective interest is exhausted the narrative dies.

The place of Thorndyke in the investigation is this. On the one hand he develops in a direct line the theme, 'You have seen, but you have not observed'. On the other he is, in himself and by his methods, a criticism of Holmes's flamboyance.

The significance of minute particulars, when they are arranged by the detective into a pattern that corresponds with the supposedly unknown sequence of events of which they are signs, is the heart of the matter. In several cases we meet Polton's delightful miniature vacuum cleaner which collects dust from clothes for analysis. The detective point in 'A Wastrel's Romance' [4] is the finding of a man who has disappeared. Thorndyke finds him by reconstructing, from particles of dust found in his coat, the neighbourhood in which he lives. The instrument appears again in 'The Anthropologist at Large' [9–307], where it is used to extract hairs from a hat, and so to help furnish a description of a wanted man. The clues to be found in different types of sand are part of the plot of 'A Mystery of the Sand-Hills' [28–814]. A special kind of dust found in another garment helps to identify the wanted man (who turns out to be beyond prosecution) in 'The Touchstone' [34–994].

Observation pure and simple, without the element of special scientific knowledge, does not usually clinch a plot. It does so, though, in 'Echo of a Mutiny' [3], where Thorndyke makes deductions from the condition of a pipe left about by a suspected smoker. And it serves its turn in 'The Mysterious Visitor' [30] and in 'The New Jersey Sphinx' [33]. Here Thorndyke simply reasons from data provided by the case, not from his specialist knowledge. But most of the time he appears as the superman whose private learning is as profound as his incidental knowledge is wide. As a specialist he is credible enough when it comes to identifying a supposedly cremated body as cooked butcher's meat ('The Contents of a Mare's Next' [14]), or when cranial measurements point to the race, and therefore the identity, of a thief in 'The Anthropologist at Large' [9]. Where it is, as it often is, medicine, chemistry, anatomy, pathology, or any related branch of applied science to which he refers, Thorndyke is credible enough to the layman. The impetus of all this private knowledge makes it the less surprising that he can spot at once the significance of a convex mirror [29], or of the special properties of binocular vision and the limitations of monocular vision ('Phyllis Annesley's Peril' [25]). Our credulity feels the strain only when we find out how much he knows about Asiatic fleas ('The Sower of Pestilence' [26]), and the ecology of various forms of duckweed ('A Naturalist at Law' [16]). The strain becomes dangerous when he says in an offhand way, 'I do just know the Japanese characters' [13–424], and, 'Now it happens that I have just enough elementary knowledge of the hieroglyphic characters' (sc. of the Egyptian language). Jervis could have been forgiven for saying with a sigh, 'Yes, you would'. It looks as if just at those points Thorndyke's creator was giving ground to romantic conventions.

At one point he is vulnerable in a way for which we cannot blame his creator, but which perhaps a longer and broader view of science might have warned him about. It reminds me of the well-intentioned poetess who, seeking to write a hymn for children which celebrated the common sights of the modern city (a laudable aim), wrote a line about 'engines that whistle', which the diesel age rendered unusable. Thorndyke's modest precision, wholly in place at the time, misfires for today's readers when he says (in 'The Pathologist to the Rescue' [20–588]), 'There is no known method by which the blood of one person can be distinguished with certainty from that of another'. This is the Achilles' heel of 'second-culture' detection. It is not likely to base a deduction on a supposed scientific dogma since proved false, but it is very likely to exclude some possibility which scientific progress has later revealed.

On the other hand, we can regard the story about a cremation [14], and that involving a phonograph ('Mr Ponting's Alibi' [17]), as celebrations of the products of technology well in keeping with the author's manifest desire to show how life's mysteries lie open when science approaches them. This phonograph, we may say, is made much better use of than the one Holmes introduced in 'The Mazarin Stone', in which Doyle sideslips badly and unsuspectingly on the banana skin of the non-existence of a record giving an unaccompanied performance of what he amiably and imprecisely calls the

'Hoffman Barcarolle'. On the whole, this is not the kind of error that Freeman makes. He stays within the limits of such scientific knowledge as was available to him and his reader, and to this end he shelters Thorndyke from all sentimentality and all mysticism. Above all, Thorndyke is modest in the manner of the true scientist. He does not indulge in any rhetoric about the boneheadedness of the police, and he is never resented by the police. His excursus on the dubious value of bloodhounds in detection ('A Case of Premeditation' [2–85, 87]) is one of the few specific comments he allows himself on the inferiority of accepted detective habits. The salutary effect that the stories had at the time when they were written was that of reminding readers that detection of crime could be carried on, and described, without the heady overtones of the Holmes stories. For this achievement he sacrificed that romantic impetus which Doyle accepted; and he was not stylist enough to sustain the technique through a story of full novel-length. But he made his gesture.

7

In the Dark

AUSTIN FREEMAN ASKED questions about Holmes's infallibility, and, by creating his dedicated scientist-physician-lawyer Thorndyke, sought to separate detection as far as possible from romance. At roughly the same time another mind of a very different sort put a new question, and the question was about Holmes's (and Thorndyke's) super-humanity. Here were these fellows, to whom no door was closed because of their almost fantastic store of knowledge and skill in deploying it. They were almost all the time deadly serious fellows, given to a certain pomposity of speech and axiomatically in command of whatever situation they found themselves in. Thorndyke has no discernible weaknesses or recorded failures. Holmes has his weaknesses and his failures, but none the less the impression which he gives is one of invincibility. The battles he lost seem to be unimportant once he has got even with Moriarty.

Ernest Bramah, that sensitive and witty writer of the Edwardian age, questioned the need for all this solemnity, and for this assumption that the hero of a detective story must be from the beginning an invulnerable person. What, he asked, if we suppose a man to be blind, and then set him up as a detective?

Carrados is the first—and I believe the only—blind detective in the literature. Other detectives after him have been placed under limitations by their authors, but the notion of a blind detective was one which it took a Bramah to conceive. Carrados was not even born blind. He became blind through an accident after reaching maturity, so it was not a case of developing the special perceptions of a blind man from birth. But he did develop his remaining senses to an astonishing pitch of efficiency. That efficiency becomes the confusion of every miscreant with whom he comes into contact. But, as his creator showed in an introductory article to one of his collections of short stories, *The Eyes of Max Carrados*, history insists that nothing in the Carrados adventures is in itself incredible. This introduction is a considerable essay on famous and gifted blind people, partly drawn from a book by one James Wilson called *Biography of the Blind* and published in 1820. It mentions Nicholas Saunderson (b. 1682), who became Lucasian Professor of Mathematics at Cambridge, Henry Moyes the blind chemist of Fife, Thomas Wilson the blind bellringer of Dumfries, John Stanley (b. 1713), one of the most eminent of eighteenth-century organists, and the fabulous John Metcalf of Knaresborough, gentleman-soldier in the '45 and thereafter road-builder, who lived to be ninety-three and died in 1810; long after conceiving the Carrados stories Ernest Bramah found that he was distantly related to this 'Blind Jack of Knaresborough'. A succession of more modern blind geniuses ends with Helen Keller.

Compensating for this affliction, Carrados is given certain initial advantages in a very acute intelligence, an enviably equable temperament, and a very substantial legacy from an American cousin which enables him not only to live as a gentleman of leisure but also to employ a personal servant (Parkinson) and a high-grade secretary. Parkinson combines photographic efficiency in observation with mechanical dexterity and a complete lack of imagination or the desire to question any judgement of his master.

Carrados has no wife, so the tradition of bachelor detectives is not yet broken. But he has a considerable house, a monumental car, and a very happy existence indeed.

His contact with the outside world is maintained through the many friends whom he makes and keeps—for it is a familiar fact that the blind are often the best of company; his contact with that world which arouses his detective abilities is made through an unexpected meeting with a struck-off solicitor turned private detective. In the opening story, 'The Coin of Dionysius' [MC 1], we get the kind of introduction we have in *A Study in Scarlet*—the manner of the meeting between the great man and the friend who becomes his Watson (though not in this case his first-person biographer). By an odd coincidence both men have changed their names—Louis Calling has become, for prudence's sake, Louis Carlyle, and Max Wynn has become, for his legacy's sake, Max Carrados, referred to confusingly as Wynn by certain of his older acquaintances.

Max Carrados, the first collection of stories, came out in 1914, the other two collections a little later.[1] The dramatic date is never stated in these stories, apart from 'The Secret of Headlam Height' [MCM 1][2] which is placed in the first week of the First World War—namely, early August 1914. (So we have two famous detective incidents taking place on the south coast within a few days of one another: this and 'His Last Bow'. Not remarkable, considering the time chosen.)

In these stories—a small collection, by the standards we have been encountering—everything is magnificently spacious. The age is the age of elegance, the culture that of courtesy. Whatever the date of their writing, the scars and sorrows of 1914 have not yet touched their world. It is rare in these twenty-five tales to meet anything within remote reach of the sordid. There are just two murders, 'The Tilling Shaw Mystery' [MC 6], in which the murderer has already committed suicide when the enquiry opens, and 'The Holloway Flat Tragedy' [MCM 3], in which the murderer does the same before its end. There is one attempted murder ('The Tragedy at Brookbend Cottage' [MC 3]), where it is not the intending murderer but the intended victim who commits suicide. There are various forms of fraud, usually connected with the somewhat rarified life of book-collectors, art-dealers and numismatists which is part of Carrados's normal field of activity. There is, of course, the unhappy business of the railway accident deliberately contrived by a disgruntled Indian ('The Knight's Cross Signal Problem' [MC 2]); there is a touch of prescience about this: it has been a later age, in Britain anyhow, that has made unhappily familiar

[1] First editions of these would be collectors' pieces of a kind to delight Carrados himself. But all three have been published at one time or another by Penguin Books: *The Eyes of Max Carrados* [EMC] as no. 103 (1940), *Max Carrados* [MC] as no. 436 (1943), and *Max Carrados Mysteries* [MCM] as no. 2158 (1964). Probably the first of these is by now a collectors' piece in itself: the price on my copy of *Max Carrados* is 'ninepence'.

[2] This story often appears in anthologies (including the Penguin edition) in an abridged form. The full text can be found in the Bramah volume in the series *Short Stories of To-day and Yesterday* (Harrap, 1929).

the destructiveness of political violence. But even here the Indian was provided with a less alarmingly high-flown motive in that, being financially embarrassed, he hoped to clean up on the railway company's shares. Thirty-five people were killed, but Carrados's business is to exonerate the engine-driver.

Some of the stories are tales of small-scale social embarrassment, like 'The Comedy at Fountain Cottage' [MC 7], which opens with a dish of kidney and liver being thrown over Mrs Bellmark's garden fence and closes with the seasonable discovery of buried treasure: or the dispute with a landlord that aroused suspicions of a 'Ghost at Massingham Mansions' [EMC 5]. On one occasion Carrados is mixed up in the curious and unkind consequences of religious fanaticism, where the supposed abduction of a child turns out to be the scheme of a conscientious doctor who finds the girl suffering from a disorder requiring an operation, but can treat her only by getting her away from her mother, who has been fed crude Christian Science by a comically sentimental American woman. This is 'The Disappearance of Marie Severe' [EMC 2]. The last two pages of this story provide a good deal of quiet fun if one is prepared to accept the serene assumptions of Edwardian anglicans about Christian Scientists from Chicago.

Carrados's part in all this is to use his highly-trained four senses to outwit criminals, or to assist the deficiencies of the righteous, who have to make do with five. Often he takes occasion to remark on the sorry plight of those who have eyes, and who therefore see so little. Sometimes the total effect is a sort of secular translation of the dark saying in St John's Gospel, 'Because you say, we see, your sin remaineth'. The most dramatic demonstration of the positive advantage of blindness is in 'The Game Played in the Dark' [MC 8], in which Carrados, trapped by criminals, manages to fuse the lights and at once has complete command over the sighted men who are in darkness.

The detective-interest in these stories is therefore somewhat limited. The surroundings are romantically spacious and peaceful. It is as much the incidents as the over-all plots that hold the reader's attention. Not infrequently they are comical—like the American who tries to steal the bones of Shakespeare from the parish church at Stratford-on-Avon ('Rigby Lacksome' [MCM 5]). We get used after a time to Carrados's ability to read ordinary print with his fingers, and to hear people's watches ticking, to shoot with deadly accuracy in the dark and to recognise voices. We are constantly surprised, however, by the sheer pleasantness with which Carrados can go one better than his sighted colleagues, and it is not difficult to accept the stories as the description of a character which makes into a gift of genius what to others would be a crippling disability.

But there is another side to all this. Bramah is a wit, a fanciful, occasionally very satirical writer, a dealer in delicacies rather than in hard earthy chunks of life: that is the Bramah we meet in *Kai Lung*, a character who became much more famous than Carrados. Once he has established Carrados as a detective, his unusual mind reaches round for strange things for him to detect. There are two places where Bramah goes clean off the puritan track into the field of the supernatural. This is to break a cardinal regulation in detective writing; its rejection of the supernatural is perhaps its most authentically puritan trait. But Bramah is not so closely wedded to the detective muse as to be incapable of two moments' infidelity.

'The Strange Case of Cyril Bycourt' [MCM 7] is a very odd business. At its opening we seem to be investigating the attempted murder of a child. What Carrados turns up seems to be a ghost story masquerading in the dress of science. The house has recently been equipped with electricity, supplied from a 'dynamo house' in the garden. This source of supply, it is discovered, has been built on what had been, two and a half centuries before, a burial place for victims of the 1665 plague, brought to the village by a tradesman. The boy had been sleeping in such a position that his nose was only a foot or so from the electric output socket. Carrados's diagnosis was that the 'dynamo, designed to transform mechanical force into electrical energy, has here in some obscure way also changed physical effect into psychological experience'. Electric wires cased in piping had been the means of conducting some nameless effluvium from the ancient burial pit into the bedroom and inducing sickness and mental disturbance in the child.

Whether this was a ghost story to Bramah we cannot tell. He probably believed (he makes Carrados say there is 'a record' of some similar supposed experience) that this could happen without supernatural interference. It is not the scientific implausibility of the story that makes it remarkable: it is rather the fact that its author had the notion of bringing a detective tale so close to what was to him the imponderable world. 'We know so lamentably little of electrical energy yet,' says Carrados. Exactly. There was one per cent science and ninety-nine per cent superstition in most educated men of letters in 1920.

That story would hardly be worth two paragraphs of attention were it not for the existence of a more remarkable story still, called simply 'The Eastern Mystery' [EMC 9]. Here a friend of Carrados (whom we have met before in 'Dunstan's Tower' [EMC 3]) calls on him with an extraordinary tale of personal deliverances and providences, the latest of which, a miraculous escape from being run down by a London 'bus, Carrados has actually witnessed. Pressed to amplify this the friend, Tulloch, tells of certain experiences which he had in India, among them the attempt of a devoted Indian whom his medical skill had saved from death to give him an object described in the native's speech as 'the sacred tooth of the ape-god Hanuman'. It was intended to be a gesture of gratitude. Tulloch refused the gift. He knew that the Indian thought it was a charm of incalculable value, and he thought it too precious in the Indian's eyes, and too trivial in his own, to accept. After much of this conversation, Carrados shows that in fact the object had been secreted in the lining of Tulloch's coat by the Indian, who was on other evidence something of a conjuror. He then propounds the theory that it was the presence of this charm on his person that has preserved Tulloch from violent death time after time. But then Carrados goes on to identify the charm.

> 'But now, what is that relic? A monkey's or an ape-god's tooth, an iron-stained belemnite, the fragment of a pagan idol —you and I can smile at that. We are Christians. No matter how unorthodox, no matter how non-committal our attitude may have grown, there is upon us the unconscious and hereditary influence of century after century of blind and implicit faith. To you and me, no less than to every member of the more credent Church of Rome, to everyone who has listened to the story as a little child, it is only conceivable that if miraculous virtues reside in anything inanimate it must pre-eminently be in the close accessories of that great world's tragedy, when, as

> even secular and unfriendly historians have been driven to admit, something out of the order of nature did shake the heavens.'
>
> 'But this . . . this—what is it then?'
>
> 'You described it as looking like a nail. It is a nail. Rusty, you said, and it could not well be otherwise than red with rust. And old. Nearly nineteen hundred years old; quite, perhaps.'

In a sense it is a pity to lay critical hands on that. You either can take it or you cannot. Carrados does not lose his head about it at all. In his matter-of-fact and unembarrassing way he goes on,

> 'It is not only possible, but in one aspect it is very natural. Physically we are dealing with an historical fact. Somewhere on the face of the earth these things must be enduring . . . And among the thousands of relics that the different churches have made claim to it would be remarkable indeed if some at least were not authentic . . . I have offered a solution that explains everything when no other theory will. But there is something else that confronts you. What are you going to do?'

He is going to throw it into the sea.

It will be evident to our reader that our story does not travel along a straight road. There must be deviations and strange scenery. My own purpose in raising this matter at all is this. We are here in something like 1920, and looking at the work of a man of letters who in his fascination with unusual things and his respect for science has constructed a short series of unsensational detective stories. And he has gone off the puritan track. We can see exactly where he left it. We can point to the line. He has written it there:

> There is upon us the unconscious and hereditary influence of century after century of blind and implicit faith.

Religious puritanism denied precisely that. Secular puritanism of the nineteenth century said rather, 'there is upon us the unconscious and hereditary influence of two centuries of rational enquiry'. Once you speak of blind and implicit faith, you are speaking of that which secular puritanism absolutely denies, and which religious puritanism, when it was really speaking authentically, denied at a deeper level. Faith may be implicit, but it is not blind. Those Christians whom Carrados quoted said, or should have said—anyhow, they were instructed by their Founder to say—that blind faith was what they were there to deliver the world from. Coming from a blind man, the defence of blind faith is the more impressive: and that is certainly how things still looked in 1920. But from other directions the argument of the century which has seen the rise and decline of the detective story has urged itself forward towards an inevitable and alarming conclusion concerning the supernatural. The essence of that conclusion is that, whatever else the supernatural has done for us, it is not there to rule men through blind faith. Throughout the ages some people have believed that men are, and always must be, blindly subject to supernatural forces which are known by the technical term 'demonic'. Superstition is the cult of the demonic. Religion has constantly been attacked by its detractors as a cult of the demonic: and its spokesmen and practitioners have given much ground upon which its assailants can stand to deliver that charge. But such speech and action are error, and are known by the genuinely religious to be error.

We have come, then, to a point at which we can establish a fresh and very firm link between the English puritan tradition and the detective story. From every point of view this story, 'The Eastern Mystery', is one which the puritan mind could neither contrive nor accept, not merely because of a puritan suspicion of relics or anything else so superficial. It is because of the puritan suspicion of 'make-believe'. Blind faith is a response to 'make-believe'—being made to believe by demonic forces. Demons are forces which constantly seek to govern human life. In the Gospels they are scattered and defeated. So a certain literary treatment of the supernatural is demonic, and in always resisting it the detective story becomes an anti-demonic gesture. It does not of itself cast out devils, but it does proceed on the assumption that they do not furnish the truth about any human situation. Bramah in nearly all his stories is faithful to that principle: in his desertion of it at this point (or perhaps these two points), he has given us the chance to see what otherwise we should have missed: which is why I keep and treasure my ninepenny volume containing 'The Eastern Mystery'.[3]

[3] In these two paragraphs I have condensed and abridged an argument which in another place I propose to pursue in detail.

8

The Art of Making Objections

AT THIS POINT I must irritate my reader, and outrage the scholars, by introducing a detective character who at first sight will certainly appear anachronistic. H. C. Bailey's Mr Fortune inhabits the world of Poirot, Wimsey and Inspector French, which is the world of the detective novel proper, and we have not really finished with the primitives. But he is relevant here because he makes up the third of the trio whom specifically I wanted to set up against the Holmes-myth.

The Fortune literature proves now (1970) surprisingly difficult to get hold of.[1] There is quite a lot of it—in full-length novels and collections of moderately short stories. He is to be found quite often in anthologies, but the fact that his more briefly recounted adventures are usually presented in some forty pages makes him difficult material for the collector. But, more than this, the 'short' stories are so condensed, and require to be read with such close attention, that they have always looked incongruous among the smoother and usually more trifling offerings in short story bargain-bundles. On the other hand, the long stories have never achieved the kind of staying power with which the Sayers novels have been blessed. Those still regularly appear in paperback editions forty years after their first appearance. So do the Christies, and so do some of the Crofts yarns. But not Fortune. One of the figures we have missed in order to come to Fortune is Father Brown. Fortune is very close to Father Brown, and in the same way elusive, and

[1] Since these two chapters were written it has come to my notice that the work of Bailey and Bramah is currently being reprinted by Lythway Press, Bath. I gladly modify my implications about the non-availability of these books in the light of this news.

for the same reason has failed to capture the popular imagination. So in a sense he is more 'old-fashioned looking' than even Agatha Christie's characters, who are somewhat senior to him but have proved to be better insurance-risks. None the less—indeed, from one point of view precisely because of it—Fortune is something of a treasure; and if you have missed him, or dismissed him in haste, there is a case for advising you to look at him again.

Anyhow, he is as good an example as I know of a rebel disciple of Holmes. Reginald Fortune is a scientist inasmuch as he is a doctor—a high-ranking consultant surgeon. He does not appear to have a West End address, nor do we hear in what area he specialises. He combines a ferocious hedonism with a surging indignation in the face of injustice. He is in many ways a self-conscious opposite of Holmes: he is plump and comfort-loving, having hobbies like designing rose-gardens and making puppet-theatres; he is profoundly lacking in bellicose instincts except when these are channelled through the mind; he is married (not when we first meet him), and he has a peculiar love for children. In this last characteristic he is well ahead of his time: the relation between children and the atmosphere of detective literature has been one of the most difficult problems for the detective novelist, and it is only the much younger contemporaries of H. C. Bailey who manage to handle it with any conviction. It is characteristic of the detective of the fifties, but not of the thirties, to have children of his own. Fortune does not have his own, but he is at his most strenuous in rescuing children from bizarre and repulsive situations when called on to do so.

Certain recurring themes at once mark out the Bailey stories from all the rest. One is children; another is his relations with the police. Always held in respect by them, he is more merciless in his criticism of them than any other amateur in the literature. There must be few stories in which he does not find the opportunity to say blistering things about the 'official mind'; and many of the stories are cast in a form that presents Fortune as the vindicator of the innocent. These stories are more suffused with purple anger than any I know: it is an incandescent passion for justice that authoritatively contradicts the efficiency of an unimaginative police force. Invariably the police apologise gracefully, and after a considerable diet of Fortune one is perhaps liable to react by judging that the police can't be quite as credulous as Bailey has made them.

This isn't the Holmes approach, or the Carrados approach, or (good heavens!) that of Thorndyke. For them it is the solution that is the thing. For Fortune it is the liberation of the innocent, the redressing of injustice, the correction of what would be fatal official error.

This is the kind of thing. (It's difficult to write about him, but ten times more difficult to quote him because he simply cannot be abridged or summarised. This comes at the end of a story in which one policeman has been cleared of corruption [Grice] and another, now dead, convicted of it [Cay]. There has been at least one murder of an underworld character in a tank of acid, and another married couple, also of the underworld, have been cleared of complicity. And so forth: see if you can pick it up.)

> Reggie sat at lunch in the little restaurant which he loves best tasting a new fantasy on the theme of sole and crayfish. 'Yes, joyful.' He smiled benignly. 'With the Montrachet,' he filled Lomas's glass. 'One of my best cases, what? In the simple style. Grice is doing nicely. Rather a mess of shoulder and collar bone. Sorry. The best way, though. It clears him clean, Cay's desperation to kill him.'
>
> 'And to kill himself,' said Lomas.
>
> 'Yes. Very successful experiment. I thought Cay was a realist. Wonder if he led the woman on or she him. Probably she. Female of the species is more dreadful than the male. Sometimes. But he has the better brain. When the wretched Chatty Brown had his mouth stopped in her infernal tanks, Cay knew the pace was getting too hot to last. Made his arrangements to vanish and let her stand the racket. Got across Fishface and Kitty affectionate in the court to fix up a scrap. Left Fishface's blood and his own dentures behind for evidence. Burnt his papers, providin' sketches of Fishface and Kitty as further clues. And retired to keep hens. No, that's not chicken I'm giving you. Veal in a cream sauce. Very able fellow, Cay. But underestimated the simple mind. My mind.'
>
> 'Devilish good your work on that yellow cloth,' said Lomas.
>
> 'You did notice that?' Reggie purred.
>
> 'I take it Cay was in at the death of Chatty Brown.'

'You can, yes. He'd been where nitric acid splashed. Let him explain. I should say the woman's husband will break and blab. If handled.'

'Don't worry,' Lomas smiled.

'I'm not. Finished. Triumph of the art of makin' objections. . . .'

Reggie came into the hospital room where Kitty Evans lay in bed. She gave him a wan smile. 'Is that the best you can do?' he sat down beside her, examined her . . . 'Not a very good girl, are you? You will worry. You shouldn't.' Her eyes filled with tears.

'Oh no. No.' He went to the door and let in a clean Fishface.

'Arty! Oh, Arty!' Kitty rose from her pillows, arms open.

'I'm out, kid,' he flung himself on her.

'Steady. She's not strong.' Reggie grasped his shoulder.

'Plenty of time. You're both out. For good. I object to the deal you've had. Fresh deal now.'[2]

This does pitch us rather suddenly into the age we have not yet quite reached in our time-sequence. Note the novelist's style of conversation. On the one hand there is the Noël Coward drawl, with phonetic affectations which were associated with the upper classes at that date and now sound as foreign as the Dickensian cockney's 'werry good, sir!'. And of course the senior policeman who is Fortune's close friend is the Honourable Sidney Lomas and wears an eyeglass. But it is the condensed, telegraphic style of Fortune's conversation that makes the point. It makes him epigrammatic and often terrifyingly penetrating. In the final conversation in the hospital ward you have his creed: 'I object to the deal you've had.' In the earlier conversation, we have him justifying the suicide of the criminal—a thing he often defends and often needs to defend to Lomas. There was another occasion of that kind which drew a characteristic epigram:

'Good gad!' Lomas exclaimed. 'You knew his heart was rotten and you drove him to it and left him!'

'Drove? Not me, no. The girl drove. Who was safe while she lived? We couldn't put her out of action. Not a chance of a case against her. I left Dean, yes. Left him to choose. He chose well. She can't kill any more. And he's gone to his boy. Best

[2] From the last paragraphs of 'The Yellow Cloth', no. 1 in *This is Mr Fortune* (Gollancz, 1938).

we could do for 'em. Not too bad. I have my uses. Alterations and repairs by R. Fortune.'[3]

That was actually a contrived murder. Mr Fortune doesn't arrange people's lives for their own good, and is quite unrepentant when he can prove the fact.

Background in these stories is always very lightly sketched in. Place names are invariably fictitious, though not insensitively coined. One remembers the industrial town of Radbury in Raddonshire, not far from the cathedral town of Raster. That, anyhow, is not illiterate.[4] And evocations of particular English districts are always powerful, especially in *The Bishop's Crime* and *Black Land, White Land*; Wales is no less pungently described in *Mr Fortune Finds a Pig*. There is much travelling in the stories: Mr Fortune has a very opulent car and a chauffeur who drives faster than anyone else on the road—except Mr Fortune himself. There is a cottage in the Cotswolds. All is ample and leisured, and we do not ever hear of Mr Fortune's being called away from any other work to help with a case; but he is usually called in by the police; he has no 'private practice' except, as it were, by social accident.

If the question were important it would be possible to show that Fortune is a religious man. But I should not go about that project by starting with the evidence of the evangelical hymns which he, like his disreputable contemporary Joshua Clunk, is so fond of quoting. In my time I have wandered about in the field of hymnology, but I have rarely been able to identify the hymns from which either of them quotes. The only one I can place for certain is one which only Methodists know familiarly.[5] The indications come more surely from Fortune's unusual avoidance of profanity in an already loose-speaking age, and from his deep-rooted horror of cruelty and injustice.

Indeed, the impression these tough, involved, convoluted plots always leave is of an unusual urge in the author to show that simple and obedient logic can in the end overthrow the

[3] The last two paragraphs of 'The Key of the Door', no. 6 in *This is Mr Fortune*.

[4] In *Dead Man's Effects* (Macdonald, n.d. [1940]).

[5] 'And are we yet alive and see each other's face': by Charles Wesley, especially associated, I am told, with the opening of the annual Methodist Conference. See 'The Football Photograph', beginning of the second part.

contorted devices of crime or perversity. Fortune, like Father Brown, cultivates an image of 'simplicity'; 'simple mind. My mind.' His constant accusation against the police is that they will not accept evidence. I do not find a Catholic background in all this, but I should defend the conjecture that Mr Fortune has associations with the Society of Friends in his mature years, and remembered these terrible hymns from an evangelical youth. That is a way of saying that I find his cult of simplicity more than a pose. But he is not a very characteristic puritan quaker in his mode of life, for in the thirties such an embracing of the pleasures of the table was not thought of as a quaker trait.

That doesn't matter at all, except for two minor issues to which it leads. One is that the factor which contradicts the puritan ideal we mentioned as being a dynamic in the detective story is, in Mr Fortune, purely foreground material; his pursuit of justice is singularly unsentimental. His sympathy is first for the wrongly accused person and second for the victim.

The other point concerns Joshua Clunk, who is a most entertaining inversion of Fortune. Fortune is all upper-middle class in his attitudes (though his situations are strictly bourgeois or working class ones). Joshua Clunk, a solicitor whose methods and deportment move all respectable solicitors to tears but who has never yet been struck off, is a very good novelist's Methodist. Probably Primitive: just possibly not a Methodist at all but a Pentecostal or Elim; certainly a lay preacher. He drips with comical, yet never really malignant, stage-piety. He has an exceedingly acute mind, and no hobbies at all but lay preaching and—this is where he meets Fortune—successfully vindicating the improbably innocent. Fortune's clients for vindication are usually put-upon people, old lags whom the police suspect in a prejudiced way, defenceless or underprivileged people of one kind or another. So are Clunk's, but usually they are people whom other laywers won't risk their reputations on. He is constantly outwitting the respectable in a maddening and complacent fashion, but one feels that his pose of lush evangelical zeal is as delusive as Fortune's pose of indolence. Both are very much on the side of the angels, and without them there would be less justice in the world—that's the message. A fascinatingly horrid little man—not repulsive like Joanna Cannan's Roger Price: only superficially repulsive; and you, the reader, feel after being thoroughly taken in that you have really been quite wrong about him and had better climb down. This is typical Bailey. You, the reader, are accused of the attitudes which the anti-Clunk, anti-Fortune characters express.

But Clunk and Fortune move in the same world—the world of Sidney Lomas (who hates Clunk as he loves Fortune) and Inspector Bell. They even meet now and again, somewhat inexplicably. They have nothing whatever in common; Fortune would shudder at any direct encounter with Clunk, who is able to sustain such dialogue as this:

> He came to feed the birds, patriotically denying them bread, but making up for it with a rich assortment of fatty scraps. Robins fought for them at his feet, blue-tits ate from his hand, blackbirds grabbed and flew off cursing.
>
> 'Sweet, sweet birds,' Mr Clunk chirped to them.
>
> 'You're just like that dear St Francis,' said Mrs Clunk.
>
> 'Our little sisters and brothers, my love.'[6]

Clunk would wag his finger at Mr Fortune and think him abrupt. But if they share no culture they share the characteristic of being their author's mouthpieces in delivering a social proposition more weighty than one expects in this sort of literature. H. C. Bailey said, 'If detective stories are concerned with crime, they're serious.' They are, when carefully read, quite remarkably serious. They yield very little to a casual reader. They're not really relaxation except for the most observant and the sensitive. If you say that the whole detective literature project is trivial, then they bore and exasperate you, because they refuse to be trivial, and thus essay to carry a weight for which, *ex hypothesi* (your hypothesis, as Mr Fortune would say), they aren't designed. But on another view they are absolutely first class engineering: spare, taut and poised.

One notices, then, how their criticisms of Holmes would run. Bailey would say, on this evidence, that Holmes and Watson were emotionally irresponsible: they had no interest, he would say, in people. Fortune doesn't gush over people, but his creator can describe a person in a snatch of sentence. 'His alarmed eyes saw a woman swelling out of a mink coat in

[6] '*Slippery Ann*' (Gollancz, 1944), p. 29.

crimson silk.'[7] Quite so. You need no more. You get one more sentence but that is all. Watson by comparison is clumsy, subjective and convention-bound in his descriptions of people. Fortune, for all his rotundity and comfortable habit, is more ruthless than Holmes, because he is more directly vulnerable to naked evil.

Thus the novelist naturally disputes with the chronicler. With Mr Fortune we are already in the novelist's age and culture. It is through character that issues are stated and clarified, not through science. And you need be no superman, only a person so ordinary that anything unusual registers at once, to assist in that clarification. But you wouldn't be doing it in that way if Holmes hadn't first done it in his.

[7] 'The Children's Home', no. 2 in *This is Mr Fortune*, p. 49.

9

The Mystery of Iniquity

IN THE YEAR in which Sherlock Holmes was fifty-seven, already retired eight or nine years from his criminal practice, a competitor appeared with whom he would have found it difficult to make conversation. A responsible reconstruction of a collaboration between Holmes and Father Brown would be something of a literary scoop. Father Brown is the first detective character to be produced by an author who was already an established man of letters in many other fields. G. K. Chesterton, thirty-seven in 1911, had already written twenty-one books, including studies of G. F. Watts, Browning, Dickens, Bernard Shaw and Blake, two important theological books, *Orthodoxy* and *Heretics*, four volumes of collected short essays, two long stories, *The Napoleon of Notting Hill* and *The Man Who was Thursday*, some short stories called *The Club of Queer Trades* and some poetry. He was one of the half-dozen best known journalists in the country, and had by this date been called on to write prefaces to no fewer than twenty-two books by other authors. His total number of publications up to the time of his death in 1936 was ninety-six, apart from posthumous matter and ninety prefaces to other works. Undoubtedly Chesterton is the most prolific author in other fields who also wrote detection on any scale. His friend and co-religionist, Ronald Knox, was prolific in other branches of literature, especially theology, although oddly enough he isn't the only Bible translator to have written detection—Freeman Wills Crofts, late in life, produced a version of the Gospels. But Knox's detection is quite insignificant in its own field, while Chesterton's not only is not insignificant—it is the most important single collection we shall be dealing with here.

Father Brown is the most mythological of all detectives. In forty-eight stories[1] published between 1911 and 1935 his creator tells us less about him than we are told about any other comparable detective hero, except possibly Austin Freeman's Dr. Thorndyke.

He is of course a priest of the Roman Catholic Church. His first name begins with a J.[2] (We do at least know that Thorndyke is John.) He manages to get involved in more or less criminal affairs in all sorts of places: but then he has had a varied life. When he was a youngish man he was a Catholic Chaplain in a prison in Chicago;[3] but also in his youth he was the guest of Aristide Valentin, the Paris police chief. Also in his earlier life he had a curacy—perhaps his first appointment—in Hartlepool.[4] A little later, perhaps, he was priest in the Essex village of Cobhole[5] which, presumably during a later London period, he revisited on holiday.[6] He had some time in a charge at Scarborough,[7] but his most active period in criminal affairs was, not surprisingly, while he was priest of St Francis Xavier, Camberwell.[8] It is clear that he paid a second visit to America;[9] and at some time made some kind of missionary visit to Latin America.[10] He seems, indeed, to have led a more restless life than parish priests in the Roman Catholic Church commonly do. And certainly in his free time he manages to get about. We find him in Scotland (*Gow*), in Norfolk (*Saradine*), in Italy (*Thieves*), in Paris (*Garden*—or is this the same visit that included *Hirsch*?), on Exmoor (*Wig*), in Cornwall recovering from an illness (*Pendragons*), near Oxford (*Boulnois*), in 'Heiligwaldstein' (*Fairy Tale*), in Yorkshire (*Dog*—the Scarborough pastorate, perhaps), in Boston, Massachusetts (*Moon Crescent*: perhaps to be tied in with Arrow), in Spain (introduction to *The Secret*), and variously in the English countryside at other times.

But that is all we know. His background when it is mentioned

[1] Most of this chapter will concern itself with only the first four of the five collections, which between them contain forty stories.

[2] *Apollo*, 31. Page references are to Cassell's second collected edition (1947); story-references are by clue word which can be explained by reference to the list on page 240.

[3] *Machine*, 221. [4] *Blue Cross*, 22. [5] *Caesar*, 233. [6] *Gongs*, 270.

[7] *Absence*, 173. [8] *Apollo*, 131. [9] *Arrow*, 333.

[10] *Arrow*, 319, and *Resurrection*.

is always that of a parish, so he is less of a free-lance than his illustrious contemporary, Ronald Knox. His very name, which often contrasts strikingly with the romantic names of his fellow-characters, is designed to suggest that commonplaceness which was his creator's stock-in-trade.

Chesterton himself was as un-commonplace a person as lived in our varied literary society of that time. Huge in person, dynamic in temperament, absolutely unrivalled in quotable wit, Chesterton made himself the champion of the common man; he crusaded for the recognition of the virtues of the common man, not for the redress of his grievances. If you want the doctrine in a nutshell it is in his essay, 'The Twelve Men'[11]—but it is nowhere far to seek in what he writes.

Father Brown is the Catholic Church impersonated as the church of the common man. The stories about him in the first four of the five collections are almost all moral theology presented as detection. It is, therefore, impossible in writing about him to avoid a certain amount of language that recalls moral theology in its popular form. Detective literature is seventy-five per cent moralism anyhow; but here it is entirely moralism.

But it is moralism of a certain kind, which Chesterton was supremely good at stating. It is the sort of moralism in which the morality of the common man is presented as contradicting the morality of sophistication, and as being nearer to that morality of eternity in which the profoundly anti-relativist (and as we should now say anti-existentialist) Chesterton believed. Himself the most sophisticated of writers and the most mannered, Chesterton succeeded in holding his readers in whatever he wrote because he was the one man alive who could write in so mannered a fashion and yet not become a bad writer. He perfected this piece of jugglery more skilfully than any writer, perhaps in any language, ever did; he was a master of fantasy and romance, and a master of literary rhythm and proportion. Consequently nearly all the best written jokes in all literature are his. 'The human race, to which so many of my readers belong. . . .'

This sophistication he turned to the purpose of championing

[11] Reprinted, for example, in K. D. Whitehorn (ed.) *Chesterton Essays* (Cassell, 1953), pp. 18ff.

the common man as citizen of state and of church. When he began to write the Father Brown stories, and up to the time when he finished the first twenty-four of them, he was already a well-known apologist for the Catholic Church, but not himself a Catholic. He was received into the Church near the end of the interval which separates the two halves of the Father Brown collection (the year was 1925). This makes no difference. So far as his interpretation of Catholicism to Englishmen went (or, as his detractors preferred to say, his propaganda), the fact of his being personally received into the Church was hardly more than an historical detail. He made it his business to represent Catholic teaching as sane, commonplace, cheerful, colourful and above all English, to a readership the majority of whom still thought of it as dark, contorted, forbidding, drab and above all foreign.

So his priest was small, inconspicuous, physically negligible, entirely ordinary. He was Father J. Brown. Whenever he was involved in a problem which people who conformed to and were misled by normal ways of thinking had mishandled, Brown cleared up the mystery by cutting through the artificialities with which misdirected thinking had surrounded it, and exposed it as something quite normal and human. He is therefore as concerned as any puritan to strip away 'the supernatural' when it means 'the superstitious' from people's view of a situation. Again and again he does that. He was liable to do it by speaking, in his flat and dull voice, some epigram which in the space of a few words upset the accepted, but erroneous, order of things. He sometimes spoke with passion. But he spoke for that ordinary person whom Chesterton wanted to liberate—for the original man hidden under the chocolate-and-biscuit dado of Victorian and agnostic convention.

What really places this humble clerical Quixote in territory all his own is that in these episodes, which may involve crimes as clear-cut as murder, his moral sense has almost nothing to do with what some believe to be the moral sense behind detective stories. Now much that is said about this is entirely beside the point. The fact that crime is inseparable from detective stories is no argument for their inherent immorality: but it is equally true to say that the fact that crime is found out and punished is not ground on which one can build a respectable argument in their favour. They are 'about' something which is not identifiable by so confined a description as that. It is true—and one can say so, provided one does not inflate the truth into a sort of virtue—that detective stories enshrine the moral axiom that it is wrong to murder, or blackmail, or steal. Father Brown, being a priest of the church of the New Testament, says, in effect, 'We know that: we assume that. But there is a great deal of another kind of wrong about; there is the wrong that preceded the crime, and there is the wrong that has so perverted people's minds that they are now looking in the wrong place for the criminal.' In all the forty-eight stories, there is just one description of even the arrest of a criminal. That is not Father Brown's business.

But then, the crime is by no means always murder. Note how often we have already said that! It is murder in twenty-four of the first forty stories, attempted murder in one; in six it is theft, in one, blackmail. There are two suicides, one case of sacrilege; in four cases no crime has been committed, and in one it is prevented. Restitution in one case annuls an actually committed theft. Two of the murders are historical enigmas solved by Father Brown in the course of conversation long after they took place (*Fairy Tale* and *Broken Sword*).

At the end of many stories you find the clue gently and often evasively given by the priest as he is turning away to go about some routine duty like visiting a deaf school (*Three Tools*). In these parting epigrams, which solve the only mystery Father Brown is interested in (that of how people's minds work), there is almost invariably exposed some error which common custom and carelessness of mind have represented among society to be an axiom. We do not here have to judge whether Chesterton's insights were always right or even whether we agree with them.

Take for example 'The Invisible Man', a story which has become so famous as to be proverbial. Here the puzzle to be solved is how a murderer entered a place into which quite positively nobody was observed to go by the only possible entrance. The answer is that it was the postman—a person whom, because of his uniform and his absolutely regular visits, nobody thought of observing. Now John Dickson Carr, that master of locked-room puzzles who owes so much to Chesterton, would have presented his solution as something which neither the readers nor the characters in the story noticed. Chesterton says, not 'You didn't notice that', but 'You wouldn't notice that'. In that subjunctive the whole business of uncovering the deeper strata of detective literature is implied.

> 'Nobody notices postmen, somehow,' he said thoughtfully; 'yet they have passions like other men, and even carry large bags where a small corpse can be stowed quite easily.'[12]

Half a sentence for moralism, the other half for method: that is Father Brown's way. The story ends not with an arrest but with (in the Catholic sense) a confession.

A similar social moralism is behind the amusing tale of 'The Queer Feet'. Here a theft is committed at a men's dinner by a first-class professional thief who relies on the fact that in evening dress he looks indistinguishable both from the gentlemen who are dining and from the waiters who are serving them. The effect of this episode (Father Brown, by the way, gets the silver back before the thief has had time to dispose of it) is that from that time the members of this particular dining club always wore green dinner jackets.

> 'I say, you really got the goods back, what do you suggest?'
>
> 'Why,' said the colonel, eyeing him with a certain sardonic approval, 'I should suggest that henceforward we wear green coats instead of black. One never knows what mistake may arise when one looks so much like a waiter.'
>
> 'Oh, hang it all!' said the young man. 'A gentleman never looks like a waiter.'
>
> 'Nor a waiter like a gentleman, I suppose,' said Colonel Pound, with the same lowering laughter on his face. 'Reverend sir, your friend must have been very smart to act the gentleman.'
>
> Father Brown buttoned up his commonplace coat to the neck, for the night was stormy, and took his commonplace umbrella from the stand.
>
> 'Yes,' he said; 'it must be very hard work to be a gentleman; but, do you know, I have sometimes thought that it must be almost as laborious to be a waiter.'[13]

[12] *Invisible*, 77. [13] *Queer Feet*, 53.

Note the repetition of 'commonplace', and the double paradox in the punch line. You, the reader, are being gently accused of being over-sophisticated, wrong about the demands of being a gentleman, and wrong about the demands of being a waiter. Chesterton usually gives his stories more than one sting to their tail. You see the same thing near the end of 'The Mistake of the Machine', which turns on the fallibility of a scientist who operates an infallible lie-detector. On the one hand Chesterton, through the mouth of Father Brown, offers comfort to any who are alarmed at the prospect of computerised civilisation (and here, as so often, he is more contemporary in 1970 than he was in his own day); and on the other hand there is the social leg-pull. Father Brown enjoys pulling American legs even more, if that be possible, than pulling English ones. At that date a certain strain in American opinion was much given to belittling English social distinctions such as those represented by peerages, but the end of the story is that Lord Falconroy, whom a certain ex-convict called Drugger Davis was supposed to have murdered, was in fact himself the ex-convict, and in that manifestation had indeed committed a murder.

> 'Why, look here, Mr Usher,' said Father Brown quietly, 'you said the machine couldn't make a mistake; and in one sense it didn't.
>
> 'But the other machine did; the machine that worked it. You assumed that the man in rags jumped at the name of Lord Falconroy because he was Lord Falconroy's murderer. He jumped at the name of Lord Falconroy because he *is* Lord Falconroy. . . .
>
> 'I think you Americans are too modest. I think you idealise the English aristocracy—even in assuming it to be so aristocratic. You see a good-looking Englishman in evening dress; you know he's in the House of Lords; and you fancy he has a father. You don't allow for our national buoyancy and uplift.'[14]

This story has many characteristic Father Brown sayings. There is, indeed, a form of Father Brown oracle every bit as distinguishable as the Sherlock Holmes 'dog in the night-time'. For example, introducing the lie-detector, the priest is heard to say:

[14] *Machine*, 231.

> 'What sentimentalists men of science are! And how much more sentimental American men of science must be! Who but a Yankee would think of proving anything from heart-throbs?' [221]

and again:

> 'What do you mean?' demanded the other. 'Why should he be innocent of that crime?'
>
> 'Why, bless us all,' cried the small man in one of his rare moments of animation, 'why, because he's guilty of the other crimes! I don't know what you people are made of. You seem to think that all sins are kept together in a bag. You talk as if a miser on Monday were always a spendthrift on Tuesday.' [229]

That last is what we now recognise as an old friend in detection —the argument from character; but let it be remembered that in 1914 the argument from character was still regarded as a slippery tool in detection, and also that Chesterton knew its slipperiness better than anybody else, and set his clerical detective to expose its misuse time after time.

Pursuing the subject of superficial quirks in human character which provide a moral pattern for some of the lighter stories in this collection, we may note the pleasant irony of 'The Oracle of the Dog', in which a dog, when invested with mysterious perceptive powers such as dog-sentimentalists are apt to bestow on him, points to one person as the criminal, whereas, when he is treated as a dog, he points to another. 'The dog knows,' says one of the characters to Father Brown; 'the dog was the only mystic in our company'. Later Father Brown says,

> 'The truth is, I happen to be awfully fond of dogs. And it seemed to me that in all this lurid halo of dog-superstitions nobody was thinking of the poor dog at all. . . .
>
> 'A dog is the devil of a ritualist. He is as particular about the precise routine as a child about the precise repetition of a fairy tale. In this case something had gone wrong with the game. He came back to complain seriously of the conduct of the stick. . . .'
>
> 'Why, what had the stick done?' inquired the young man.
>
> 'It had sunk,' said Father Brown.[15]

[15] *Dog*, 64–5.

It had sunk because it was a sword-stick, and the man who threw it into the water, not the one whom later on the dog barked at in the garden, was the guilty party.

Again, there is a world of social and psychological comment in the climax of 'The Man in the Passage', where a series of witnesses at a trial are invited to describe a strange-looking person whom they claimed to have seen in the dark passage behind a theatre. Father Brown demonstrates that what they saw was their own reflection in a mirror which had been slid out into the passage (part of the mechanism of an ingenious crime).

> The judge leaned forward, his old eyes yet more brilliant, and said in specially distinct tones: 'Do you really mean to say that when Sir Wilson Seymour saw that wild what-you-call-him with curves and a woman's hair and a man's trousers, what he saw was Sir Wilson Seymour?'
>
> 'Yes, my Lord,' said Father Brown.
>
> 'And you mean to say that when Captain Cutler saw that chimpanzee with humped shoulders and hog's bristles, he simply saw himself?'
>
> 'Yes, my Lord.'
>
> 'And can you tell us why you should know your own figure in a looking-glass when two such distinguished men don't?'
>
> Father Brown blinked even more painfully than before; then he stammered: 'Really, my Lord, I don't know . . . unless it's because I don't look at it so often.' [220]

At times Chesterton uses the same ironic technique to take us into deeper waters. There are occasions, for example, when Father Brown has to indict his witnesses of insular prejudice against foreigners before he can get at the truth. The most elaborate of these constructions is 'The God of the Gongs', which at its climax produces this.

> 'Malvoli has nothing to do with it. I dare say he has some Italians with him, but our amiable friends are not Italians. They are octoroons and African half-bloods of various shades, but I fear we English think all foreigners are the same so long as they are dark and dirty. Also . . . I fear the English decline to draw any fine distinction between the moral character

> produced by my religion and that which blooms out of voodoo.' [281]

What the later twentieth century knows as 'colour bar' prejudice had no interest either way for Chesterton. What was thoroughly topical (what, for example, is especially conspicuous in Wilkie Collins) is the English assumption that Voodoo and Roman Catholicism are all one. That was topical enough.

'The Salad of Colonel Cray' plays the same tune in a different key—the presence of a foreigner (an Indian this time) who generates an atmosphere of superstition in the military mind of a typically insular Englishman, and the passion of an author who believes in the equality of the rights of all men to deny the equality of religions. The crime which he manages to avert is, the priest insists, 'the crime of a white man', for all the suspicions, in which a good churchgoing woman has shared, that it was the crime of the Indian [291].

Bogus religion, or the belief that all religions or any mixture of religions are as good as Catholic Christianity, forms the surprising background of several other stories. 'The Wrong Shape', which contains some pleasant Holmes-like detection through detail, contains also an indictment of nature-worship and humanism, and, for good measure, it brings in a mysterious Indian for the usual purpose of throwing mystical dust in the reader's eyes. 'The Hammer of God' is an unusually grave and haunting exposure of the symbolism of towers—the exaltation of a church spire perverted into the kind of pride which William Golding so memorably handled in his novel *The Spire*. 'The Eye of Apollo' is a commentary on that sun-worship which formed the background (to mention only one very distinguished example) of the religion of Constantine the Great. In this story the high-priest of a revived sun-worship gains such ascendancy over a naïve woman that he persuades her to stare at the sun until she goes blind.

> 'It came with this precious prophet, or whatever he calls himself, who taught her to stare at the hot sun with the naked eye. Oh, if these new pagans would only be old pagans, they would be a little wiser! The old pagans knew that mere naked sun-worship had a cruel side. They knew that the eye of Apollo can blast and blind.' [142]

'The Secret Garden' is, of course, based on the fanatical and materialistic anti-clericalism of classical post-Revolutionary France. The chief of police has murdered a millionaire who was about to make a dramatic donation to the Church. The millionaire is a 'scatterbrained sceptic' but is 'drifting to' the Church; as for Valentin, the murderer, 'he would do anything, *anything*, to break what he called the superstition of the Cross. He has fought for it, he has starved for it, and now he has murdered for it.' Only by understanding what a man of this temper would do to bring down the Church could the priest solve that particular mystery [38].

Then there is that hilarious business called 'The Resurrection of Father Brown'—the first of the 1926 stories. Outwardly this has something of the Reichenbach Falls in its atmosphere; for a few pages we are in no doubt that Father Brown is dead, murdered at the mission station in Latin America where he is doing special duty. During the ceremonial lying-in-state he comes to life and sits up comically in his coffin, and everybody thinks that he has indeed risen from the dead, to which, as soon as he can find a voice, he can only splutter, 'Oh, you *silly* people . . . God bless you and give you more sense.'

It turns out to have been a hoax. Drugged, given out to be dead, he 'comes back to life': the people take it for a miracle: then the sceptical enemies of the Faith will expose the whole story and show the whole town how the church has deceived it. Behind it all is (guess what) an American journalist [320]. But what the journalist managed to use as part of the equipment for his conspiracy was one of Father Brown's rare essays in clerical journalism; it seemed that in some peppy article, desiring to illustrate the strength of his purpose in getting rid of gross corruptions in that land, he had written, 'I am ready to die and come back to life again like Sherlock Holmes, if that is the best way'. Considering all the circumstances, this is perhaps the most remarkable thing that Father Brown ever said, and if his grotesquerie was not pointed out to him by his bishop, he did at least have ample chance to repent it. He only just managed to get the truth exposed and the record set straight.

All this indicates that in Chesterton's stories there is a very powerful religious interest. This need be no disadvantage in the secular age which during Chesterton's lifetime was beginning, and which has since his death thoroughly set in. For the message always is that true religion is as rational and as human and as popular as a detective story, and that its business is to release the truth from the prison in which bogus religion has locked it. In the books which he was writing at the same time as the Father Brown stories, Chesterton was constantly saying that religion is not an esoteric activity proper for specialists or the bourgeois or the anti-socially pious, but a commonplace thing as familiar, as rugged, as uncompromising and as admirable as the common man himself. As might be expected from a Catholic apologist, the English puritan habit of mind was often his target, and surface-puritanism was normally the best example for his purpose of bogus religion. Chesterton rarely expressed a hatred of Protestantism such as his friend Hilaire Belloc constantly expressed, but like Ronald Knox he was really angered by what he took to be puritanism. In one weird and terrible story, 'The Sign of the Broken Sword', Father Brown demolishes the reputation of a local hero by examining his character, starting from his puritanism.

> 'Sir Arthur St Clare, as I have already said, was a man who read his Bible. That was what was the matter with him. When will people understand that it is useless for a man to read his Bible unless he also reads everybody else's Bible? A printer reads a Bible for misprints. A mormon reads his Bible and finds polygamy; a Christian Scientist reads it and finds we have no arms and legs. St Clare was an old Anglo-Indian Protestant soldier. Now just think what that might mean; and for heaven's sake don't cant about it. It might mean a man physically formidable living under a tropic sun in an Oriental society, and soaking himself, without sense or guidance, in an Oriental book. Of course he read the Old Testament rather than the New. Of course he found in the Old Testament everything he wanted—lust, tyranny, treason. Oh, I daresay he was honest, as you call it. But what is the good of a man being honest in his worship of dishonesty?' [153]

This is one of the best Father Brown stories, partly because of the effortless and inevitable inclusion of so many memorable sayings. To put together two separated passages in it:

> 'Where does a wise man hide a pebble?'
> 'On the beach.'
> 'Where does a wise man hide a leaf?'
> 'In the forest.'
> 'But what does he do if there is no forest? He grows a forest to hide it in. A fearful sin.' [146, 149]

But as the story goes on it provides two false solutions to the mystery (which is the reason for the legendary broken sword always associated with General St Clare and reproduced on the statue they are standing under). Flambeau, Father Brown's closest friend, proposes first that the General went mad. The priest replies:

> 'A horrid story . . . but not the real story . . . Yours is a clean story, a sweet, pure, honest story, as open and white as that moon. Madness and despair are innocent enough. There are worse things, Flambeau.' [148]

Second, when it is made clear that St Clare had reason to seek the death of one of his officers who could expose him, Flambeau suggests that he murdered him under cover of battle.

> 'You are still full of good and pure thoughts,' said the other. 'It was worse than that.'

Then follows the passage about ignorantly reading the Bible—the attack on puritan values; then the truth—that St Clare murdered his enemy first, then arranged a suicidal battle to cover it, thus planting the forest in which to hide his leaf.

That is a dark business in which we are told that Father Brown was 'deeply moved'. A much more light-hearted affair, but one whose narration uses the same technique of 'false solutions', and the same background of ignorant Protestantism (but this time honest protestantism), is 'The Honour of Irsael Gow', which is the only story situated in Scotland. The strange secret burial of the last of the Glengyles and the weird collection of miscellaneous treasures laid out in the house by the half-witted gardener, Gow, provide the starting point. Father Brown, challenged to show any rational connection between some heaps of snuff, some torn manuscripts, the inner machinery of a clock and a collection of jewels without their settings, produces offhand two plausible explanations neither of which he supposes for a moment to be the right one. He is up to that point urging his hearers not to be over-hospitable to mystery and spookery. But the true explanation is a story of literal honesty, beginning with an illiterate village lad who, given a sovereign for a tip in mistake for a farthing, returned with nineteen shillings and elevenpence three farthings change, and ending with that same lad in old age, having been left for his pains 'all the gold of the Glengyles', systematically removing the gold from every object Glengyle had—even the gold from his teeth—and leaving in the house everything that the removal of the gold had left—the machinery of gold watches, the stones that had gold settings, the pages that had gold illuminations, the snuff that had been in gold snuff boxes. It is a study in fundamentalist honesty, beginning with a nobleman's obsession with it and ending with a peasant's response to it [88]. There is no crime. The literalism of the Scottish presbyterian peasant is followed to its lunatic conclusion: it looks fantastic, but not ignoble.

Coming back to that which, being English, can receive the epithet 'puritan', we have another story in the darker tone in 'The Three Tools of Death'. The mixture here is complicated by its central character's being once again a Scot, but the scene is English. Of a certain Sir Aaron Armstrong (Scottish with a dash of the Old Testament, no doubt), whom we are about to meet as a corpse, we are told this:

> Although Sir Aaron was a philanthropist, and thus dealt with the darker side of our society, he prided himself on dealing with it in the brightest possible style. His political and social speeches were cataracts of anecdotes and 'loud laughter'; his bodily health was of a bursting sort; his ethics were all optimism; and he dealt with the Drink problem (his favourite topic) with that immortal or even monstrous gaiety which is so often the mark of the prosperous total abstainer. [158]

For Chesterton, if puritans were a vile kind of protestant, the total abstainer was the vilest kind of puritan. He continues:

> The established story of his conversion was familiar on the more puritanic platforms and pulpits: how he had been, when only a boy, drawn away from Scotch theology to Scotch whisky, and how he had risen out of both and become (as he modestly put it) what he was . . . He was, one felt, the most seriously merry of all the sons of men. [*Ib.*]

The solution of the problem set to Father Brown lies in the improbable fact that this cheerful and self-confident person committed suicide. The unlikeliness of this, which led others to suspect that he had been murdered by a person towards whom circumstantial evidence pointed, was exploded in a series of moral fireworks. Having established that the presence of a noose, a knife and a pistol implies not a direct lead to a murderer but a mysterious superfluity of 'tools of death', and shown in what other ways these were actually used, Father Brown says—

> 'All these grisly tools, the noose, the bloody knife, the exploding pistol, were instruments of a curious mercy. They were not used to kill Sir Aaron but to save him.'
>
> 'To save him! . . . and from what?'
>
> 'From himself. He was a suicidal maniac.'
>
> '*What?* . . . And the religion of Cheerfulness——?'
>
> 'It is a cruel religion.' [167]

Father Brown all through has been sceptical about the cheerfulness which others took for kindness. 'Was anyone in the house cheerful but he?' he asks [159], and a little later he says, 'People like frequent laughter but I don't think they like a permanent smile. Cheerfulness without humour is a very trying thing' [160]. The story, in which Father Brown shows how everybody hated this universally and publicly benevolent man, proves that the only possible solution that covers the moral facts as well as the physical ones is suicide. The moral and pathological clues are perfectly recognisable by any reader who seeks to anticipate the solution. Chesterton is justifiably sure that few will, for how many people in those days had the least suspicion that anything was wrong with radiantly benevolent Christianity?

10

The Fairy Tale and the Secret

> 'I won't discuss whether we can be killed by something that happened in the thirteenth century; but I'm jolly certain that we can't be killed by something that never happened in the thirteenth century, something that never happened at all.'[1]

SENTIMENTALITY ABOUT HISTORY and religion is inevitably attributed by Chesterton to Americans, but a readiness to believe in mystery and the supernatural intervention of irrational forces is the chief impediment to the rational explanation of problems wherever anybody lives. That is what Father Brown firmly believes. There is a close connection, his theology teaches him, between error and unreason. Some of the stories naturally emphasise the error, some equally naturally the unreason, but in the best of them the two are joined. Just as in his argumentative and polemical books Chesterton constantly exposed the error of popular assumptions by showing them to be emotional and irrational and usually generated by groundless fear and ignorance of the way in which people's minds work, so in the Father Brown stories he traces every crime, or supposed crime, back to the same sources. And when he has finished the reader finds that it is not now the punishment of the crime that interests him; he has been given a new and alarming light on universal human nature, and that is what sticks in his memory.

The conversation with Flambeau that ends 'The Flying Stars' contains the conversion of Flambeau from a life of romantic Robin Hood lawlessness to a life given to the prevention of crime; and this is achieved by simply pointing out that

[1] *Golden Cross*, 402.

Robin Hood, whatever the romancers say, will certainly descend from the heroic to the mean before he has finished [64]. The point of 'The Sins of Prince Saradine' is, characteristically, the danger of morally, as well as intellectually, underrating an enemy [117]. The point of 'The Head of Caesar' is the power of greed to corrupt, which is concealed by the apparently blameless pursuit of the 'collector', who can turn out to be no better than a miser [244]. 'The Vanishing of Vaudrey' is a study in hatred, and in the cure of hatred [540]. Here the point is a simple moral one, without much subtlety but with sufficient unexpectedness to get home to the reader.

Two American stories in *The Incredulity* have usually searching moral implications. 'The Arrow of Heaven' is very subtle, and builds up to a devastating moral climax. It is a 'locked room' case, and, as often in these tales, the people concerned are inclined, from an irreligious or superstitiously agnostic background, to invoke the supernatural as the only cause. Gradually it appears that a socially negligible person is the murderer, upon which vengeance is called for by the American devotees of justice. The priest, who has resisted their notions of justice, in the end insists on common justice. The negligible man (Daniel Doom) and the eminent man (Brander Merton) have been shown to be the same person, and so—

> 'No!' Father Brown cried, in a voice like a pistol shot. 'There shall be no difference. I gave you your chance of pitying the poor devil when you thought he was a common criminal. You wouldn't listen then: you were all for private vengeance then. You were all for letting him be butchered like a wild beast without a hearing or a public trial, and said he had only got his deserts. Very well, then, if Daniel Doom has got his deserts, Brander Merton has got his deserts. If that was good enough for Daniel Doom, by all that's holy it's good enough for Merton. Take your wild justice or our dull legality: but in the name of Almighty God let there be equal lawlessness of equal law.' [351]

'The Miracle of Moon Crescent', another story set in America, makes in the end much the same point. The physical circumstances are, indeed, somewhat bizarre and demanding of credulity. But the moral punch-line is here:

> Fenner laughed, and then looked puzzled. 'I don't understand one thing,' he said. 'If it was Wilson, how did Wynd come to have a man like that on such intimate terms? How did he come to be killed by a man he'd seen every day for years? He was famous for being a judge of men.'
>
> Father Brown thumped his umbrella on the ground with an emphasis he rarely showed.
>
> 'Yes,' he said, almost fiercely; 'that was how he came to be killed. He was killed for just that. He was killed for being a judge of men. . . . What is any man that he should be a judge of men?' [386]

Contempt is a quality hateful to the common man, and therefore to Chesterton and to his priest. It is the clue to the character of the criminal in 'The Man with Two Beards' [496]. But contempt, double standards, hypocrisy, and the perversion of charity itself are all brought together in the climax of the last of these stories, which in most ways is the finest of all—'The Chief Mourner of Marne'.

There is nothing for it but to quote a passage from this story at some length. I call it the finest of the stories because it seems to me to contain all those qualities and devices which distinguish the Father Brown stories; to those to whom Father Brown is rarely interesting or entertaining, this is the most boring of the tales; to those who find them remote and unrealistic, this is the remotest; to those who are exasperated by their Christian emphasis, this is the least tolerable of all because its theological content is more uncompromising than that of any of the rest.

This is 'The Arrow of Heaven' over again, but more violently presented. It is a story to be savoured. Its central figure, the Marquis of Marne, has shut himself away in a remote castle. His personal name, as we gather, is James Mair. He is popularly believed to have become a recluse because of the guilt he feels at having killed a brother to whom he was devoted. He killed him, according to the story, after a duel. A certain ruthless Canadian newspaper reporter with violently anti-clerical views is determined to release the story that this sense of guilt has been fostered by priests of the Catholic Church, of which, unlike most of those close to him, the Marquis was a member. Father

Brown, who comes into the story by plausible courses, is determined not only to prove that the newspaper proprietor (Sir John Cockspur) is about to disseminate a malicious lie, but that the whole story is based on an error.

He finds that the relatives of this mysterious and melancholy marquis are anxious to be reconciled to him, and increasingly indignant that he should be incarcerated in his own castle by a sense of guilt which they are prepared to absolve. Father Brown, after making enquiries, begs them not to attempt it. He insists that unhappiness will come of it. As the story works towards its peak, he meets the family outside the castle, about to go in and force reconciliation on its unhappy owner.

> 'Look here,' he said in his simple, bothered, fashion, 'I told you you'd much better leave him alone. He knows what he's doing and it'll only make everybody unhappy.'
>
> Lady Outram, who was accompanied by a tall and quietly-dressed lady, still very handsome, presumably the original Miss Grayson, looked at the priest with cold contempt.
>
> 'Really, sir,' she said, 'this is a very private occasion, and I don't understand what you have to do with it.'
>
> 'Trust a priest to have to do with a private occasion,' snarled Sir John Cockspur. 'Don't you know they live behind the scenes like rats behind a wainscot burrowing their way into everybody's private rooms? See how he's already in possession of poor Marne.'
>
> 'Oh, that's all right,' said Father Brown, with the impatience of anxiety. 'I've talked it over with the marquis and the only priest he's ever had anything to do with; his clerical tastes have been much exaggerated. I tell you he knows what he's about, and I do implore you all to leave him alone.'
>
> 'You mean leave him to this living death of moping and going mad in a ruin?' cried Lady Outram, in a voice that shook a little. 'And all because he had the bad luck to shoot a man in a duel more than a quarter of a century ago. Is that what you call Christian charity?'
>
> 'Yes,' answered the priest stolidly; 'that is what I call Christian charity.'
>
> 'It's about all the Christian charity you'll ever get out of these priests,' cried Cockspur, bitterly. . . . [579–80]

The occupant of the castle, we later learn, is not James Mair at all (the supposed remorseful duellist) but his brother Maurice, who, pretending to have been shot in the duel, shot his brother while he was bending over him hoping to revive him. The shock of discovering this, which the priest had sought to spare them, brought out in the relatives a torrent of vindictiveness. Upon this Father Brown takes up the tale again.

> 'Are you sure of this?' asked Sir John at last, in a thick voice.
>
> 'I am sure of it,' said Father Brown, 'and now I leave Maurice Mair, the present Marquis of Marne, to your Christian charity. You have told me something today about Christian charity. You seem to me to give it almost too large a place; but how fortunate it is for poor sinners like this man that you err so much on the side of mercy, and are ready to be reconciled to all mankind.'
>
> 'Hang it all,' exploded the general; 'if you think I'm going to be reconciled to a filthy viper like that, I tell you that I wouldn't say a word to save him from hell. I said I would pardon a regular decent duel, but of all the treacherous assassins——'
>
> 'He ought to be lynched,' cried Cockspur excitedly. 'He ought to burn alive like a nigger in the States. And if there is such a thing as burning for ever, he jolly well——'
>
> 'I wouldn't touch him with a barge-pole myself,' said Mallow.
>
> 'There is a limit to human charity,' said Lady Outram, trembling all over.
>
> 'There is,' said Father Brown, drily; 'and that is the real difference between human charity and Christian charity. . . .'
>
> 'But hang it all,' cried Mallow, 'you don't expect us to be able to pardon a vile thing like this?'
>
> 'No,' said the priest; 'but *we* have to be able to pardon it.' [582–3]

There is some danger, I am aware, that the reader will by now have become sated with the implied moralism of all this—mine, I mean, not Chesterton's. Without reprinting the whole Father Brown series *in extenso* I see no way of demonstrating beyond question Chesterton's innocence of the charge of dragging moralism in so that Father Brown may be given a chance to preach. But innocent he is. The artistry of the stories is not in their moralism, but in the skill which makes the reader miss the moralism altogether until his third or fourth reading. That is why the Father Brown stories are almost universally misunderstood.

Some time about 1950 Christopher Bush wrote a comical detective story, *Case for Four Detectives*, which set the scene for a criminal puzzle and then brought in four characters, each of whom tried to provide a solution, and all of whom were beaten to the truth by an imperfectly educated village policeman. The four characters were Christopher Bush's re-creations of Sherlock Holmes, Lord Peter Wimsey, Hercule Poirot and Father Brown. In each case the author endowed the character with what he had recognised as the outward qualities that his originator had given him—Holmes's feverish activism, Poirot's indolent sedentary reasoning, Wimsey's modish clubmanship, and Father Brown's talent for obscure and oracular epigrams. It was a frivolous lampoon which assumed that these characters could be re-created by dressing puppets up in their clothes. The point it made about Father Brown, however, was that this was how a casual reader saw him. In consequence not a single thing he said made sense. The careless reader finds his paradoxes tiresome, and the reader who neither shares nor accepts his values is at a loss to understand what he is talking about, and is mystified by the notion that it can be important. It is nonsense to say that Father Brown reaches his solutions by the exercise of some esoteric, even psychic, gift that can express itself only in oracular utterances of delphic ambiguity. I know of a few unsafe paradoxes in Chesterton's more exuberant essays: I can find none in Father Brown. He represents not paradox but plain dissent. He firmly rejects what is bogus in humanistic and materialistic thought, representing Catholic doctrines as, precisely, common sense. It is found always to be sentimental materialism which has thrown people off the track. It is always entertaining, therefore, when materialists in the stories are prepared to invoke the supernatural, only to be brought back by the priest of the exotic mysteries of the Church to an earthly, natural, solution. This takes us back to 'The Miracle of Moon Crescent':

> 'You all swore you were hard-shelled materialists; and as a matter of fact you were all balanced on the very edge of belief—of belief in almost anything. There are thousands balanced on

> it today; but it's a sharp, uncomfortable edge to sit on. You won't rest till you believe something; that's why Mr Vandam went through new religions with a toothcomb, and Mr Alboin quotes Scripture for his religion of breathing-exercises, and Mr Fenner grumbles at the very God he denies. That's where you all split. It's natural to believe in the supernatural. It never feels natural to accept only natural things.' [386]

But the balance against an over-moralistic appreciation of these stories is restored by recalling that in several of them the leg-pull is almost entirely intellectual. I have already stated my preference for the last of the stories over any of the others, but in another mood I might well select the very first, 'The Blue Cross'. Nowhere else does Father Brown indulge in such epic clowning as in that heroic chase of Flambeau which is made to appear like a leisurely excursion through London. There are moments here that the creator of Holmes might well have given a year's royalties for.

> ' "Here," I says to the chap, who was nearly out of the door, "you've paid too much."
>
> ' "Oh," he says, "have we?" . . . "Sorry to confuse your accounts, but it'll pay for the window."
>
> ' "What window?" I says.
>
> ' "The one I'm going to break," he says, and smashes that blessed pane with his umbrella.' [17]

That is the stuff out of which *The Man who was Thursday* and *The Flying Inn* were made. It introduces Father Brown as an inconspicuous little Quixote who is going to be one too many for the magnificent Flambeau; it introduces Aristide Valentin, Chief of the Paris Police, who is chasing Flambeau but cannot find him without encountering Father Brown and using Father Brown's clues. It is the very next story in which Valentin's materialistic passions bring him to his death, and the next but one after that brings Flambeau on to the side of the angels. But that opening story is symbolic of the principle of dissent from the obvious and accepted conventions of life that is the junction between the Father Brown stories and the main line of detective fiction. Father Brown is in his way as romantic (by the same canons we used in judging Holmes romantic) as Holmes himself. The décor is rarely anything but distant, impressionistic, and slightly uncanny. The names are as evocative as Doyle's, 'Pendragon', 'Saradine', 'Boulnois', 'Bohun', to say nothing of Flambeau himself. It is the 'dissent against convention' colour in romanticism that Father Brown supplies in his own person, leaving the rest to the subsidiary characters and exotic background of the scenes into which he makes his way. For Chesterton human life always was like that—a counterpoint between the familiar and the fantastic. (His devotees will remember his special love for such adjectives as 'wild' and such images as 'sword'); and indeed the Church and its faith were likewise for him a counterpoint between reason and romance—the reason of St Thomas Aquinas and the pageantry of the Mass.

So when the dogmatic content of the stories is relatively distant, they usually turn on the detective writer's device of 'misdirection', which is almost universal, and on secular detection, which it is only Chesterton's distinction to have related so intimately with morality. In 'The Duel of Dr Hirsch', 'The Perishing of the Pendragons', 'The Strange Crime of John Boulnois', 'The Song of the Flying Fish' and 'The Worst Crime in the World' the point is entirely gained through misdirection. Nobody is made to appear a moral illiterate because he did not see the point; Father Brown is no more than the only person present who follows the Holmesian maxim of accepting the improbable as true when every alternative is clearly impossible, and he does not need to be a priest to do that. On two occasions only do we get anything approaching the '140 varieties of cigar ash'—the display of special knowledge. In 'The Actor and the Alibi' the solution is plain to Father Brown because he alone of those present sees the suggestiveness of the play's being *The School for Scandal* (in which one actor is for some time on stage but invisible), while in 'The Doom of the Darnaways' the title of a book on a bookshelf, 'The History of Pope Joan', suggests, because of its non-existent subject, a non-existent book, a dummy bookshelf, and a secret passage. (This was a shade risky: some people have believed in the existence of a Pope Joan, and Brown's disbelief was dogmatic rather than historical.) But those two very mild displays of special knowledge are the only examples of their kind, and the Father Brown stories are therefore the purest examples in the whole field of detection through faculties which are common to everybody.

Lest there be any residual doubt in the reader's mind about the interpretation of the stories which I am here offering, two more brief quotations should resolve it for good. Half-way through that passionate tale about justice and double standards to which we have already referred, 'The Arrow of Heaven', a sceptical character says this to Father Brown:

> 'You're very smart, but there's more to you than smartness. Somehow you're the sort of man to whom one wants to tell the truth.' [339]

And in that introduction to the fourth series, called *The Secret of Father Brown*, the priest is found among a gathering of people who are leading him on to explain by what kind of intuition he produced so many solutions to puzzles that baffled the experts; they have spoken of the literary detectives, Dupin and Holmes, and the subject of the occult and of 'second sight' has begun to rear its head. Somebody says that some crank has been giving lectures on second sight with illustrations from the Father Brown cases. 'Oh, I say,' says the priest, 'this will never do.' Then the secret:

> 'It was I who killed all those people.' [464]

A long explanation follows, which is the purest moral theology you could find.

> 'I try to get inside the murderer. . . . Indeed, it's more than that, don't you see? I am inside a man, I am always inside a man, moving his arms and legs; but I wait till I know I am inside a murderer, thinking his thoughts, wrestling with his passions; till I have bent myself into the posture of his hunched and peering hatred. . . .' [465]

There we go beyond even moral theology; we go direct to the central theology of redemption and atonement, and there is no more to be said about that in this place.

What does concern us is the implications of the statement that this is something you cannot imagine Holmes or Dupin (or Thorndyke or Carrados) being made to say. We have here entirely departed from the 'superman' tradition of detection. Father Brown neither looks nor behaves like a superman, and any attempt to build him up into a superman arouses his alarm and anger (as in 'The Resurrection'). He does not detect crime by making himself larger than the criminal, nor confound the established police force by demonstrating greater skill or education than its members have. There are two layers, as it were, in the structure of thought he always erects to solve a mystery. One is common to him and Holmes—reason, but Father Brown's reason is far less vulnerable than Holmes's. He certainly protests against the distortions of reason which lead others to false conclusions, and this is what all the other classic detectives do. That is one layer. But the other is this direct contradiction of the superman tradition; he pursues his object by making himself less, not greater, than the criminal, by 'getting inside him', as he puts it: by never allowing himself to say, 'That's a thing I could never have done'.

This isn't a brilliant *tour-de-force* by Chesterton; it is no more than an accurate observation of human nature and human communications. You may outwit a criminal by superior skill, but you do not identify him or vindicate an innocent person by superior moral goodness—the very idea makes nonsense. This is the same kind of operation that Chesterton was engaged in in all his other writings. At the bottom of it is a comprehensive cosmic optimism which has its roots in the eighteenth century and which he shared with nobody else in the twentieth. He really did believe in the fundamental goodness of the common man. Evil in the common man was an exception to the design. That was what nobody else really believed, and what to a much greater extent everybody positively disbelieves now. The normal belief is that man is evil and that goodness is an exception or an accident. To Father Brown any criminal is a good man gone wrong. He is not an evil man who has cut himself off from the comprehension or sympathy of those who labour to be good. Consider the laborious rectitude of all the characters in 'The Chief Mourner of Marne', and how vulnerable and brittle the priest shows it to be. The way he talks makes it perfectly plain that if they were the people accused of a crime his patience with them would be as unflappable as is his patience with the man they are now accusing.

One effect of noticing this is to explain the unusual attitude to violence which these stories show. Violence is the ground on which many well-intentioned and sentimental critics attack the detective story. Here anyhow is the evidence for saying that it is an accident of such stories, not a property; for here there is virtually none, apart from that which produced the crime. Who could be less of an apostle of violence than Father Brown? Where in all the literature is violence so certain not to be met with violence? As I shall later argue, the 'violence' argument against detective stories is the weakest link in the case brought against them. But even Holmes was a good boxer, and Carrados knew where to lay hands on a revolver.

But there is more to say than simply that Father Brown was non-violent. Chesterton himself was a study in controlled and directed violence. His writing is full of the imagery of war, wildness, and power. Himself a massively peaceable person, he was called by the Pope himself at the time of his death a 'Defender of the Faith' (an expression used in a Papal pronouncement only once before in history, and then of an equally corpulent but less felicitous character in Catholic history, King Henry VIII); but in that 'Defender' the militancy of Chesterton's crusade against error and despair was by design implied. Neither he nor his creature, Father Brown, was incapable of anger, or of courage, or of decisive dissent from a popular view. They were both men of violent passion and of controlled moral strength. Their violence was harnessed to actions that were palpably and unquestionably peaceable: the author's in his emphatic and polemical prose (to say nothing of his poetry), the creature's in his passion against hypocrisy and distorted thought.

Chesterton, we said, was the only author of detection who has written so much else in so many literary forms. Other detective authors have written non-detective fiction, and one or two others have written even theology; and a few people have written one or two detective tales as a sideline from the main track of quite different work. Only with Chesterton do we have a major contribution to detective literature which is doing the same thing as his other work is doing—using fantastic means instead of argumentative means to get the same thing said about something of primary importance, in this case his optimism about the common man's common sense. Father Brown's arguments against the erratic judgements of those whose company he kept are the same kind of argument which Chesterton used against the moral cranks of his time (as he judged them); without entering into debate here on the question whether he was right about eugenics, the Suffragettes, or the then modernistic theology of the Bishop of Birmingham (Dr Barnes—a special enemy of his), it is clear that the people who are made to look ridiculous in the stories are the same people who are pulverised in the essays.

I have often wondered, therefore, why the Father Brown stories of Chesterton are of so different a quality from the detective stories, long or short, of Ronald Knox. Knox (1888–1957) was Chesterton's younger contemporary, and an equally brilliant essayist, equally committed to the defence of a Catholic Church which was still subject to much sentimental and ignorant popular calumny. Knox was as entertaining as Chesterton in his way, as popular a writer, and a far more sought-after public speaker. His detective stories are as workmanlike and unmemorable as a hymn-tune by Elgar. They show all the surface excellences of good writing (and in the 1920's, when he wrote them, that was surely something), but there was not a character in them who stayed in the mind after the book was closed, neither was there a plot or situation which anyone remembers with any sense of revelation. So far as they are anything, they are late classical rather than high romantic in style—Thorndyke rather than Christie or Sayers. But I fancy the reason can be extracted from what we have just said. It is a matter of history that Knox wrote his detective stories to get funds to furnish the new Catholic Chaplaincy at Oxford. They had nothing more than that to do with what in the rest of his literary work he was about. Moreover, Knox's was a colder, more analytical mind. He was a wit, not, like Chesterton, a humorist. He could compose Ximenes crosswords and write those brilliant 'Essays in Satire'; he could burlesque and parody in more languages than one; in these ways he could do things that Chesterton could not have done if his next meal depended on doing them. This meant that he was one of those writers—and this is not to say a word against them—who in their writings can switch out or switch in their personal convictions as the subject requires. Such men are usually better writers than those who cannot switch their convictions out, but Chesterton was of the other kind, and the gravamen of the charge that his detractors bring against the highly idiosyncratic manner of his writing is precisely that.

It was this, then, that made Chesterton, through the accident of his hitting on a successful detective form, a major contributor to the literature. Having found his way into this field, he managed in the Father Brown stories to raise all the most awkward questions which make it difficult to dismiss the form as a trivialisation of the novelist's art. Having said that, I should be prepared to defend the proposition that his lighter tales, *The Club of Queer Trades* and *The Paradoxes of Mr Pond*, are just as much 'pure' Chesterton as Father Brown is. They, like the last, and in some ways (compared with the earlier ones) apocryphal Father Brown stories, *The Scandal of Father Brown*, are amiable intellectual leg-pulls, studies in the resolution of incongruities, fantasies in logic that nobody else could have written. At the same time it has to be said that had he written them but not created Father Brown, Chesterton would not have qualified as a detective writer, while had he written the Father Brown tales but not those others, he would not have diminished his reputation as a crusader against humbug.

No: there is humbug in Holmes, but there is none here. It will remain an open question whether the Father Brown stories lifted themselves, by their own distinction, clean out of the detective field, or whether we may use them as evidence for arguments yet to come about the literature. I am assuming the second answer to be right, but having done so I have made everything much more difficult than it otherwise would have been.

III

PURITANS AND ROMANTICS

11

Coming of Age

IT WAS NOT surprising that the detective story should for the first generation of its life be confined to the short story form. Detection pure and simple would not stand the strain of a three-volume novel. True, there were the two masterpieces of Wilkie Collins, and there was the unfinished *Edwin Drood*, but these have special qualities which will have to be discussed later. These were real novels of character, and once the detective story had taken off on its new course, following a limited form of plot and leaving character to take care of itself, it was just right for publication in full in literary weeklies. A series of self-contained stories bringing back each time a central character but each making its point quickly and decisively was just what would keep the reading public cliff-hanging. Attempts to draw the detective story out to full length were bound to collapse without the skill of the genuine novelist to sustain them. Doyle managed it only once, in *The Hound of the Baskervilles*, and even that is very brief by the standards of the novel of its day. The other long stories in the Holmes saga are really novelettes running in multiple-unit. Such other attempts at longer detective stories as were made have long since been forgotten.

The breakthrough that opened the road for the full-length detective novel came from an unexpected quarter, when it occurred to E. C. Bentley, a professional man of letters and a friend of Chesterton, to write a full-length detective story which should at the same time show how it could be done and expose the humbug in the older classics. Here is his own account of it:

> Sometime in the year 1910 it occurred to me that it would be a good idea to write a detective story of a new sort. . . . I found

> the austerity of Holmes and the rest a little wearisome. It should be possible, I thought, to write a detective story in which the detective was recognisable as a human being and was not quite so much the 'heavy' sleuth. . . . It was not until I had gone a long way with the plot that the most pleasing notion of all came to me: the notion of making the hero's hard-won and obviously correct solution of the mystery turn out to be completely wrong. Why not show up the fallibility of the Holmesian method? . . . In the result, it does not seem to have been generally noticed that *Trent's Last Case* is not so much a detective story as an exposure of detective stories.[1]

By 1940, when Bentley wrote those words, reaction and counter-reaction originated by the Holmes orthodoxy had been too frequent for anybody without a keen historical sense to notice the irony of *Trent*. Readers of that age (or this) would also need to be told how new was the idea of introducing a conventional love-interest into a tale of detection (Holmes's 'most dismal groan' disposed of Mary Morstan as 'love-interest'). But this was, eccentric exceptions apart, the first real detective novel. And what a beauty! Its narrative is conducted in perfect and unaffected English, neither casual nor pompous, as befitted a man whose trade in 1910 was writing. It is sufficient measure of its literary craftsmanship that for the sheer pleasure of reading it you miss the irony of its author's intentions (even the *Last* in the title is an irony).

The rest of its inner history can be read in the very entertaining pages in Bentley's autobiography from which the quotation was taken. It was not published until 1912, after a number of miscarriages, and it was an American publisher who first risked it. The publisher made one historic amendment. Bentley had given his hero the unattractive name 'Philip Gasket'; the alteration of that to Trent was a considerable service to literature—and no doubt to the book's sale (*Gasket's Last Case*!). As it eventually stood for the printer, the story marked the coming of age of the detective story; it planted the seeds of humanity, humour and irony which were the qualities it needed to deliver the style from stuffiness. The symptoms of coming of age are all connected with the principle of reacting

[1] E. C. Bentley, *Those Days* (Constable, 1940), pp. 249–54.

against one's father while remaining one's father's son. What can be changed, the second generation is prompted to change; what is essential, unless things go badly wrong, he is content to retain. Bentley did a very neat job in reacting without graceless-ness. He stepped in at exactly the moment when the detective story was due either to degenerate into inbred affectation or to establish a true principle of originality.

He did not complete the job; that would have been too violent. But he did ask whether the amateur detective must necessarily be a celibate superman, and whether situations must needs be macabre, grotesque and in the ancient sense mysterious. Having said 'No', he set his story in as ordinary a situation, and among as ordinary people, as his imagination could contrive. He made his story as like a novel of 1910 as he could make it.

This, not unnaturally, meant that he wrote, not about fantastic people, but about his own kind of people. In the romantic school of detective writers which he here inaugurated it was the custom for authors to set their scenes in a stratum of society just above that in which they themselves moved, and this is a fashion which Bentley set. (In the Holmes stories there is a certain movement towards high society, which is a product of the romantic element in them against which their immediate successors reacted.) By later twentieth-century standards Bentley's characters are not as ordinary as all that. The assumption that people of this sub-aristocratic, articulate, well-provided kind were the people to whom things worth writing about happened was taken over from the nineteenth-century romantics. But little else was. The detective was so little of a superman that he gets the solution wrong and falls in love with the heroine; and the villain is so far from being a villain that he isn't even punished. (There is another villain who, in the kind of story Bentley was reacting against, would have been the murderer.)

Now this is to question, at an early date, the dogma that detection leads either to legal process or to the death by other means of the culprit. This was a sacred dogma: for the detection reading public was a puritan public and its morality did not wish to be made uncomfortable. In other words, the Bentley reaction against the classical pattern was the opposite of

Chesterton's. Chesterton and Bentley between them demonstrate the essential mediocrity of the popular puritan ethic of 1900. Chesterton criticises it by going beyond it to the ethic of the common man, which he equates with that of the Church and claims to be universal where the puritan ethic is sectional and ill-adjusted. Bentley appeals from it not to a more universal ethic but to an individual ethic. The murdered man was a swine—anybody can see that. The murderer (who eluded the detective) was a nice fellow—anybody can see that too. Then judge for yourself, says the author; and in saying that he knocks down one wall of the traditional structure, for the traditional structure is partly supported by the axiom that crime is wrong and punishable. Yes, Holmes did it once or twice (in 'The Blue Carbuncle' and, in a matter of killing, in 'The Abbey Grange'), but Bentley does it for a quite different reason. Father Brown would not lift a finger to deliver a guilty man from punishment —but then he would say that a man was marginally better off if he died penitent than if he lived with the memory of a crime, and that is a different world again. Bentley is a liberal who believes that a man need not die for a justifiable murder, the opinion on the justification being his own and that of like-minded men.

Bentley did write other detective stories. The only other full-length one was written twenty-six years later, in collaboration with H. Warner Allen, and called *Trent's Own Case*; it lacks the distinction of the earlier one and respects more orthodoxies. The corpse here is a highly religious person of repellent habits (named as a Congregationalist and stated to have bequeathed a fortune to the London Missionary Society, a body associated with that denomination until 1966). In the end it turns out not to be murder, so everybody is happy. There are also some short stories, collected under the title *Trent Intervenes*, published in between, which are harmless diversions. The plot of one of them, 'The Clever Cockatoo', collides head-on with one of Dorothy Sayers's, written about the same time, called 'The Incredible Elopement of Lord Peter Wimsey': this is a strange coincidence which suggests that some real-life episode must have given the idea to both authors, but we do not know what that may have been. In his autobiography Bentley is tantalisingly silent about his later detective writings, but clearly he was less impatient about detective stories once he had created Trent than he was before the process began.

The appearance of Trent, anyhow, generated a fairly strong growth of amateur detective characters, of whom the earliest was probably Philip Macdonald's Anthony Gethryn. The milieu was primarily amiable and conventional. The heroes are not eccentric, they are decently well off, they mix in reasonably civilised society, and they bring to the business of detection no special knowledge, but rather a gentlemanly concern for justice and a readiness to do hard work. It is all very sane and stable, provided that the world of decent men stays put.

One remarkable thing we are about to notice is that the First World War seems to have had no effect whatever on the development of the detective story. We shall find that the effect of the Second World War was catastrophic. I think that the reason is not far to seek. The First World War was unexampled for its accumulation of suffering, while the second was unexampled for its accumulation of evil. So far as the English were concerned, the suffering released into their world by the events of 1914–18 was something to which they knew how to respond, and something which in retrospect generated a sense of real victory. They were more convinced at the end than at the beginning that they knew what was right and what was wrong. It may have made us insufferably self-righteous and dangerously romantic about our virtues, but the testimony of the sense of achievement which followed the misery of those years is the continuing interest in the literature and history of that conflict on the part of two generations who never witnessed it. Its veterans are now very old, but some of its songs are still sung, and in 1964 I was told by a bookseller that books about the First World War were commanding as lively a sale as those in any other field of non-fiction.

This was good fortune for the detective story. The puritan values of right and wrong, law supreme over lawlessness, had been vindicated in a big way (or so people generally thought). Everything we say in that sense about World War I was contradicted by World War II, which really did rock the moral foundations of western society, letting loose a desperate anger and a fatalistic sense of guilt in which detection could not flourish because the people who wrote it and those who read it were precisely the people who suffered most from the effects of this moral tornado. All that we shall come to later. For the present we are launched out, on the conclusion of the war, into the cheerful springtime of detection, whose chief characters seem to be Freeman Wills Crofts and Agatha Christie.

Freeman Wills Crofts, perhaps the greatest puritan of them all, made his first appearance in 1920 with *The Cask*, a year after Agatha Christie had led off with *The Mysterious Affair at Styles*. Crofts (1879–1957) was an employee of the railways, brought up at a Methodist school, who wrote a great deal of his work after he had retired at fifty in order to do it. Among his other works was a translation of the New Testament—and that is about all he has in common with Ronald Knox.

He was as regular and industrious in his methods as Trollope, and scrupulously fair in his laying of clues. He was ruthless in disposing of his murderers, who were never in any circumstances attractive or deserving of the reader's sympathy. Their motives were sometimes passionate, but far more often associated with greed, a vice peculiarly hated by puritans. There is no levity in his work. It is all sober, systematic slogging. And that is why he is the creator of the first great policeman in the business.

Good policemen who take the centre of the stage are sufficiently familiar now (Ngaio Marsh and John Creasey show other ways of handling them) to make it necessary to remind the reader how relatively rare, taking the literature as a whole, the good policeman is. There are several possible ways of using the police in a detective story. They can be well-meaning perpetrators of injustice, corrected by the superior intelligence of an amateur (like Lestrade or Sidney Lomas); they can be a team of technicians who are grateful for the assistance of a brilliant amateur but do not look as if they would have ultimately gone wrong without him (like Stanley Hopkins and Charles Parker); they can be ruffians and incompetents—and this really didn't occur to any author as a possible line to take before the 1950s; or they can be simply the people that the story is all about.

Now if you are writing a police-novel about detection you have little room for romance. Give your policeman too much character and you'll soon get a protesting reaction from the reader's sense of credibility. Pack the story with too much incident, and you will get the same reaction from people who are persuaded that police work isn't like that. You are almost forced into writing straight documentary (like Creasey's 'Gideon' series). Your long suit must be the response you get from the readers to any writer who can make some well-known profession interesting by making use of the fruits of the most precise and sensitive observation. Given that, you can get away with a good deal. Novels about doctors have a long tradition of acceptability because they are bound to bring the reader into tense human situations, and they are always the better for precise observation of medical life. Court-room scenes are the best material for those who would present lawyers in novels because they can be dramatic, but again they are much better value if the author knows his law. (I was distressed and disillusioned to hear, in 1955, the comments of an eminent Q.C., now a Lord Justice of Appeal, on the court-room scene in Margery Allingham's *Flowers for the Judge*.) Novels about solicitors are rarer than those about barristers: the solicitor becomes easier material if he is something of a dissenter from established values, like Joshua Clunk or Arthur Crook. And of course it has been shown that it is possible to get insurance-men or business tycoons into sensational situations: but on the whole it is the inherent drama of the doctor's or the criminal barrister's life that the novelist welcomes most.

It is like that with the police, and either you must romanticise them (as Creasey does with Inspector West, or Ngaio Marsh, more winningly, with Alleyn) or you must hold the reader's attention by engaging his sympathy with the policeman as he is, taking the rough with the smooth. It was Crofts who showed how this might be done. His feet are firmly on the earth. He writes like an educated clerk. He gets his effect, like his famous Inspector French, by plain puritan hard work.

As a professional railwayman, Crofts was naturally the most eminent of railway-minded detective writers, and his timetables are one of the most conspicuous features of his stories. There is nothing sedentary about any of his policemen, who are never happier than when they are dashing about the country or the continent of Europe, always by train. Trains, symbol of the counterpoint between authority and adventure, appeal naturally to the puritan temperament of enterprise and moral rigour

(I am told that in any railway society two of the best represented professions are likely to be low-church clergy and church organists).

The Great Train Robbery of 1963 was a pure Crofts situation, not least in that its motive was crude gain. That is his favourite motive, and murder, when we get it, is incidental to that: sex is usually secondary to it. And if anybody wants a two-page guide to the modern English puritan mind, he has only to study, or recall, the reactions of public opinion to the two major national scandals of that summer—the train robbery and the Profumo affair. The Profumo scandal generated a sense of helplessness (nicely expressed in the then Prime Minister's own words in Parliament)—a sense of being caught in a kind of epidemic: nothing to be done, and even a court case frustrated by a suicide. The train robbers, on the other hand, got considerable applause from the country and thirty years from the judge. You knew where you were with that: it was, in a sense, a 'good clean crime', almost a relief, so public comment seemed to imply, from the sinister implications of corrupt high life. All that is necessarily and designedly a trivial comment, but it was the comment of society. It exposes both the character and the limitations of the ethos which the Crofts detective tale assumes. There is no high life, apart from high business life, in Crofts. 'He was hanged on the 14th' is a perfectly possible final line in a Crofts short story. His accounts are unsensational enough to have pleased Holmes himself. And there, just as much as in Noël Coward, you see the spluttering bravura of the twenties. Coward is all style and champagne: Crofts is all no-nonsense moralism. It's all, to jaded eyes of the present, too good to be true, but in its way it's good all the same.

The Cask was a new kind of sober masterpiece, one of the finest first novels in detective history. Inspector French did not appear until 1925, in *Inspector French's Greatest Case*, which was quickly followed by *The Cheyne Mystery* (1927) and *The Starvel Tragedy* (1927). If you want the best example of the technique of arousing and holding a reader's interest in a specialised work-situation, worthy to stand alongside the best middle-period Sayers, it would be in *Death of a Train* (1946), one of his last books. Crofts found his length at once and held it. He knew just how to work within his limitations. He set many of his scenes in

London or near the town where he lived (Guildford). With him you get moral relaxation in an ethical armchair that will never let you down, and a celebration of ordinariness that supplies adventure without any reference to Ruritania.

Between him and the throne of the Queen of Crime, to whom homage becomes due in a moment, stands the more modest figure of 'John Rhode'—one of the first pseudonymous detective writers of considerable output. His real name was C. J. C. Street and he was a well-known journalist. Rhode was a disciple of Austin Freeman, and some of his short stories have the authentic Freeman atmosphere and might indeed have been thought of by him. His tales have suffered an eclipse as unaccountable as the unavailability of H. C. Bailey, but in their time they were worthy to be called classics. The amateur tradition returns with him—but with a new twist. His detective is a peppery retired professor of physics, Dr Priestley, who was a stickler for professional and social etiquette and among other things probably invented the hoary situation-cliché, 'No talk of business over dinner'. (Working lunches are unknown to classic detective amateurs.) In a time when 'science' was strictly a 'mystery', a cult demanding the uncritical admiration of the uninitiated, Priestley's deductions and adventures made an immediate appeal to people brought up on Latin and Greek. Everything was puritanically masculine, and nearly all the meat of the stories is in lectures by Priestley to two favoured friends, an inspector of police and a doctor. But Priestley was no 'grey cells' aesthete. He believed in inspecting the scene of the crime, and especially in reconstructing crimes. *The House on Tollard Ridge* (1925), one of Rhode's best stories, is a masterly combination of the frightening and the technological. Technology has now gone so far that there is little with which an author can surprise his reader (unless you count 'The Mistake of the Machine', I cannot at present recall a detective story about a computer, but no doubt it will come); but in his day the ceremonious Priestley cashed in on the mystery of science in a manner satisfactory to any reader who was as content as Inspector Hanslet not to ask tiresome questions. The very good craftsmanship of these stories does not seem to have saved them from oblivion in a later age; this may be because 'science' now means strictly that discipline in which there is no bamboozlement, no humbug and no romance. In the post-Snow era a scientific superman becomes distasteful.

One or two other attractive authors of the twenties seem to have shared the same fate. 'George Birmingham', otherwise known as Canon J. O. Hannay, D.D., wrote very acceptably and was one of the earliest and most successful clerical authors. He was better than Ronald Knox, and his *Wild Justice*, a detective story in an English village with Irish associations, made a quite memorable novel. There was also John Ferguson, who introduced a rather Holmes-like practitioner of formal logic in his McNab, who punctuated his expositions with the technical jargon of deductive logic but always got his man. Beneath these a large underworld of thriller-writers flourished, whose work is now less regrettably forgotten, but whom one still occasionally meets in the anthologies, and a fashion of detective plays developed which made work for the West End stage in a period when English drama was otherwise somewhat becalmed. Anthony Armstrong's *Ten Minute Alibi*, also published as a novel, was among the cleverest of these. But there was no doubt whatever who was making the best speed as a detective creator. With something of a fanfare we must announce our first encounter with a woman novelist who really captured the detective market.

12

Quartet of Muses: First Pair

Agatha Christie, who has (1970) written over eighty detective stories of full length and countless short stories, not to mention the longest-running West End play in history, spans the whole of the period which is left to us to explore. She has earned the name of 'Queen of Crime' by maintaining a certain standard, without the least sign of falling off, through a total number of pages which can have been exceeded, if indeed it ever has, only by writers whose standards were lower. Some thriller-authors have covered more paper, but we are not concerned with thrillers. The only other detective writer within sight of her for combined standard and output must be John Creasey under his various names; but the distance in character between even them is very great.

The secret of her success is just the same as that of a successful eighteenth-century musician. Like such a musician, she writes to amuse, not to involve. And if you are to pour out tolerably good amusement for fifty years without taking a rest and without outstaying your welcome, you must find your style early and stick to it. Like Crofts, she did. It has to be a style which does not make excessive demands either on writer or on reader. There must not be too much originality or you won't be able to keep it up. (Doyle was vulnerable to that weakness.) You must accept certain clichés, and work within a pattern that does not include any agonising self-criticism. But if you suspend self-criticism, will you not write trash? Not if within the prescribed pattern you observe rigid professional reliability of performance. That is where Agatha Christie has her secret: the whole job is invariably done to professional standards.

Looking over her great output it's remarkably difficult to say of any one book, 'That's a winner', or 'That's a weak one'. With most authors you can do this very easily. There will not be much difficulty in making such judgements about Dorothy Sayers or Margery Allingham or Michael Innes and getting them agreed with. But Agatha Christie, more than anybody else in the true detective tradition, and as much as anybody in the thriller tradition, runs like a train. Her apparently effortless regularity in delivering the required goods is something we have to go to a lower level of literature to find repeated.

She rigorously cuts out anything that strays from the classic detective technique. She hardly ever challenges herself by putting a story in a specialised milieu; the nearest she comes to that is in one or two written in the thirties against a background of archaeological exploration, which was one of her special interests. She never arouses in the reader the least personal interest in character—this would distract him as it would distract a good policeman. The setting of the stories, although she allows herself just enough variation not to become wholly boring, is always some permutation of an agreed system of clichés.

She began in 1919 with *The Mysterious Affair at Styles*, a competent story set in a country house, and as she started, so she went on. The country house, or the country village, is the norm from which just often enough, especially in the urbanised sixties, she allows exceptions. If it is not a country house it is likely to be a big London house—a house in any case big enough to have a library for the body to be found in.

Thus she accepts the convention of providing romantic escape for groundling urban commuters. She peoples her country houses with stock characters—the baronet, the major, the well-to-do elderly couple, the well-to-do younger couple, and the scholarly and absent-minded parson. She gets her puppets out of a box, draws a ring round them to represent the stage on which they are to perform, puts them through their paces, and returns them to the box.

Yet just as you pick up the next Christie with a lurking fear that it will be another butler-baronet affair, it turns out to be *The Murder of Roger Ackroyd* (1926), which by common consent is the finest tour-de-force in detective surprise in the whole field. And just as you are sure that this, once done, can never be done again, you run into *Endless Night* (1967), which contradicts every cliché assumed in the earlier novel, and repeats the same device of surprise. Or it may be *Murder on the Orient Express* (1934), set entirely in a train, or *Ten Little Niggers* (1939), on Lundy in a storm, or even *Death Comes as the End* (1945), set in ancient Egypt.

In her output of eighty stories she keeps always within the world she knows; but (as in a moment will be demonstrated) when knowledge of a new world is needed, she is ready to do the necessary work to acquire it. In the early novels a socialist life-peer isn't possible—but then in those days they didn't have life-peers. You cannot be quite sure that in the next book you won't meet one.

One way of putting it is to say that Hercule Poirot was really an unconscionable time a-dying. (If he's still alive he will probably have had a centenarian's telegram by now.) Poirot was an alien force against which all the surrounding characters in his situations reacted with stern conventionality. Should a reader begin to take the butlers and barts too seriously, it is Poirot who will administer the necessary pinprick. But this in itself soon became a cliché. He's a stage-foreigner all the time, and in the readers' sympathies the colonels and squires usually win. Poirot seems to have been in active practice as a consultant from the end of the First World War until at least 1960. In *After the Funeral* (1953) he is said to have retired, but in 1919 he had already retired from the Belgian police force. But while he is about he is the only unconventional figure on the stage.

He is, of course, a gesture against the activist detective. He believes that observation of character gets you home quicker than crawling about with a magnifying glass or categorising cigar-ash. Hence the foreignness, the Gallic logic, the French tags and the moustaches. But he kills his secondary characters stone dead.

It was, then, a mercy that Agatha Christie managed to handle more than one detective in her stories. At a fairly early stage (1929) she introduced Miss Marple in *Murder at the Vicarage*, and look what happened. Miss Marple in that book starts out as a stage village spinster, and you place her at once as a talkative and officious old pussy among several other old pussies with too much time on their hands. But before you are at the end of the story you realise that that assessment won't quite do. And what is more, you at once get a number of quite memorable secondary characters, not least a parson who isn't absent-minded at all but knows his business quite well and qualifies to be the narrator. Miss Marple has much more both of brains and of charity than you expected, and in subsequent books village scenes construct themselves around her with a good deal more verisimilitude than the Great House permitted.

But Miss Marple and Poirot share the same view of the art of detection. Miss Marple's favourite formula—usually met with in the short stories about her, but never really absent—is, 'Now that reminds me of poor Billy Bell the grocer's boy at St. Mary Mead'. Both of them study behaviour. Poirot dignifies this by the name of psychology, and in doing so tickles the fancy of a readership for whom 'psychology' is still something of a mystery, beginning to usurp the status of 'science'. It is a pretty crude and unsubtle behaviourism, owing nothing worth mentioning to Freud or Jung, and amiably lampooned by Bertie Wooster and Jeeves in their conversation back and forth about 'the psychology of the individual'. It is bound to be crude simply because those characters whose 'psychology' is exposed by Poirot are usually so stiff and forbidding in their communications with the reader.

You don't read the Christie stories as studies in psychology; it's the last thing you would do. You read them because with unfailing efficiency they solve problems and present you with a solution that in the end you know you ought to have seen. It is always a matter of 'the least likely person'—but note how Agatha Christie does it, and you see at once the need for keeping this unlikelihood strictly in the reader's mind. It is cheating, and the reader feels let down, when the criminal turns out to be a person who *really* wasn't 'likely', whom you still can't believe to have done it. It must be the reader alone who regarded the detected criminal as 'unlikely'; in the end he must be shown to be the inevitable criminal. This Agatha Christie invariably achieves.

Miss Marple doesn't go in much for drama, and neither she nor Poirot seem to get into many situations in which the reader is cliff-hanging in sympathy with a wrongly suspected person. There is no passion anywhere—but with Poirot there is plenty of stage-climax; his favourite way of ending a case is to assemble everybody in conference, and then either physically or verbally reconstruct the crime. There is plenty of 'ham' in these scenes, and now and again the reader's credulity would be strained to believe in the docility of the audience were it not for the masterly rhythm of the build-up.

Poirot doesn't arouse any affection in the reader. He is competent and assured, but never kind or attractive. Miss Marple manages to arouse a sort of mild pleasure. Among subsidiary Christie characters who remain in the mind—a small company, I suspect, in anybody's book—I should certainly place that 1950-ish professional home-help in private practice who appears unexpectedly in *4.50 from Paddington*, and Mrs Ariadne Oliver, who is either a self-portrait or a self-caricature. A certain Mr Harley Quin appears in a few Christie stories, and seems to be her one concession to the mythological; he is decidedly phantasmal, like his name—nobody knows whence he comes or where he goes. He never achieved the success of Poirot or Miss Marple and looks a bit as if he were the one person Agatha Christie could write about when she couldn't stand the sight of either of the others.

She did begin, by the way, by adopting a 'Watson' technique. Watson thus proved himself a subtler character than first appearances suggest. Most Watsons aren't much good, but this one was peculiarly foolish. Captain Hastings, who moved Poirot to so much wrath, was too obviously the stage chump, and his creator got rid of him by matrimony. And this was just an example of what is always true of Agatha Christie: the beauty of her technique (which is quite compelling) is entirely in technique, never in style. No writer worth attending to has used more stock phrases in dialogue than she did. How many times does a lawyer say that a fresh point of evidence 'throws a new complexion on the case'? Oftener, much oftener, than the occasion in *Sad Cypress* which fell open for a spot-check. The devotee of Michael Innes would find her style as exasperating as the lover of Ngaio Marsh or Thurman Warriner would find her people. The time had hardly yet come when the detective tale essayed an encounter with *belles lettres* or with the serious novel, and the habits formed in 1920 persisted beyond 1960. Nobody minded, because she did it so well. She made the detective story an institution. She is the most frequently named of all detective story writers. She is the *Hymns Ancient and Modern* of detection.

Yes: Hymns Ancient and Modern—traditional, innocent of style and social criticism, middle of the road, indispensable to the old English rustic scene. It will do very well: and by the same token (though it will be tedious to press the analogy much further), *English Hymnal*, high-toned, high-church, slightly intense and intellectual, scholarly, business-like—that, when we get to her, will do for Miss Dorothy Sayers.

And yet—one must be careful. There is a resilience and flexibility about Agatha Christie in her later work which it would be fatal to overlook. Her later work shows a certain awareness of the changing social scene, a broadening of observation quite remarkable in one who had already been writing for forty years. *The Pale Horse* (1961) is full of unexpected things, and I ask leave now to quote an extended passage from it which shows that by that date Agatha Christie was prepared to share some secrets with her readers. In this passage the reader will notice many things: it hardly matters whether the central figure in the scene is a detailed self-portrait; what does matter is that the authoress here exposes her methods of working, and, with that, the limitations of which she is conscious. I don't think one can get hold of the total impression without reading through the entire scene.

> I mounted two flights of stairs, tapped lightly on a door, and walked in without waiting for encouragement. Mrs Oliver's workroom was a good-sized room, the walls papered with exotic birds nesting in tropical foliage. Mrs Oliver herself, in a state apparently bordering on insanity, was prowling round the room, muttering to herself. She threw me a brief uninterested glance and continued to prowl. Her eyes, unfocused, swept round the walls, out of the window, and occasionally closed in what appeared to be a spasm of agony.
>
> 'But why,' demanded Mrs Oliver of the universe, 'why doesn't the idiot say at once that he *saw* the cockatoo? Why shouldn't he? He couldn't have helped seeing it! But if he *does* mention it, it ruins everything. There must be a way. . . . There must be. . . .'
>
> She groaned, ran her fingers through her short grey hair, and clutched it with a frenzied hand. Then, looking at me with

suddenly focused eyes, she said, 'Hallo, Mark. I'm going mad,' and resumed her complaint.

'And then there's Monica. The nicer I try to make her, the more irritating she gets. . . . Such a stupid girl. . . . Smug, too! Monica . . . Monica? I believe the name's wrong. Nancy? Would that be better? Joan? Everybody is always Joan. Anne is the same. Susan? I've had a Susan. Lucia? *Lucia*? Lucia? I believe I can *see* a Lucia. Red-haired. Polo-necked jumper. . . . Black tights? Black stockings anyway.'

The momentary gleam of good cheer was eclipsed by the memory of the cockatoo problem, and Mrs Oliver resumed her unhappy prowling, picking up things off tables unseeingly and putting them down again somewhere else. She fitted with some care her spectacle case into a lacquered box which already contained a Chinese fan and then gave a deep sigh and said:

'I'm glad it's you.'

'That's very nice of you.'

'It might have been anybody. Some silly woman who wanted me to open a bazaar, or the man about Milly's insurance card which Milly absolutely refuses to have,—or the plumber (but that would be too much good fortune, wouldn't it). Or it might be someone wanting an interview—asking me all those embarrassing questions which are always the same every time. What made you first think of taking up writing? How many books have you written? How much money do you make? Etc. Etc. I never know the answers to any of them and it makes me look such a fool. Not that any of that matters, because I think I am going mad, over this cockatoo business.'

'Something that won't jell?' I said sympathetically. 'Perhaps I'd better go away.'

'No, don't. At any rate you're a distraction.'

I accepted this doubtful compliment.

'Do you want a cigarette?' Mrs Oliver asked with vague hospitality. 'There are some somewhere. Look in the typewriter lid.'

'I've got my own, thanks. Have one. Oh no, you don't smoke.'

'Or drink,' said Mrs Oliver. 'I wish I did. Like those American detectives who always have pints of rye conveniently in their collar drawers. It seems to solve all their problems. You know, Mark, I really can't think how anyone ever gets away with murder in real life. It seems to me that the moment you've done a murder the whole thing is so terribly obvious.'

'Nonsense. You've done lots of them.'

'Fifty-five at least,' said Mrs Oliver. 'The murder part is quite easy and simple. It's the covering up that's so difficult. I mean, why should it be anyone else but you? You stick out a mile.'

'Not in the finished article,' I said.

'Ah, but what it costs me,' said Mrs Oliver darkly. 'Say what you like, it's not *natural* for five or six people to be on the spot when B is murdered and all to have a motive for killing B—unless, that is, B is absolutely madly unpleasant and in that case nobody will mind whether he's been killed or not, and doesn't care in the least who's done it.'

'I see your problem,' I said. 'But if you've dealt with it successfully fifty-five times, you will manage to deal with it once again.'

'That's what I tell myself,' said Mrs Oliver, 'over and over again, but every single time I can't believe it, and so I'm in agony.'

She seized her hair again and tugged it violently.

'Don't,' I cried. 'You'll have it out by the roots.'

'Nonsense,' said Mrs Oliver. 'Hair's tough. Though when I had measles at fourteen, with a high temperature, it did all come out—all round the front. Most shaming. And it was six months before it grew properly again. Awful for a girl—girls mind so. I thought of it yesterday when I was visiting Mary Delafontaine in that nursing home. Her hair was coming out just like mine did. She said she'd have to get a false front when she was better. If you're sixty it doesn't always grow again, I believe.'

'I saw a girl pull out another's hair by the roots the other night,' I said. I was conscious of a slight note of pride in my voice, as of one who has seen life.

'What extraordinary places have you been going to?' asked Mrs Oliver.

'This was in a coffee bar in Chelsea.'

'Oh *Chelsea*!' said Mrs Oliver. 'Everything happens there, I believe. Beatniks and sputniks and squares and the beat generation. I don't write about them much because I'm so afraid of getting the terms wrong. It's safer, I think, to stick to what you know.'

'Such as?'

'People on cruises, and in hotels, and what goes on in hospitals, and on parish councils—and sales of work—and music festivals, and girls in shops, and committees and daily women, and young men and girls who hike around the world in the interests of science, and shop assistants—'

She paused, out of breath.

'That seems to be fairly comprehensive to be getting on with,' I said.

'All the same, you might take me out to a coffee bar in Chelsea some time—just to widen my experience,' said Mrs Oliver wistfully.[1]

It still remained to be proved that the detective story could be a novel. It now had commercial success and respectability; it had shown itself at its best and at its worst. We knew, by 1925, what its weaknesses were liable to be, and how persuasive it could be when it was on form. But could it ever be describable as a serious novel? Bentley's *jeu d'esprit* did not carry enough weight to force that proposition through. Was it not inevitable that its cut-and-dried morality and its highly formalised plot would prevent it from doing what a novel must, as a most elementary duty, do, namely, show us how people's minds work? Your idea of a good novel will differ from mine—granted; but we all demand that it should arouse in us an interest in people as whole people. Make the situation too vivid or too frightening, or too incredible, and you will not be attending to the people. Whoever is hanging on the cliff, you want him to get back safely, whether he is saint, sinner or plain Jones. Can an author portray a whole person in the presence of murder. Can he divert your obsessional interest from the hazard to the person?

Three women writers set themselves to show how this could be done, and in the end it is fair perhaps to say that one of them got away with honour once, and all of them scraped through. Some may think that their combined assault on the preserver of the novel adds up to a near miss: it is an open question. I am thinking here of Dorothy Sayers (1893–1956), Ngaio Marsh (1899–) and Margery Allingham (1904–67).

These three are fascinatingly diverse, yet they have certain things in common. Roughly speaking they are contemporaries, and two are no longer alive, having died at the same age. Dorothy Sayers and Margery Allingham both had East Anglian

[1] *The Pale Horse* (1961), pp. 12–15.

connections. Both were married, Margery Allingham to a well-known artist. Ngaio Marsh is a New Zealander and unmarried. Dorothy Sayers lived a busy professional life as a writer, and described herself not as a novelist but as a playwright; she was also a much sought-after lay theologian. Only Margery Allingham had children; she and Ngaio Marsh would be little known if they had not written detection.

They come close together in their detective writings, and the first amusing coincidence is one which I do not think other commentators have brought into prominence. All three of them give some indication (Dorothy Sayers and Margery Allingham positive indication) of the ages of their central figures. Lord Peter Wimsey was born in 1890, three years before his creator; Albert Campion was born in 1900, being four years senior to his; and Roderick Alleyn's date of birth is demonstrably 1894–5, making him about five years older than Ngaio Marsh. If you pursue this interesting statistic you soon discover that five to ten years senior to the author is a fairly reliable rule. Conan Doyle was born in 1859, Sherlock Holmes, we are all sure, in 1854. It is natural that an author should make his detective more or less his own contemporary, if only because it will be very inconvenient, if everything goes well and the author wants to keep him alive, when the time comes to make the choice between retiring him at a credible age or continuing his activities into a less and less credible dotage. Agatha Christie's Poirot (as we said) becomes an incredibly aged detective if he is regarded as a fully drawn character and not as a mythological one. Father Brown's age is as irrelevant as the age of Ulysses. Holmes's is deducible but doesn't affect him (he is the kind of person who would retire at 48). But when your character is fully drawn, then he has a biography and you are stuck with it. This did not matter to Dorothy Sayers, whose hero disappears from the scene altogether at 45; Ngaio Marsh slipped a few cogs in portraying Alleyn after indiscreetly indicating at an early stage that he was 41 in 1935;[2] Margery Allingham's Campion is always very slightly mythological—he has a title which we are never told, and an air of detachment which would sit easily on a man of thirty and no differently on

[2] *Enter a Murderer*, ch. 2 (1935), Penguin ed., p. 13. 'Twenty years ago next month I came down from Oxford.'

a man of sixty. The one author who arouses our imagination and then strains it badly is John Dickson Carr, whose two heroes are based on living characters of great fame and are therefore a whole generation older than he. Dr Fell is G. K. Chesterton, and so goes back to 1874, which makes him pretty ancient in the later tales; while Sir Henry Merrivale, who is Churchill and therefore was born in the same year, suffers more because he is much less sedentary. That is what happens when your hero is thirty-two years your senior.

All this is not merely statistical; it shows what happens when a detective story becomes a novel, and sets aside the legendary or mythological technique. Characters in novels have biographies; they get married, or show cause why they shouldn't, they grow middle-aged, they may have to hang on as long as you need them in a series of novels; but they mustn't die while they are commercial. It turns out to be very difficult for an author to create a detective character younger than himself and get away with it. His first central hero must be to some extent heroic: it is not easy to find him a successor. When we come to Michael Innes we shall see a very deft transition from the kind of story appropriate to the young Appleby to that appropriate to the distinguished and retired Appleby; and Margery Allingham was a good example of an author who could find a new character to go alongside an old friend, which in her case was the result of making the original one a very lightly sketched character who left room for a brilliant new colleague when the time came.

The first of the really successful detective novelists who operated on anything like a large scale was Dorothy Sayers, and it is she who gives us the richest character study of her hero, about whom, by the time we have read three or four of her sequence, we know a great deal, quite apart from the fictitious biography she supplies in her later editions. She introduced Lord Peter Wimsey in 1923 in *Whose Body?*, and with him inaugurated the vogue of the aristocratic detective. We have had professionals—doctors, lawyers, academics, but not, up till now, a full-blown lord. For making him one she was castigated by the puritans, who were sure that her motive was snob-appeal. Obviously it was nothing of the kind. It was much more prudential. Consider the great advantages of this scheme. If you want something different from an eminent doctor, lawyer or what not, why not have a peer? The great question for the author is how, if the detective is not a policeman, he is to find time and money—which means freedom of action—for detection. Earlier answers had been to create either a Holmes, who made his living by detecting, or a Frenchman who was a policeman, or somebody at the top of his profession who in the course of his career had assembled the finance, and because of his eminence could organise his own time. (Therefore it must be a consultant rather than a G.P., a barrister rather than a solicitor, an academic scientist rather than a boffin.) The Oxford and Cambridge dons had not yet been thought of. Who else was there who would have the time? Well, one very plausible answer is the man of leisure (at another level Bulldog Drummond was the most famous of these). Peter Wimsey, the younger son of a duke, had half a million in his own right and all the leisure of Dornford Yates's Pleydells. He also fits happily into the heady romanticism of the Noël Coward era.

So far, excellent. But if this Wimsey is to dabble in criminology he must be something of a dissenter from the values of Duke's Denver. All right—let him dissent. This was possible in the 1920s in a way in which it simply wouldn't have been for Trollope. His values are contrasted early on with those of his ducal brother and his terrible sister-in-law, and in the second book in the series they are vindicated by placing the duke himself in a position from which only the detective ability of Wimsey can rescue him. Where does he get this streak from? From his mother—a lovable character if ever there was one. What else do we need? Some evidence of abnormal sensitiveness to offset the emotional frigidity of the hereditary aristocracy. Easily done by the instrument of the First World War, in which Wimsey is buried in a trench and rescued by his batman. He never quite got over the experience and is liable to be emotionally upset by the consequences of his own detection.

The batman becomes his Jeeves. In Bunter there is about 70 per cent Jeeves, and indeed in a good deal of the background situation and dialogue there is a good deal of Wodehouse. Dorothy Sayers borrowed extensively from the vocabulary of the immortal Bertram in her earlier books: it didn't quite transplant in the way she hoped for, and this effect becomes less noticeable in the later books.

Wimsey is absolutely bound to marry a commoner. We get no Barsetshire family conspiracies to marry him off to a ducal daughter; what we do get is a social misalliance with the vindicated prisoner in *Strong Poison* (1930), the sixth book, which is not brought to the point of marriage until the very end of *Gaudy Night* (1935), the eleventh. This provides a counter-subject that appears in some but not all of the intervening stories. For good measure Wimsey's sister Mary is also married off to a commoner—a policeman. In both cases the family top brass are suitably scandalised. It is all a process of combining the piquancy and the simple usefulness of the lordship of Wimsey with a humanity that both reader and author need to make him credible as a detective. Of course he's no Francis of Assisi; he is a clubman and a dilettante, a better pianist than his background would lead you to expect, a bibliophile and a collector of unconsidered things and people. There is nothing surprising in the ease with which he mixes in all kinds of society. Once you have accepted his background and met his relatives as rarely as is decent, you have heard the last of English high life. Not one of the stories is placed in a country house, and there are fewer aristocratic titles per story than there are in the Holmes or the Poirot adventures.

What gives Dorothy Sayers a place in the novelists' stakes at all is the success of her subsidiary characters. One reading of the complete series leaves a handful of excellent and memorable additions to anybody's literary acquaintance. There are Charles Parker, the CID man from Barrow Grammar School with a non-conformist background, Katherine Climpson, as lovable a spinster as Miss Marple, Marjorie Phelps, the pleasantest ordinary young woman you ever met in a few pages of fiction, the Reverend Mr Venables of Fenchurch St Peter—the parson who is decidedly not a stage parson—and (a particularly haunting one) the tortured Tallboys in *Murder Must Advertise* (1933). As she goes on she becomes better at this, and in *Gaudy Night* she shows how she can handle a large crowd of equally important characters without making the reader feel oppressed with noise.

The other thing she developed as she went along was a

remarkable technique for creating credible specialised environments. I should judge three of her four best stories to be *The Five Red Herrings* (1931), a beautifully poised evocation of the artists' colony in Galloway, *Murder Must Advertise*, set in an advertising office (she worked in one to get copy for it), and *The Nine Tailors* (1934), which deftly and gracefully brings the science of campanology into a story that also celebrates the special culture of the English fenland. These three are masterpieces. *Gaudy Night* is the most famous of quite a string of Oxford detective tales, but its detective interest is really a subordinate theme.

Her first story, *Whose Body?*, is quite clearly an experiment in the use of a deracinated aristocrat as a detective; equally clearly the next, *Clouds of Witness* (1926), comes of saying, 'Let's get the Duke into a scrape'. From then on it is easy to see how each plot formed itself, and also how the old principle of puzzling the reader about method gave way to the new principle of fascinating him by the reactions of people to each other and to a crisis. Having established the ducal family in the first two stories the author seems to have become interested in constructing stories round curious scientific or situational notions. The third story, *Unnatural Death* (1927), is a bad story with a creaking plot; its double source was a legal point (argued out in a nearly unreadable chapter) and a medical curiosity about the lethal properties of an empty hypodermic. *The Unpleasantness at the Bellona Club* (no. 4, 1928) introduces the idea of committing a murder and using the two minutes' silence on Armistice Day to cover it up (it dates from the time when this observance occurred on whatever weekday was November 11th); and the best of the science-based tales (no. 5, *The Documents in the Case*, 1930), written in collaboration with a scientist, Robert Eustace, combines a hair-raising climax with an epistolary narrative (admirably handled) and a remarkable debate on science and religion that involves a credible parson. It was in the sixth, *Strong Poison* (later 1930), that the romantic interest was heightened by the arrest and trial of Harriet Vane, who in the end became Lady Peter. We hear a little of Harriet Vane in later books until we come to *Have His Carcase* (no. 8, 1932), which is probably the least satisfactory of all the series, and shows in its laborious plot (the scientific germ here is haemophilia) the embarrassing encounter between pure detection and the detective novel which was working itself out throughout the thirties. Romance wins in the end with *Busman's Honeymoon* (1937), which is an account of Lord Peter's marriage and honeymoon containing a reasonably competent detective sub-plot. The sub-plot by itself would have made quite a good short story in its own right.

For really satisfying reading, I should myself choose the three 'situation novels' plus *The Documents in the Case*, for in these the two crafts of detective writing and novel writing seem to be best matched. The appearance of Harriet Vane put a strain on the author as well as on her hero. That torrid love affair seemed to throw the pictures out of drawing. There is much more real compassion for the condition of the tortured criminal in *Murder Must Advertise*, much more interest in subsidiary characters in *The Five Red Herrings*, and far better straight detective thrill in *The Documents* than in the two longest, latest, and best known of her stories.

Usually a single idea generates a better short story than full-length novel. *Unnatural Death* would have been a good short story. Those short stories that Dorothy Sayers did write are very good value. Not all of them feature Lord Peter (but no long story features any other detective). *Lord Peter Views the Body* is all Wimsey, and he appears a few times in *Hangman's Holiday* and *In the Teeth of the Evidence*. 'The Incredible Elopement', in the first of these, is the story that seems to be repeated by E. C. Bentley in 'The Clever Cockatoo'; 'The Cave of Ali Baba' corresponds to Doyle's 'The Final Problem' and 'The Empty House' combined, giving us a fictitious death and resurrection of Wimsey calculated, like Holmes's, to catch a criminal gang. There is much quiet fun in 'Uncle Meleager's Will', 'The Stolen Stomach' (another Galloway story) and the long-short tale, 'The Bone of Contention'; and as a makeweight the slightly absurd Montague Egg provides light entertainment.

I think that Dorothy Sayers was right in the end not to call herself a novelist. But her contribution to the evolution of detective literature was greater than the actual quality of most of her stories. She showed that you could hold detective interest without losing style, even if the love-interest in the end provokes Holmes's comment, 'I really cannot congratulate you'.

There is plenty of humour, and plenty of tension, in the best of the stories: the dialogue is so good that people used to identify Dorothy Sayers's tastes with Lord Peter Wimsey's. It is said that she was constantly offered port wine, which she could not drink, because of Lord Peter's taste for it, and long dialogues between men run so naturally in her books as to demonstrate that nobody need actually go into the smoking-room to know how men talk to one another. The Wimsey idiom is in itself so powerful (such a 'strong English accent', as an American character puts it on one occasion) as to sound forty years later as foreign as Mr Fortune's. But there is a solid integrity and credibility about all the characters which provides a real platform for later writers to work from.

There is no more social judgement in Sayers than in Christie; she takes the world very much as she finds it. The assumptions are that decent people are peaceable, extrovert and anglican; there is little sign of any sympathy with dissent from the puritan values of hard work and integrity. Lord Peter is accepted because he does, when he is under the reader's eye, do his job, and take trouble over it, and respect professional standards. His family (apart from his mother) are rejected because of their idle snobbery, and people like Goyles in *Clouds of Witness* (whom Lady Mary didn't marry) and Philip Boyce in *String Poison* (from whom Harriet was rescued by his death) get short shrift as wasters or dreamers. It's a secure and predictable world in which all will be well if people respect their betters; and our friend the suburban commuter was grateful for its friendliness and moral rectitude.

One is bound to say that Wimsey is not to Dorothy Sayers what Father Brown was to Chesterton. In the 1940s Sayers was not much less famous as a theological writer than Chesterton had been thirty years earlier; but she made her name as a detective writer before becoming a popular religious apologist. During the years of World War II, when C. S. Lewis and Charles Williams were for a short time the arbiters of responsible lay thinking about religion, Dorothy Sayers made a third with them as a lay theologian, writing many articles, doing a number of broadcasts, putting on several plays with religious themes and crowning it all with the astonishing (and thoroughly deserved) success of *The Man Born to be King* (1943), a dramatisation of the Gospel story in twelve broadcast episodes originally designed for children but rating annual repeats for several years from its first broadcast in December 1941. This was what, in the 1940s, Dorothy Sayers was perhaps best known for. She does not make Wimsey say any of these things. Wimsey is a diversion, and all the religion one gets in his short series of stories is the production occasionally of thoroughly acceptable and capable clergymen, which is something most detective writers either wisely avoid trying to do, or attempt with abysmal failure. It is characteristic of her nicest parson, Mr Venables, that *The Nine Tailors* would be just as good a detective story without him, but not half so persuasive a novel.

13

Quartet of Muses: Second Pair

MISS NGAIO MARSH has attempted slightly less than Dorothy Sayers, and achieved, in detective writing, a great deal more. She is a specialist in this art, and her output has now spanned a whole generation. Less prolific than Agatha Christie, she resembles the older writer in having found her length early and having held it consistently. Every one of her detective tales is a novel, and from the beginning she shows a gift equal to that of Dorothy Sayers for communicating character. Like those other two, and like Margery Allingham, she is primarily a London writer, although two of her stories are set in her native New Zealand. She favours, and constantly returns to, two kinds of setting: the English upper class milieu and that of art, chiefly painting and drama. There is a markedly theatrical background and emphasis in *Enter a Murderer* (1935 her opus I), *Vintage Murder* (1937), *Final Curtain* (1947), *Opening Night* (1951), *False Scent* (1960) and *Death at the Dolphin* (1967). The world of painting is personified in Agatha Troy, whom we first meet in *Artists in Crime* (1938) and who becomes Mrs Roderick Alleyn: she has a significant part, and so does her painting, in *Final Curtain*, *Spinsters in Jeopardy* (1953) and *Clutch of Constables* (1968). Miss Marsh does not deal much in macabre situations: her murders are straightforward killings for passion or gain, taking place in such English country homes as we are allowed to enter in *A Man Lay Dead* (1935), *Death and the Dancing Footman* (1942), *Off with his Head* (1957), *Hand in Glove* (1962), or such London inter-war high life as provides the setting for *Death in a White Tie* (1938). But there are occasionally excursions into the romantically queer, as in *Death in Ecstasy* (1936), in the folkery of *Off with his Head*, and in the orgiastic climax of *Spinsters in Jeopardy*.

She is an excellent craftsman; you do not catch her out in details, and what she writes about, she knows about. The total effect of her stories is quite remarkably peaceful and urbane, and we owe that mostly to her two policemen, to whom she has remained faithful from the beginning.

Roderick Alleyn, we must suppose, is the last romantic hero in detective fiction. He is a policeman, a professional inspector (then superintendent) of magnificent appearance—a mixture of the grandee and the monk, Miss Marsh says quite often—and of aristocratic connections, who, I fancy, does not live on his pay. He makes Lord Peter Wimsey look like a frivolous neurotic. His creator does not often involve him in hair-raising physical crises out of which he has to fight his way; what is perhaps her greatest distinction is that she communicates so much of Alleyn's character through his conversation. His conversation is apt, unaffected, economical, humorous and authoritative. I am afraid he is quite incapable either of making a mistake in deduction or of dropping a clanger at a dinner party. Like Wimsey, he is over forty when he marries. We have not yet got to the point where it is safe to introduce a married detective with a number of children to the detection-reading public. He is, up to about 1937, a dedicated bachelor. He then enters upon a stormy courtship of Agatha Troy, which he believes himself to be handling clumsily but in fact conducts with unexceptionable chivalry (*Artists in Crime*). He really is a very satisfying and amiable kind of superman—the sort of person it is worth trying to keep on the right side of. We all know somebody who looks just like him.

I don't believe it was really difficult to create him, although he is most skilfully made credible. The character in Ngaio Marsh who gets my vote every time, however, is Edward Fox. Fox is Alleyn's right hand man: unambitious, contented, courageous, efficient, and marvellously communicated from the very first. In the early books Alleyn has an amateur 'Watson' in Nigel Bathgate, a personable young journalist, but like Poirot's Hastings he soon gets caught up in matrimony. It is Fox who lives to provide a setting for Alleyn, and the relation between the two is the best thing Ngaio Marsh has done for the reader; it was fortunate indeed that the chief cornerstone in her plot-construction was such a sound one.

In the collaboration of Alleyn and Fox, not to mention Messrs Bailey and Thomson, who grow grey in the service of fingerprints and photographs, you have the zenith of what we now call the Dixon of Dock Green tradition. Nowhere is the integrity and honour of the police force so generously celebrated. This supplies what was lacking in Inspector French's cases to make them into novels. It is all absolutely central to the detective tradition, and Miss Marsh shows the detective novel at its most reliable and well-founded. Others rose higher but they were less reliable; others asked questions which Miss Marsh has never asked.

This leads to the other outstanding characteristic of Ngaio Marsh. In this she is different from both Dorothy Sayers and Margery Allingham. She is never oppressed by any sense of the evil which righteousness is at war with. Dorothy Sayers more or less leaves us with the notion that unrighteousness is irreligious and rebellious and undisciplined, and that a person of right habits and mind and the necessary gifts of industry will be able to circumvent it. Margery Allingham, after a blithe start, entered more fully than any such writer before or since into the dark mysteries of evil. For Ngaio Marsh it is an aberration, but the optimism impersonated by Alleyn prevents our ever being really upset by it at all. When you look over her output between 1935 and 1970 what you chiefly remember is pleasant characters and pleasant situations—nice English places, friendly London corners, agreeable English people, inviting New Zealand scenes. You remember with more difficulty and searching who was murdered and why, and what kind of pressure the murderer was under. Not that you aren't told, and told quite fairly, all these things. They simply don't seem to be their author's preoccupation. True, they very rarely are in this kind of literature, but this is the difference between Ngaio Marsh and H. C. Bailey, and, as we shall in a moment see, between her and Margery Allingham.

It is reasonably certain (though I invite correction here) that Ngaio Marsh is an agnostic. Alleyn has to admit that he is, in *Singing in the Shrouds* (1959), where he meets an impressive and sensitively-drawn priest who looks as if he was inspired by Father Huddleston (now Bishop of Stepney) in the *Nought for your Comfort* days (1956). The last thing I would wish to say is that better detective stories are written by Christians than by pagans or agnostics—the evidence is all against it anyhow. But the point about Ngaio Marsh is that she stays completely and obediently within the humanist tradition of human perfectibility: and this makes it possible for Alleyn to be what he is, and for anybody who looks for social judgement or political sensitiveness in her work to be entirely frustrated. She writes police novels, not thrillers, with a modest but rarely startling detection plot, balanced between the psychological and the physical. On this pleasant equilibrium, with no intrusions from ethical doubt, she has sailed through thirty-five years of calm water. There is not a prickle, not a rough surface, to spoil the gloss of the finished article. She knows exactly what her craft is and what her limitations are, and she does her job as well as Roderick Alleyn does his. If you want to see her at the top of her form, read *Surfeit of Lampreys* (1941), her longest and I think her richest story. There's a child in that story—one of several children—who grows up to become Lord Michael Lamprey and, for a while, a constable in the metropolitan police.

But sooner or later we have to wake up. We are bound to say that Margery Allingham was more adventurous than Ngaio Marsh. Did she in the end achieve more?

Margery Allingham opened her detective writing career with *Mystery Mile* (1930) and closed it with *The Mind Readers* (1965) and the posthumous *Cargo of Eagles* (1968), completed after her death by her husband, P. Youngman Carter. Like Sayers and Marsh, she created a detective with aristocratic associations, and like them she wrote mostly London-based novels. She started out with 'Mr Campion', whom she surrounds with mystery. She allows us to know that he is at least a baron, perhaps something more exalted than that, going under an assumed name. Yes, he too is forty before he marries, and has a fair run as a bachelor before he meets Amanda Fitton. He must have run into Lord Peter Wimsey, because Wimsey lived at 110a Piccadilly while he lived round the corner at 17 Bottle Street, Piccadilly (no: unhappily no Bottle Street is marked on contemporary London maps). What on earth Bunter would have thought of the ex-cracksman Magersfontein Lugg, who looked after Campion's comforts, we will not pause to speculate. But here is Margery Allingham's version of the uprooted nobleman, complete with off-beat valet, with a mischievous and adventurous temperament. Where Wimsey is flamboyant, Campion is pale and withdrawn, designedly difficult to get to know.

This cheerful spectre is launched in a series of Buchan-like adventures, several of which are associated with the romantic countryside of East Anglia. Suffolk goes in for no oppressive grandeur, but the little hills and the hedges and the trees can hide things, and the gradual disappearance of the land into the North Sea provides endless opportunities for evoking gull-screaming desolations. Quite sinister things happen to Campion in these quiet places, not without violence here and there. It is all very much in the tradition of high romance; all slightly mistier and more allusive than the Ngaio Marsh scene. You don't feel that you are nearer the centre of things than a bystander who isn't of the same social group as the participants; most of them have their backs to you, but what you overhear is very entertaining.

At this stage she is writing thrillers and not much more. A little later she moves on (after an excursion to Cambridge, in *Police at the Funeral*, 1933) to that part of London known as 'Little Venice', where artists at that time were to be found, and there she introduces us to artists and 'arty' people, and a little later (*Flowers for the Judge*, 1936), to a publishing firm. The Allingham artists are just like the Allingham country bigwigs—cheerful, crowded, talkative, and attractive. *Death of a Ghost* is the characteristic story of this kind (1934). All the pre-war stories were written strictly for amusement—they move fast, become less and less violent, and are noticeable for little beyond a talent for creating suspense.

By 1939 Campion meets the girl he is going to marry. Having done so he hauls off and marries her between books—none of the agonised courtships of Wimsey or even of Alleyn. It is quite a long time (*The Fashion in Shrouds*, 1939) before we learn that Campion has a rather brilliant sister. Margery Allingham likes unusual and brilliant twentieth-century women. Campion's sister Val runs a successful and very prosperous costumier's in Mayfair; Amanda Fitton designed an aeroplane and helps her brother to run a factory for making it. In 1945 Campion, returning via an unexpected case from work during the war (*Coroner's Pidgin*, 1945), turns up after several years' absence at his home, and has the first sight of his first child. 'Meet my war-work,' says his wife—one of the great exit-lines in the literature.

This measured casualness is pure blue-blooded stuff. It is the Georgian equivalent of the Victorian stays and quadrilles. Only the top brass can really rise to it. He may call himself Mr Campion, but he and his associates are as lordly as if they all wore their titles on their sleeves (we except Lugg, who was the only class-conscious person present in most of these gatherings).

But things changed quite abruptly, and Margery Allingham seemed after the war to make a new start. *More Work for the Undertaker* (1948) introduces us to the possibility of a change of tone. This is set in a new kind of London, more silent and more sinister, of which we are to hear more. But what is more important—vastly more important—is that it introduces us to Inspector Charles Luke.

I cannot but believe that Margery Allingham said to herself, 'This is the nuclear age, the post-Auschwitz age. I'm sorry, Campion can't really cope.' She doesn't drop Campion, but he gradually moves towards the edge of the stage to make way for the most staggeringly professional policeman to have found his way into fiction. Pause, please, for Mr Luke.

Inspector Charles Luke, when we first meet him, dashes into the picture as six foot four of pure Cockney policeman. I have my own theory about the origin of Luke. To me, Margery Allingham's descriptions of him, with his flashing dialogue, his irrepressible dramatic gestures while he talks, his unusual accent, recreate the poet Charles Williams who died in 1945. Williams's accent, his vividness, his astonishing gift of gesture and drama in ordinary conversation, even the appearance of his features, everything except his normal human height, so precisely correspond to Luke that all Miss Allingham had to do was to add six inches to his stature and a proportional measurement to the width of his shoulders. Whether she meant it or not, Charles Luke is Charles Williams talking prose—and one wouldn't insist on the prose, so powerful is Luke's gift for saying more than the words.

> 'Well now,' said Charlie Luke, his eyes snapping and the trace of a country inflexion creeping into his voice, which was

> as strong and pliant as his shoulders, 'I don't know what you've heard so far but I'll rough it out as it's come to me. It began with poor little old Doctor Smith.'
>
> Campion had never heard before of this particular Doctor Smith but suddenly he was in the room with them. He took shape like a portrait under a pencil, vigorous with the startling vividness of truth.
>
> 'A tallish old boy—well, not so very old, fifty-five, married to a shrew. Overworked. Over-conscientious. Comes out of his flat nagged to a rag in the mornings and goes down to his surgery-room with a shop front like a laundry. Seven-and-six for a visit, half-a-dollar for a squint at your tonsils or a thorough once-over if he isn't sure, and a bottle of muck which does you good. Stooping. Back like a camel. Loose trousers, poking at the seat as if God was holding him up by the centre buttons. Head stuck out like a tortoise, waving slightly. Worried eyes. Good chap. Kind. Not as bright as some (no time for it) but professional. Professional gent. Old school, not old school tie. Servant of his calling and don't forget it. He starts getting poison pen letters. Shakes him.'
>
> Charlie Luke spoke without syntax or noticeable coherence but he talked with his whole body. When he described Doctor Smith's back his own arched. When he mentioned the shop front he squared it with his hands. His tremendous strength, which was physical rather than nervous, poured into the recital, forcing the facts home like a pile-driver.[1]

This was exactly what was wanted: but the inspiration filled the need with generous measure to spare. In the post-1945 world into which Margery Allingham dives in her greatest stories, one is quite convinced that even Superintendent Alleyn would have been out of his depth. Luke's wide tolerance can encompass Campion and Oates and other characters from earlier stories, but he brings to these new situations a titanic anger that no other fictional detective comes near, except possibly Mr Fortune. Here at last is the one thing that detective literature is always short of—human passion of the relevant sort.

The apotheosis of Luke is in *The Tiger in the Smoke* (1952). Here we are swept down from London's artists' quarter to London's 'square mile of vice' in the Paddington district, and everything except the last episode happens in that London

[1] *More Work for the Undertaker*, pp. 31–2.

which is adequately evoked by its popular name, 'the Smoke'. The story has every quality that a detective tale of any period needs, plus a sense of moral collision which is always unusual and at this date quite new. A key figure is an anglican clergyman who is one of the few vicars worthy to stand alongside Mr Venables—who, indeed, far outruns him. He is entirely unpretentious, as unaffected as Father Brown, entirely devoted to the pastoral 'way of Exchange' (to use Charles Williams's phrase). The sense of brooding evil, as opposed to irrational and self-indulgent terror, is kept up throughout the story. That dreadful street-band, the cellar, the fog, the understated deadpan monstrousness of Jack Havoc, the sad and sinister parish woman—and Charlie Luke sparking through it all like an electric current at 132,000 volts: it is all there, and it comes to a climax in, of all places, the local parish church, where the priest is in conversation with just about the most evil rogue ever invented by an author of fiction. Any detective story frightens us at some point: the distinction of this one is that we are frightened by what is really the most frightening thing in the world—not suffering but evil. I suppose we have come as far as we can here from the intellectual relaxation of the primitives, but equally we have come as far as we can from the settled bourgeois assurance of the earlier romantics, indeed of the earlier Allingham.

It is difficult to judge how much of all this Margery Allingham really intended. This evocation of naked evil was certainly not accidental: we have it again at much the same pressure in *Hide My Eyes* (1958), and there is more than a touch of it in *The China Governess* (1963); we can say she meant that. Whether she also intended the extraordinary effect which the last scene in *The Tiger* produces is less certain. That scene is on the north coast of France, and it's a matter—in the style of the earliest Allingham—of discovering buried treasure. It is there that Jack Havoc, now known to be Johnny Cash, is finally defeated. But whereas in the sort of story she wrote in the thirties it would be a thrilling climax, in this story it's a sort of appendix. After my first reading I had entirely forgotten that this was how it ended.

What about that, then? A detective story whose *ending* you forget? One in which you forget that the villain was defeated at all? This sudden transition from the depths of metropolitan realism to the images of high romance is almost bathos. I believe it isn't bathos, but the consequence of the author's suddenly realising that the end of the story is not the end of the story. Jack Havoc may be gone, but who comes next? It is not enough to kill Moriarty, or even Sebastian Moran. Not really.

It is Campion's unmemorableness, his self-effacing flexibility, that makes it possible for him to survive into this sort of story at all. To put the same character in *Look to the Lady* and *The Tiger* is a staggering risk. Margery Allingham can't have seen *The Tiger* coming when she first invented Campion. But she did invent him in just that way, as something of a reply to the traditional superman, and it turned out to be a wise decision.

When you read *The Tiger*, *Hide My Eyes* and *The China Governess*, you are brought to a point from which you can look from a new angle at the writing of Miss Allingham's contemporaries. You see what most detective writers think crime is, and what in *The Tiger* it is shown to be. Take as a test the criminals in Dorothy Sayers's short series. In order of appearance they are (1) an eminent surgeon, (2) a brutal Yorkshire farmer, (3) a greedy woman who wants to steal an inheritance, (4) a medical consultant, (5) a 'little man' who is tired of his wife, (6) a defaulting solicitor, (7) a painter, (8) a sinister foreigner (in that awful dreary book), (9) a hard-up underpaid advertising copywriter, (11) a mentally disturbed Oxford female servant and (12) a mechanic. Number (10) was unintended and an accident. It's all a matter of punishing, or at least exposing, somebody who at bottom has moral standing enough to 'take it'. You simply say, 'He shouldn't have done it.' He is in a community of people who accept their disagreeable but hardly tragic duty to dispose of the criminal. What has the situation of Jack Havoc in common with any of that? What has it to do with Holmes's master-minds of crime, or with Crofts's endless string of naughty-respectable thieves and killers? They shouldn't have done it. But Havoc leaves us helpless, because he is helpless. He is as helpless in his monstrous pride as we are in our inefficiency. He is the product of and the natural inhabitant of the world the war left; more the post-Auschwitz world than the post-Hiroshima world. The traditional criminal has a touch of Milton's Satan; but this one has the whining arrogance of Screwtape. Father Brown alone would understand Havoc. 'I killed all those people,' said he. Fine. He's in a book. Margery Allingham leaves me helplessly saying, 'But I'm Jack Havoc. I'm Jack Havoc's victim. I'm Jack Havoc's creator.'

As if that weren't enough, there is this somewhat less harrowing but hardly less interesting thing that the Allingham stories from *More Work for the Undertaker* onwards tell us; and that is what a problem the love-interest turns out to be for detective authors. Campion, we remember, was married between books. So, heaven help him, was Charles Luke. Now the book that immediately followed *The Tiger* was *The Beckoning Lady* (1955), and it happened to appear just during the two years when I had a locum appointment (unpaid) reviewing novels for an improbable journal: and I shan't soon forget the feeling with which I opened it. I give you my word, I found it unreadable. I still do. I think I said at the time that it left you, the reader, with the feeling of being shut up with a great crowd of people all of whom were talking at once, so that you found yourself almost physically putting your fingers in your ears. We were right back to the old style of people talking with their backs to you.

This, to follow *The Tiger*—well, it is the fact that it did that made me hesitate to be sure of how much of the effect of *The Tiger* was forseen by its author. But the most dreadful thing about *The Beckoning Lady* was what happened to Charles Luke, for, behold, he is in love—with a terrible stick of a woman called Prunella; and in consequence he is entirely extinguished. Had some lunatic told Margery Allingham to tone Luke down? It's not improbable that so vital and devastating a character should be attracted by somebody who was about as warm as a marble statue, and Margery Allingham was entitled, within the canons of her art, thus to throw her new hero among the ghosts; but the result was so appalling that within a year or two she had to contrive the death of Prunella to deliver Luke at all.

This raises a question which we will discuss a little later. But the fact that this happened in the works of the authoress of *The Tiger* does oblige us to notice the one clue we are likely to get to the moral puzzle of detective fiction. No novel without passion is really a novel, and detective fiction doesn't lend itself to passion. Very well, the easy option is to impose passion on it by getting the central character involved with a woman. Again I cannot say that Margery Allingham fully intended this, but what she tells us is that if you want passion in a detective story it must be, if it is brought to the centre, not this passion but the other one: Luke's passion against evil, Luke's capacity for suffering with those who are surrounded by and assailed by evil.

It looks as if it will be demonstrable that the married state is no impediment to the efficiency of the detective in fiction, professional or amateur; but I don't think that the combination of detection with a major treatment of the crisis of courtship has ever succeeded. Some may say that Ngaio Marsh got away with it. Yet where the hero is the sort of superman who can't possibly fail to get both the criminal and the girl you have melodrama of the facile sort. Both Dorothy Sayers and Margery Allingham made it a little more difficult than that for their heroes: Wimsey had to work hard for his marriage; Luke, from the reader's point of view, made a failure of his. And the courtships spoiled the books (I have never thought *Gaudy Night* to be Dorothy Sayers's best book). Elsewhere, then, we shall find either the secure marriage or the American convention of the accepted non-marital association between a hero and his female Watson. There are not many more attempts to combine a courtship-agony with a detective crisis, and it is just as well.

I doubt whether the detective story has ever reached a point of maturity higher than that to which Margery Allingham brought it. She seems to me to stand on higher ground than either Ngaio Marsh or Dorothy Sayers. But each of these three contributed something of indispensable importance to the scenery, and none of them, perhaps, would have attempted anything of the kind had it not been for the example set by Agatha Christie.

14

Politeness and Protest

ONE OF THE events that made history in detective fiction was the foundation of the publishing house of Victor Gollancz. That extraordinary genius set up his press in the late twenties primarily to further the publication of progressive literature with a political emphasis. It became famous at an early age for its promotion of 'The Left Book Club', and for a long time it clothed most of its publications in yellow, black and magenta jackets, which were both economical and eye-catching. The yellow jacket is not now invariable but it has never been dropped. Gollancz, who died in 1967, was a latter-day puritan with a powerful social conscience and a great personal gift for writing. He also had an eye for a forward-looking novel, and the scope of his list quickly widened to include a very rich collection of worthwhile books on most accepted subjects.

It was he who first gave Dorothy Sayers great encouragement, persuading her to continue writing when she was despondent about the success of her early novels, which had been published by Fisher Unwin. When Gollancz left Benn in 1927 to start his own firm, Dorothy Sayers took him her volume of short stories, *Lord Peter Views the Body* (1928), and hers must have been the first detective stories he promoted. Even in the later days of decadence, a Gollancz detective author remains somebody who must not be ignored. Four Gollancz authors now come up for consideration, of whom the first is a well-known Oxford don, in the English faculty, who writes novels and academic non-fiction under his own name of J. I. M. Stewart and detection under the pseudonym of Michael Innes.

Innes is the writer who celebrates the academic in detective fiction; and that is to use the word 'academic' in its proper sense, which is not the pejorative sense often given to it in journalists' English. The Innes story, which has now been appearing pretty regularly for over thirty years, is written with a precision appropriate to its author's craft, and draws on the largest vocabulary of any author in the business. Innes takes a fastidious pleasure in long and perfectly balanced sentences, in the rhythms and values of words and syllables, and in the employment of such pleasingly antiquated expressions as 'well seen' meaning 'knowledgeable'. He is almost as skilful as Leo Rosten (a Gollancz import from America and the creator of Hyman Kaplan) in transliterating dialect, and he knows the difference between a phonetic transcription of its sounds and a true communication of its rhythm. Some of his later stories clearly bring in the European art-critic Braunkopf merely for the pleasure of hearing him speak, and of writing another few pages of his delicious barbarisms. And Innes's one Scottish story is a masterpiece in communicating educated Scottish speech. The impression you always get is that of a first-class senior common room raconteur with a sense of humour, to whom you listen just for the pleasure of hearing it happen.

He began with three winners. *Death at the President's Lodging* (1936) was a very good start indeed—as good an Opus 1 as that of Freeman Wills Crofts. It introduces an educated and alert policeman, John Appleby, who has remained with us throughout the succeeding years. And it is set in an Oxford college. The second was *Hamlet, Revenge!* (1938), for which he appropriates not merely a country house, but (more or less) Chatsworth itself; Scamnum Court, once visited, proved to have a great fascination for him and we hear of it again in later stories. The background here is very High Life indeed, and the profusion of sculptures in the park round the house proves to be something more than mere background décor. The people in the story include an Oxford don and a Privy Councillor, and various other characters appropriate to the romantic thirties. It is a very good tale indeed.

His books have had wide sales and plenty of reprints, but his Opus 3, *Lament for a Maker* (1939) disappeared most mysteriously.[1] Despite the long run of excellent stories he has produced since, I still think this was the profoundest plot he ever con-

[1] It was reprinted in paperback in 1965.

structed. In many ways it achieved things which Innes never came near again. It is set in the Scottish lowlands, and has an important Australian sub-plot (Innes spent a few years in Australia). The sheer beauty of the long narratives of Ewan Bell, in faultless Scottish prose, the powerful evocation of the presbyterian grimness of a Scottish castle, the quite distinguished communication of the narrator's integrity and moral agony, are all at a level which the author doesn't seem to have wanted or tried to repeat. The whole narrative is supported by the grumbling ground-bass of a sinister poem, 'Lament for the Makarys', by William Dunbar (a 'Maker' in this sense is a poet). People who read it when it first came out must be getting quite middle-aged by now, but they have found it impossible to forget.

The sustained literary allusion in *Lament for a Maker* is a device which Innes naturally uses quite often. We keep encountering bibliophiles and art connoisseurs and people of that description in his stories, and not a few are concerned with thefts of works of art.

The next Innes is in a wartime setting. A series of books, indeed, ensued which are thrillers that have a great deal in common with Buchan. A short stay at the University of Leeds gave him copy for a curious tale, *The Weight of the Evidence* (1940), probably the first detective story located in a 'redbrick' university, and certainly the only Innes to contain a palpable lapse in dialect-transmission: his Welsh Vice-Chancellor's speech is entirely unconvincing. He takes us to the South Pacific with *Appleby on Ararat* (1941) and to South America for *The Daffodil Affair* (1942). We return to simpler things and older customs with *Appleby's End* (1945).

By this time the industrious author has given us ten books, and this one becomes a landmark and gives us opportunity to pause. John Appleby appears in most but not all of the stories: and as time goes on he mellows, matures, gets promoted, gets knighted, and retires. He also gets very amiably married (right here, in *Appleby's End*). I fancy that he is less than five years older than his author: probably he is just about contemporary. So in *Appleby's End* he is thirty-nine, just approaching the accepted time for exalted detective characters to marry. All very suitable. But Innes's description of the East Anglian dynasty into which he marries is the first sign we get of an increasingly free-ranging wit, and the description of the train journey with which the story opens is characteristic of that quite remarkable narrative distinction and attention to detail which support all the rest of the stories. This book is lighter and more detached than *Lament for a Maker*. It almost looks as if Innes thought that if he went further along the line indicated by that third story he would get into deep waters where he might flounder. From here on the whole business becomes more a matter of high-grade entertainment and less a matter of the serious pursuit of crime or evil.

The enduring thing, right down to the present day, about all the rest of these stories, which often show a tendency for the probabilities to be stretched beyond breaking point, is Innes's increasing capacity for being extremely funny. There is another epic train journey in the West of Ireland in *The Journeying Boy* (1949)—and, incidentally, in the same book there is the longest passage of straight narrative, without dialogue, covering a moment or two of time, which I know of in the literature (chapter 15). Innes delights in fantastic incongruities, in people with very odd but just possible names: his names are some of the best since Doyle—Umpleby, Hissey, Prisk, Pluckrose, Dromio: Hudspith, a subordinate detective, indicates that Innes had met a Northumbrian, as do one or two other distinguished names. But he is also capable of creating the all-too-probable Australian barbarism, Joyleen. Some of his names would have made the author of *The Screwtape Letters* envious. He enjoys creating scenes of rabelaisian extravagance, though not of rabelaisian outspokenness, for all is understated and measured. He introduces you to a demure little scholar and hangs him up on a travelling bucket on a mechanical conveyor system, of criminal relevance, in Sutherland. The beauty of the thing is in the juxtaposition of this Stevensonian prose with situations of riotous comedy or of far-flung geographical trajectory.

His deliberate espousement of mental aristocracy has made him many literary enemies. One hears the heavy-footed tramp of Lord Snow coming up the common-room stair, and expects a pronouncement from the creator of *The Masters* and *The Affair* about the political and moral irresponsibility of the traditionally cultured. The occasional political judgement, presented as acceptable, indicates little sympathy with progressive socialism, still less with sentimental communism. Yet there is the occasional lift of the political eyebrow. I thought *Operation Pax* (1951) a pleasant sort of political allegory—though whether he meant it so I do not judge. The idea of a research station somewhere near Oxford devoted to painless experiments on human beings with a view to eradicating all their pugnacious instincts by injecting them with something extracted from (of all things, Innes-like) jerboa, is piquantly sinister. That story, incidentally, ends with a chase through (guess where in Oxford?) the subterranean bookstacks of the Bodleian. That is pure Innes. Perhaps the classic irony of the notion of the criminal pursuit of peace is pure Innes also. I am in less doubt about *Hare Sitting Up* (1959), which makes no bones at all about its author's views on nuclear research.

After a middle period especially notable for a superabundance of fantastic situations, in which there was a tendency for plots and situations to overlap [sculptures come to life at Scamnum, and also in *What Happened at Hazelwood* (1946), and a picture comes to life, Ruddigore-like, in *Old Hall, New Hall* (1956); there is a tendency for a plot to turn on the indistinguishableness of identical twins, and those triplets Dromios take the joke altogether too far], Innes has lately come out into calmer water. He keeps to situations of a far more commonplace kind, leaving his energy for the description of scenery and character. *A Connoisseur's Case* (1962) is a good example of the 'third period' Innes—more demure but in some ways more friendly and satisfying.

There is no more passionless detective writer than Innes, except Agatha Christie herself. Passion is out of place in the Senior Common Room. So is anything so obvious as a detective who analyses dust or fingerprints; so is a policeman who does not know what he ought to know about port wine. For the old intellectual puzzle Innes substitutes intellectual wine-tasting, the pleasure of the story rather than the pleasure of the chase. In his celebration of good conversation he is the most puritan of detective novelists. For him narrative is vastly more important than plot and character. One recalls very few of his characters (for me the memorable ones are nearly all in *Lament for a Maker*, and the rest are Ravens). The recurrence of literature and art as the only important variations on the country-house theme places a fairly restrictive fence round his field of social exploration. There is nothing to this but literary pleasure and an evening's good entertainment—but one always gets the latest Innes from the library to see how those very nice Applebys are keeping in their elderly years.

In a sense Michael Innes took off from Dorothy Sayers (who, we remember, finished her cycle of novels in Oxford). Another Gollancz writer, Edmund Crispin, clearly took off from Innes. He, like Dorothy Sayers, had much more to do than write detective stories, and indeed he made only a short foray into the field. Like Michael Innes, he writes under a pseudonym; otherwise he is known as Bruce Montgomery, one of our more accomplished musicians. He was born in 1920, and published eight detective novels, the first in 1944, the last in 1951.

Crispin shares Innes's style and bent, but he is demonstrably of another generation. His first, second and fourth stories are all set in Oxford, and his detective is an Oxford don. Gervase Fen appears in all the books, and he is something of an exception to our statistical rule. Possibly Crispin knew he would not write a long detective saga, so he felt it was safe to use for his detective a Professor of English. Now, no detective writer has been so boldly topical as Crispin in introducing into his books real places and real people. He makes something of a point of snatches of conversation like, 'There goes C. S. Lewis; it must be Tuesday'—which, by the way, was a perfectly well-observed point. For years it was known to which pub C. S. Lewis would go on a Tuesday. That kind of thing adds piquancy to his narratives (and they tend to need it). However, Crispin has allowed it to be known whom he took to be the prototype of Gervase Fen. It would not quite do to divulge the secret here, and it will have to be enough to say that those of us who knew both the fictional and the real-life characters received a massive surprise when the information leaked our way The prototype is a distinguished, able and modest person, about as unlike the flamboyant Fen as he could well be. This happens to be the only case in which I can speak from personal knowledge (as to Charlie Luke, as I explained, I was guessing: and we all know about Dr Bell and Father O'Connor). Possibly it's a case of undergraduate romanticising; perhaps Dr X really did look to

Bruce Montgomery like Gervase Fen when Montgomery was an undergraduate at St James's. But there it is. It's a mystery to me because I am much nearer the age-group of Crispin than that of the *Ur*-Fen.

Howard Haycraft, in *Murder for Pleasure*, a learned and comprehensive history of detective fiction, produced a formula for the writing of this sort of story which was, broadly speaking, '50 per cent good detection, 25 per cent character, 25 per cent what you know best'. It is a formula which covers very well the technique that the romantic writers employed. The way it comes out in Crispin is interesting. Crispin was an Oxford undergraduate and an organ scholar (he composed some good church music as well as some very good film music). In his first book, *The Case of the Gilded Fly* (1944), much of which is very good, he brings us into the chapel organ loft for the climax and then lets us down resoundingly with a totally improbable and grotesque scene based on what he knew best—the names of organ stops. One of the sources of the let-down is the almost complete absence of normal organ stops beginning with 'E'. It's as good an example of the mishandling of special knowledge as you could have in a respectable detective story. *Holy Disorders* (1945), his second novel, is gathered round a west country cathedral and there's a good deal of church music in the surrounding scenery. It was a good point for him to catch out a rascally publican by mentioning the non-existent 'Stanford in E flat', and indeed none of the musical references goes wrong in this story. But what is far worse, he gives us a textbook example of how not to build up to the 'least likely person' solution of a crime. His criminal is altogether too normally attractive until the moment of revelation. The clue of character is totally and unforgiveably hidden.

As he went on he got much better. *Swan Song* (1947) was the best of his 'Oxford' stories—his special knowledge of opera got its chance there. *Love Lies Bleeding* (1948) is perhaps the best of them all: there is some quiet fun in the naming of all the principal characters after church musicians, and in an interview with a thinly disguised impersonation of the Most Important English Musician of that time.

The Long Divorce (1951), his last story, shows perhaps even better what he might have become as a novelist had not other pursuits claimed him. He gives himself a chance to assert a political position in *Buried for Pleasure* (1948), in which Gervase Fen's crazy intention of getting into Parliament is brought to success after the most offensive speech he could devise for his constituents, and frustrated only by the annulment of his claim on the grounds of irregular operations by his agent. This is reasonably comical: the election anti-speech on the frivolous values which pass for politics in a rustic electorate's mind is a construction worthy of Innes.

It's largely soufflé, beautifully cooked, rarely descending to amateurish sogginess. Crispin has the odd mischievous touch—like Michael Innes (in *The Daffodil Affair*) he mentions his own name once; and in an early chapter of *Frequent Hearses* (1950), which, again from personal experience, is capitally drawn, he mentions the name of another very well known English musician, Geoffrey Bush. That reminds me not to overlook the most important thing to record about Crispin; it is that in a short story, in which he collaborated with this same Geoffrey Bush, he produced the best intellectual leg-pull I have personally met since Agatha Christie's *Roger Ackroyd*. It is called 'Baker Dies', and may be found in some anthologies, having been originally published in the *Evening Standard*. Crispin, more than Michael Innes, excelled in short stories. At least two of his full-length books would have gone better as short stories. But one thing can be said of him: he writes like a master, and he has the edge on Innes when it comes to creating characters.

* * *

Appleby is one of the most comfortable of policemen, and Fen one of the most amusing of amateur detectives, and in the post-war era both contributed a good deal to the relaxation of those who would otherwise have been short of it. But if we here bring in evidence two other Gollancz authors we are in for a rude shock. Hindsight makes us able to see it as inevitable that there should be a reaction against all that the detective story stood for; and that some of that reaction should appear within the detective story itself.

By way of astringent antidote to Innes and Fen, then, I must commend Joanna Cannan and John Bingham. Both of them have written genuine detective tales which question something that almost nobody had hitherto questioned with any seriousness—the validity of the friendly image of the policeman.

Joe Orton has this fragment of dialogue in Act 2 of *Loot*:

> 'The British police force used to be run by men of integrity.'
> 'That is a mistake which has been rectified.'

Miss Joanna Cannan's Ronald Price is not a policeman whose integrity one could fault, but there is precious little else to be said for him. He is designed as the ultimate answer to Alleyn and Appleby—meagre of mind and body, committed to all the attitudes of the post-war English petty-bourgeois, married to a shrewish, self-pitying woman with a mania for hygiene and a fear of everything natural. He and his wife between them are the unlovely products of the modern city, hiding a cringing outlook behind a bullying or whining manner. It's difficult to understand how Ronald Price ever solved a case, and in fact he usually needs help from unwelcome amateurs before he is delivered from the results of his bottomless stupidity. Now we have plenty of ill-educated and obstinate policemen in the literature from Lestrade onwards, but we have never met anything as slimily malignant as this until Joanna Cannan conceived him. It is, in the few stories which feature him, a brilliant evocation of all that is nasty in materialistic modernity. This, from *Long Shadows* (1955), gives his manner:

> 'They just went off, sir. I couldn't—er—detain them. I ran them into the village and when they got into Mrs Fairlie's car and drove away they had answered my questions. I had no reason to stop them.'
>
> 'You've worked with me now how long, Sergeant? Seven or eight months at least, but it is evident that you have failed to note how I terminate my interviews with suspected persons or unwilling witnesses. Do you recollect any occasion on which a person I was speaking to "drove away" or "went off" before I had finished with him? I shall be surprised if you do. Now why is that? Don't bother to set your brain in motion. I'll tell you why. It is because I am the dominating personality, and the interview, whether it takes place in a village street or on top of a mountain, terminates at *my* volition. It's a strange thing, a

dominant personality. With me it's a gift, but I suppose it can be learned,' said Price doubtfully.[2]

And this, from the same story, gives his outlook:

> 'Whew,' said Price in the police car. 'Preserve me from foreigners. Granted they look clean, but I shouldn't care to employ them in my home, especially in the preparation of food—no foreigner has the faintest conception of what to us are the elementary principles of hygiene. Once on a day-trip to Boulogne I happened to obtain a view into a hotel-kitchen—what I saw beggars description. A basket containing a cat with new-born kittens was the least of it—and I could not fancy a mouthful until I had regained the shores of Albion.[3]

All this is uncomfortably well-observed.

John Bingham (Lord Clanmorris) takes a rather different line. Here what he questions is the accepted notion that with the police you are safe if you are innocent and will receive justice if you are guilty. That is something which, you would have said, a detective story can hardly do without. But Bingham's stories are especially concerned with the mind of the hunted man, or with the revealing of a character about whom the reader was in the beginning mistaken. He is a pessimist. It is a matter of revealing the badness of a character you thought was good, rather than of vindicating a good character who was in jeopardy. *Marion*[4] (1958) is a sensitive book about a central character who is dead before it opens. But the most characteristic Bingham device, which he has made particularly his own, is the terrifying interview conducted by a police inspector assisted by a subordinate.

> 'I thought you said she was unwell?'
>
> 'She had *been* unwell,' I answered in an exasperated tone. 'Why do you keep trying to tie me up in knots? What the hell are you getting at?'
>
> 'The Inspector's not tying you up in knots,' said the sergeant. 'It's you who's doing that.'
>
> 'I've got more important things to do than try and do that,' said the Inspector. 'Not that it'd be very difficult,' he added, as if to himself.

[2] p. 142. [3] Ib., p. 62. [4] Gollancz, pp. 124–6.

'Oh, all right, all right!'

They both simulated astonishment.

'There's no need to get huffy, sir,' said the sergeant.

'I'm not,' I sighed. 'It's just that——'

'It's just what?' asked the Inspector. 'After all, if you're seen on the premises at the time of Miss Grant's murder, and seen sneaking out by a side entrance——'

'I wasn't *sneaking out*, as you call it,' I said violently. 'It just happens to be the quickest and most convenient way out.'

'And the quickest and most convenient way in, I suppose?' said the sergeant. He looked at the Inspector.

'You wouldn't think Mr Shepton'd lose his rag over a little thing like that, sir.'

'I expect he's tired,' said the Inspector, in a mock sympathetic tone. 'What with having been up so late last night talking with his great friend.'

After one or two passages like that (part of a longer scene) your basic securities are badly shaken. In a later story, *Fragment of Fear* (1965), the central character is left in an unresolved situation of pure terror.

I doubt if Gollancz has a single detective writer, English or American, in his list who fails to write to a high standard. Bingham is one of the most engaging. But he is a true Gollancz product of the later years. He pays his tribute to Gollancz by actually putting him, with his real name, in one of his thrillers, *Murder Plan Six* (1958). It is the logical end of Gollancz's progressivism that these questions about assumed values should be asked, and these realisms faced.

It must at once be said that the question about the friendliness of the police towards the innocent is not associated in any way with the occasional police scandal which during the past twenty years has received special attention in the press. There have been hints of police violence, and revelations of police venality. These have been nothing like frequent or widespread enough to justify any failing of confidence in the force. There is a failure of confidence, but it is the antecedent to these specialised events, not their consequence, and this is what it is important to understand.

During the 1960s the fashion of producing police serials on television in England generated a great deal of activity and attracted a peak audience. There has been the 'Dixon of Dock Green' series, and, by way of reply to that tradition, 'Z Cars' and 'Softly Softly'. 'Dixon' itself grew out of a commercial film which was really a police documentary called 'The Blue Lamp', in which a P.C. Dixon, played by Jack Warner, was killed in the execution of his duty. Ted (later Lord) Willis found it necessary speedily to arrange a resurrection for him, and the low-pressure friendliness of Sergeant Dixon answered very well, in several long series of episodes, to the needs of those who wished to think of the police as always the friends of the innocent. Dixon was always fatherly, never violent, a decent old stick who did his job, and policemen, we all said, are like that. Which is fine as long as you are secure in your certainty that you're innocent.

The answer to that was in the toughness of Barlow, first of 'Z Cars', later of 'Softly Softly', and the bitterness of Sergeant Watt. On the whole, I understand, members of the police force who have any opinion in these matters prefer this series—not least, as one of them remarked to me, because they meet more senior officers who are like Barlow than like Dixon. In these the police are primarily tough and frowning, and there is very little grace at all. But they still get their man. Most recently, in what looks like the best series of the sort so far, we have had 'The Expert', in which the police, assisted by a married doctor couple, are involved in various episodes of malfeasance, but in which the chief point is not usually the solution of a mystery, but rather the portrayal of the magnitude of the problem of public and social evil.

Now at bottom the real question raised by detective writers who write in this wry and protesting style is a question to the reader, which, put faithfully if inelegantly, amounts to this: 'Who the hell are you, to enjoy the security of being innocent?' That's it: the pleasure of reading a detective story is very frequently to be found in the identification of oneself with the innocent person—so that after your cliff-hang, while you wonder if the innocent person is going to be vindicated, you rejoice with him when the true solution is found. Or when you see a villain punished you say, 'I'm with the innocent: serve him right for being guilty'.

One way of putting that 'Who the hell are you?' question is

simply to pull the rug out from under the reader: to switch off his sense of security. It's time, say such writers, that people stopped being so sure that crime and violence are things that happen to other people.

This, I say, is typical modern Gollancz writing. It couldn't be further away from Innes and Crispin, or from Ngaio Marsh and Agatha Christie. There is nothing inconsistent in Gollancz's having earlier published detective tales which were strictly cultural and consenting. But it is not in the least difficult to imagine the eager welcome which Victor Gollancz would have given to writers who are prepared to bring such radical questions as these out into the open and insist on the reader's examining them.

15

And a Large Supporting Cast

WE HAVE NOW followed the perimeter fence right round the field of detective literature. This does not mean that there aren't gates here and there in that fence, providing rights of way to other, associated fields. But I do not think we have now overlooked any of the major constituents of detective fiction, any of the primarily inventive authors, or any of the important questions they raise. We have seen the detective story as romantic and thrilling: we have seen it as moralism: we have seen it as a celebration of science: we have seen it as a kind of novel, exploring human and social situations and attempting to reveal character as well as solution. We have pursued it to the point at which some of its authors suddenly found that the solution was as unimportant as their literary ancestors had held it to be indispensable.

What the supporting cast of detective story writers can do for us is simply to populate the scene we have set. I think it can be found that this cast falls into groups that gather round one of the leading figures, or into one group already formed within the circle of leaders; and I am going to hazard the guess that the much larger number of detective writers whom I shall not be mentioning would, if they were all brought on, do no more than increase the scale of the picture without altering its proportions.

First, we can briefly pay our respects to what we may call the 'mainliners'—authors who are best known, or even only known, for their detective work. At the head of this line we must place Anthony Berkeley (A. B. Cox), who, beginning in the middle twenties, wrote many very satisfying and entertaining books, and conducted some of the earlier experiments with form and content. His 'straight' detection is very much in the climate of St John Ervine among Noël Coward characters. The detective is an amateur on friendly terms with the police: sometimes a rather oppressive young man about town called Roger Sheringham, sometimes a 'little man' called Chitterwick who reflects the curious vogue in minor drama of the time for small, henpecked, ridiculous but improbably triumphant males. Just occasionally a Berkeley made a really good novel—*The Second Shot* (1938) was certainly one; and *Murder in the Basement* had a credible evocation of an English public school—than which there are many worse and one or two better. Usually Berkeley's corpse was a fairly disposable character for whom the reader could have little sympathy; and indeed his liberal attitude towards the punishableness of murderers led him into some very interesting experiments in following the chain of events up to the crime (instead of beginning with the crime), which he usually wrote under the name 'Francis Iles'. From the same source came unusual things like *Mr Priestley's Problem* (1927) and *Trial and Error* (1937), in the second of which an elderly man under medical sentence of death looks for a person whose murder would be a great benefit to society—and then, having done his murder, has great difficulty in persuading the jury not to convict the wrong man. In assessing the merits of this 'supporting cast' I attach some importance to the readiness with which, after some considerable lapse of time, I can recall a character or two from their works. Berkeley's are occasionally very good indeed—I should recommend *The Second Shot* and *Jumping Jenny* (1933) for quality of character. But there is one way in which Berkeley did what I doubt if anybody else has done at all, and I am sure nobody else did quite so persuasively. This was to write the same story twice, as a short story and as a long story, and give it different solutions in the two versions. This is a bit of history which gives pleasure to the collector of oddities. The short story is called 'The Avenging Chance', and the long version *The Poisoned Chocolates Case*. In the long version six solutions are propounded in turn by members of a detection club. The solution given in 'The Avenging Chance' is the fourth, and one of those shown to be in error, in the longer version. Did Mr Berkeley get this criticism from a reviewer of his short story and answer it in a long one?

I think this is probably unique, although those references to Holmes, placing him in error, in other Conan Doyle stories referred to earlier are not unlike it. Both show an unexpected but pleasing objectivity in their authors towards the infallibility of detectives and of their solutions.

The other figure jostling with some impatience and sense of injury at the head of the queue is John Dickson Carr, and he has a right to ask why he wasn't selected to travel first class in this carnival. It was impossible to get even this far without mentioning him; but although he has written so much, and with such distinction, and has taken so prominent a part in the critical assessment and promotion of detection at a high level, I am almost disconcerted to have to insist that you could tell the main story without mentioning him. Yet it was so. I do not know what Dickson Carr has contributed that made any real difference to the direction in which detective literature went. It is no discredit to him to say that what he did, like many other prolific and celebrated authors (and at a higher level than most of them) was to establish and give impetus to the detective story as a serious form of literature. At that level I doubt if anybody did more.

For although I don't call him an inventor, when you stand him alongside his eminent contemporaries of the thirties (which decade was his formative period) you find that he most certainly didn't copy any, and equally certainly cannot be called derivative.

Put him alongside Agatha Christie, who had been writing detection for eleven years by the time Carr's first book appeared (*It Walks by Night*, 1930), and at once you see in Carr a superior gift for character, a deliberate cult of the exotic and macabre, and a sense of humour, none of them directions in which Agatha Christie distinguished herself. (She didn't want to be macabre: she had no gift at all for humour.) Put him alongside Dorothy Sayers and he looks a professional and makes Dorothy Sayers look a learned amateur. Put him alongside Michael Innes, and Innes looks loquacious and long-winded, Carr taut and businesslike. Put him alongside Josephine Bell or Ngaio Marsh and he suddenly shows you the simple difference between what a man tends to write and what a woman tends to write. Margery Allingham in her greatest moments alone manages to achieve and transcend the Carr technique of controlled thrill, masculine energy, and professional manipulation of plot. Carr's books are very masculine indeed. Dr Fell and Sir Henry Merrivale are both larger-than-life figures of masculinity. Carr's women are as stereotyped as Buchan's; all his memorable secondary characters are men. And above all his strong suit, after humour (and, especially as Carter Dickson introducing Merrivale, he can be very funny), is the professional construction of a story, the precise disposition of clues, the inevitability, along with the shattering surprise, of the solution. He loves a locked room mystery, the thing that just couldn't happen but did, and no supernatural cheating either. He is a master of misdirection, of making the reader kick himself for being deceived. Take *The Judas Window* (1938) from the Carter Dickson series, or *The Problem of the Wire Cage* (1940) from the orthonomous one: both are beautifully set out, magnificently surprising, without the least blemish in counterpoint from beginning to end. So it goes on. Not infrequently he jogs the reader's elbow with footnotes, as in *The Nine Wrong Answers* (1952), letting him know that this, where he's got to at the moment, however plausible as a solution, isn't the right one.

And possibly this is where Carr commits himself to following the vocation of technician and interpreter rather than of inventor. He is the virtuoso pianist but not the composer. By heaven, he can play! But just occasionally you get the feeling that it's a bit of a lecture-recital. Partly that pedagogic impression is conveyed by those amusing footnotes, but partly also it appears through one or two affections of style which are just too frequent to pass unnoticed. You *know* that just as tension is building up and a revelation is about to come, the telephone will ring or a shot will be heard or a door will open. The device of interruption is all very well in *Macbeth*, but one could offer a prize to the reader who could identify a Carr novel in which it didn't happen once, and consolation prizes to any who found novels in which it happens less than three times. That and the curious italicised parentheses (*Steady! Steady!*) are effective, but hardly susceptible to repetition. Carr's contribution to the select shelf of historically-imagined detection is significant. His first and best essay in that form was *Bride of Newgate* (1950), set in the seventeenth century, and this was shortly followed by *The Devil in Velvet* (1952), a Regency story. At the end of the second of these he demonstrates in a philological note that the vocabulary he has used is entirely and unexceptionably within that which would have been used by his characters in the 1820s; and the same Ronald Knox-like faculty for writing the speech of other days (some readers may know Knox's *tour-de-force* in this line, *Let Dons Delight*) made *Bride of Newgate*, which is anyhow a slightly better story, a distinguished piece of literary pastiche.

Of all those authors who took innocent delight in setting themselves and their readers puzzles, Carr is the one who has given most simple pleasure. He falls entirely into the simplistic category of detective writers: the thing is a puzzle and capable of solution—every time. There are no draughty windows and doors left open. It's as predictable as Wodehouse, and, seen from one angle, hardly more substantial. But it's professionally done.

Then I observe three lady-writers, bound together by having affinities with medicine. Josephine Bell, a doctor in her own right, has a pleasant though not heavily weighted series featuring a doctor-detective, David Wintringham, his wife who was formerly a nurse, and their children. The stories began well, but there was a tendency in the later ones to drift down dangerously near to the style and attitude which is unkindly attributed to women's magazines. The dialogue was never very compelling, nor were the characters memorable, especially when she pensioned off the Wintringhams. The most interesting thing about Josephine Bell is probably that she was one of the earliest writers to face without turning pale with fright the idea that children could possibly appear in a novel dealing with anything so serious as detection. I shall have to come back to this, but the unwelcomeness of children in the stories of the early and romantic period is a new and persuasive confirmation of the argument that this is a puritan symptom that we are dealing with. However, in post-war years, when the whole tradition of segregating upper-class children in nurseries had disappeared, and you simply didn't have a household with a parent of Scotland Yard or Campion-Wimsey age without children asserting their rights, detective authors bowed to the storm and brought the children in, Innes leading the way with his schoolboys. Inspector Handsome-Hunk-of-Man West has two intelligent, sensible and very pleasant youngsters (a wife ditto ditto) who are always courteously mentioned and given walking-on parts. Even the awful Ronald Price has whining twins who were all but born out of a can. The Campions have a family, the Applebys have at least one son; but it seems to have been Josephine Bell who first established the possibility of the normal bourgeois family as a part of a detective novel.

Gladys Mitchell is an altogether more formidable proposition. She has written a substantial series of books featuring, from the beginning, a frightening female professor of psychology called Mrs (later Dame Beatrice) Lestrange Bradley, who has a distinguished son at the bar, and a reptilian fascination that freezes all manner of miscreants in their tracks. There's no danger of confusing what Mrs Bradley calls psychology with what Hercule Poirot calls it. Mrs Bradley is both more professional in her use of terms and less exclusive, less bumptious, in her claims for the omnipotence of her trade. She has a breezy and capable approach to things that comes off in the stories because her creator is quite unusually good at secondary characters and the description of backgrounds. Gladys Mitchell is obviously a person with a generous faculty of inquisitiveness, and what she finds out she shares. One of her early, and most attractive, stories was *Death at the Opera* (1934), set in a progressive school; she wrote this shortly after becoming interested in the theories of A. S. Neill at Summerhill. Later she returned to the educational background (her own) with a teachers' training college (*Laurels are Poison*, 1942) and an agricultural college (*Spotted Hemlock*, 1958). She does homage to orthodox detective-piety in *Watson's Choice* (1955), set in the usual country house, but diversified by a real 'Sherlock Holmes' dinner party.

Mrs Bradley has made many enemies in the detective-fanciers' world, but I must confess that I have in the end fallen for her heavily. She has to last thirty years from a beginning, in which she is already called an 'old lady' and can't be less than fifty-five; so she stands in the same tradition of imagination-straining longevity as the giants of Carr. She is the cerebral 'super-woman' detective, with her razor-like brain, her alligator-like smile, her alarming strength of wrist, and her unexpectedly beautiful voice. In her very first case she defies orthodox moralities by faking evidence to get the criminal off (*The Devil at Saxon Wall*), but she manages to keep on speaking terms with one of the most credible and sensible clergymen in the literature in *Death at the Opera*.

For Gladys Mitchell as for John Dickson Carr, human error can be put right, contrived mysteries can be solved, and whether or not criminals are punished, the enquiring mind is restored always to a state of rest by the explanation of what was alarming and mysterious. For Mrs Bradley the equipment is all there—the doctor's degree, the high professional standing, loads of money, the freedom to dress scandalously and get away with it. Given that sort of equipment you can solve mysteries: that is the assumption that puts Gladys Mitchell in the middle of the detective mainstream. Being a good writer she keeps her place there.

The third medical lady is easily the most captivating of the three. Christianna Brand also has a nursing background and married a doctor; and she has the distinction of having written one detective story which climbed right out of the lower leagues and made the charts through being quite admirably filmed. This was *Green for Danger* (1945)—one of the really great detective novels of all time. It is set in a hospital and is packed with characters who refuse to leave you when you've put the book down. It is, moreover, an unusually good reproduction of the atmosphere of the Second World War years in England. This was not her first book: that was *Death in High Heels* (1941), a skilful study in the manners of a West End fashion shop of which the author of *The Fashion in Shrouds* (see above) would have approved. That is set in wartime England too—and so was *Heads You Lose* (1941), Christianna Brand's concession to the 'country house' convention.

It is in *Heads You Lose* that we are introduced to Inspector Cockrill. In inventing him Christianna Brand throws in her lot with the 'father figure' detective authors. 'Cocky' is not in his first youth when we first meet him. But he is a very rich and salty character. Slight, energetic, vinegary and loyal, this strange little widower combines in equal measure pathos and rugged courage. The best place to look for the essence of his character is the climactic scene of *Death of Jezebel* (1950). He is remarkably lovable in his prickly remoteness.

Green for Danger remains the best thing she did, and one of the dozen best which anybody did. It was not particularly easy for detective writers to react positively to the conditions which World War II imposed on Britain; and although those who were building up chronicles had to do their best with the situation, there are hardly more than a handful of stories which really do bring back the hectic spirit of that time. One which in my view stands right alongside *Green for Danger* is *Murder on Leave* (1956), by C. V. Galwey, an author whom otherwise I do not know at all. That has the same haunting blacked-out quality, the same feeling that characters are being drawn by the light of naked bulbs in corridors.

It is still not quite time to discuss in any depth the fact that novels about murder can give pleasure; but there is no doubt at all that the writers of the 1940s who succeeded in breaking into the established circle of crime and detective fiction were mostly people who had this particular gift. There is a kind of story that leaves you at the end with the feeling, not that an awful thing has been done and avenged, but that something you can't now quite remember (but important) happened to some very good friends of yours. This is the sort of way in which I remember what I have read of that very pleasant author, Glyn Carr, whose series of detective novels about mountaineering is about as far as anything could be from the dark and deep things to which Margery Allingham was attending. Glyn Carr runs on predictable rails: there are the mountains of Cumberland, and those of Caernarvonshire; and then there are the Alps, and then again the Himalayas. His amateur detective is an actor-manager of fifty-plus (the statistical rule broken again) who in his earlier days was somewhat unwisely liable to quote Shakespeare in every other sentence. Then there is Thurman Warriner, who, besides having a well-developed faculty for the compassionate depiction of pathos, has an even greater gift for introducing you to people you are glad to meet and go on sending Christmas cards to for ten years. I am slightly less sure about his retired gentleman Mr Ambo and his energetic and unorthodox archdeacon Toft (a sort of clericalised Dr Fell), than I am about the quite superb Scotter, who in his classless efficiency and energy is the one product of the fifties to make a permanent impression in detective fiction. Scotter is rather like, though less socially alarming than, Arthur Crook, Anthony Gilbert's aptly-named lawyer, who spends his time vindicating clients whom the more respectable men of business have written off. Crook again is vulgar but lovable, and Gilbert communicates him with disarming skill.

Another novelist of the fifties and sixties who has managed to hold an audience without committing himself to a central and recurrent character is Andrew Garve, who is always good for an evening's entertainment. Garve's earlier books were more like detective stories than his later ones. But from the beginning he went in for the 'vindication' pattern of story—that is, the detection of the truth in order to correct an error which was dangerously likely to be acted on. *The Cuckoo Line Affair* (1953) was a very satisfactory early one—about an elderly gentleman 'framed' for sexual assault in a train; another good one was *The Galloway Case* (1958), in which a man actually convicted and imprisoned was proved, by a loyal friend, to have a clean and honourable record. A more famous one, *Prisoner's Friend* (1962), was about the framing of an ex-convict, and *Death and the Sky Above* (1953) about an escaped prisoner who had been wrongly convicted.

A second line he likes to follow is to reveal (in that sense detect) the weaknesses of human character. *A Hole in the Ground* (1952) was a frightening story about a pot-holer who lost his head and caused his companion's death, the story being built up on the effect of his attempts to conceal what he had done, and leading to a gruesome but inevitable atonement; *The Sea Monks* (1963) is a suspense story in a lighthouse, while *The Golden Deed* (1960) explores the consequences of a man's rescuing a child from drowning—for ends that turn out to be surprisingly disreputable. His background interest in boats (which he shares with many of his literary colleagues) comes out in several of his books, most winningly, perhaps, in *The Narrow Search* (1957), a story about the kidnapping of a child which brings in the scenery and navigational hazards of the English canal network. *A Very Quiet Place* (1968) has its scene mostly in his favourite Essex marshes, in a disused and made-over windmill. He rarely slips, but in *The End of the Track* (1955) he hung too much weight of the plot on a decision whether an embarrassing secret should or should not be revealed. He doesn't there carry the reader with him in his conviction of the inevitability of the consequent crisis.

Garve (in real life Paul Winterton) is a good example of the detective moralist who has as little as possible to do with violence, and as much as possible to do with the knots produced by weak, prejudiced or misguided human nature. Another pseudonymous detective writer who is like Garve in his good humoured approach to life is Cyril Hare, who as Judge Gordon Clarke was well known in the county assizes of the southern circuit up to his death in 1959. He is always witty and urbane, and his detective is a self-depreciating barrister called Pettigrew who is introduced in his middle age and very suitably married (in *With a Bare Bodkin*, 1943) to a wife with considerable musical talent. In *When the Wind Blows* (1948) the plot gives itself away prematurely to the musically knowledgeable though the solution is legitimately hidden from everybody else. Once the Prague symphony was as much as mentioned you knew you had to watch the clarinettist. ('But there are no clarinets in the Prague.' 'That, Watson, is why you must watch the clarinettist.') The best, and best known, of Hare's stories is *Tragedy at Law* (1942), another wartime story of English civilian life, and a very good description of life with a judge on circuit, narrated by a judge's marshal. Hare's short stories were unusually pungent, and they strayed well beyond the conventional detective field. The pious should on no account miss 'The Markhampton Miracle', to be found in his collected short stories: it is a very neat exposure of religious blarney.

We have now moved from what we may call the 'mainliners' to the 'part-timers'; many detective stories of distinction were written by people who either did not write for their living, or who were better known as writers in other forms. Not all such stories are memorable; I have already expressed a somewhat cool opinion of the stories of Ronald Knox. Nobody would consider that C. P. Snow's *Death under Sail* (1932) showed any of the qualities which gave such resounding success to his Lewis Eliot series. No: but there is a good deal of entertainment to be had from the detective work of some writers who were normally employed in more serious styles (or who would anyhow have thus spoken of themselves).

Nicholas Blake, who is C. Day Lewis and the Poet Laureate

who succeeded Masefield, proved to be a gifted if somewhat unreliable writer. As might be expected, he can handle the language, and he is good at character, and apt in communicating the specialised backgrounds convincingly. His amateur detective is a journalist called Nigel Strangeways, happily married in an early story, later losing his wife in an air-raid, subsequently living with a gifted and attractive sculptress who likes to be called a sculptor, but not Mrs Strangeways (see *The Worm of Death*, 1961). These stories are usually straight 'situation' novels with mild detective interest, and not without well-managed thrills. One remembers details: the delightful Irishman, Fergus O'Brien (*Thou Shell of Death*), who makes the rather good remark (for 1936), 'We cartholics are the only ones who can joke about our religion'; the pleasant comedy of *Malice in Wonderland* (1946), set in a holiday camp (especially, if you can take vulgar slapstick, the scene at the camp concert), and, very memorably, the shrewd introduction of the abominable Bunnett in *There's Trouble Brewing* (1937)—which is not only a good description of a brewery but a well-observed collocation of sentimental literary taste and villainy. From Bunnett's first mention of Tennyson there's no doubt that we shall find him a cruel and unscrupulous man. The first detective story of 'Blake' was *A Question of Proof* (1935), which makes him more or less a contemporary of Michael Innes in detection—as indeed he is biographically. He is less adventurous, less literary and precious, but he moves in the same literary world of good taste and intellectual gentility.

Josephine Tey, whose real name was Mackintosh and who was also known as a playwright under the name Gordon Daviot, made a small contribution to the literature that was always of high standard and in one case uniquely memorable. Her first story is dated as far back as 1927—*The Man in the Queue*, originally published as by Gordon Daviot. Probably her best known story, which is hardly a police novel at all but is certainly a novel of character vindication, was *The Franchise Affair* (1947). She is very much of the non-violent school, depending rarely on murder for her plots. *Brat Farrar* (1949) is about impersonation, and *To Love and Be Wise* (1950) also avoids bloodshed. On the other hand *A Shilling for Candles* (1936), *Miss Pym Disposes* (1946), set in a college of physical training, and *The Singing Sands* (1955), a celebration of her native Scotland, all have violent death at their centre. Character is always very well drawn in her books and a restrained sense of drama gives them a nice poise of credibility. But it is *The Daughter of Time* (1951) for which she deserves to be most honoured. Here her detective-inspector (Alan Grant, who speaks, as is proper, with a slight Scottish accent) is in hospital for an extended stay, and he turns his attention to the detection of the truth about the murder of the Princes in the Tower of London in 1483. With the help of a friend who looks up references for him in the British Museum, and a pile of books for his own researches, he comes to the conclusion that the culprit was not Richard III but Henry VII. It is in this book, which recounts the exposure of a whole system of falsified history commonly accepted as true history, that she coins the beautiful and valuable word 'Tonypandy' for all fraudulent history, taking the word from the famous Tonypandy incident of 1926. The whole thing is a masterly piece of historical detection, using the same processes which she would expect her detective characters to use in conventional situations, but here producing the vindication of a real historical character. Josephine Tey died in 1952, just as her detective stories were becoming very popular and receiving substantial reprints. All the current editions of her detective stories are posthumous. They now probably receive as wide an acceptance as did the plays *Leith Sands* and *Richard of Bordeaux*, which made her known in her lifetime.

Another author who combined historical fiction with a sideline in detection was Georgette Heyer. Her long series of historical novels has aroused contradictory opinions: it probably depends on what you think history is. If you feel that history is best related by reference to the more articulate and influential sections of society in whatever age is being put under review, then the Heyer novels give a faithful enough record and an adequate impression of their subjects: it is when one seeks a view of history that includes other people besides Regency bucks who were alive in 1815 that impatience begins to rear its head. She is probably better than her enemies suggest, and less admirable than her immense popularity implies. Anyhow, what is interesting from our point of view is what she made of the detective story. She certainly tells a good story in the small handful she wrote in this form: but she stands with Agatha Christie as an assistant priestess of the cliché. Agatha Christie gets away with it (we have said) because she is such a fiendishly clever and formidably just plot-maker. Georgette Heyer's stories are as countrified and as county as the Poirot situations of 1920, but the detective interest that kept Mrs Christie running never really gets off the ground in Heyer. For the rest—think of any detective-story cliché, any stock character, and you'll find it in her stories: the not-too-well educated policeman, the over-sophisticated policeman, the country vicar with the neurotic wife, the fast-talking competent sister of a heroine goaded near insanity by her husband's brutality, the exotic and outrageous Spanish dancer (called, of course, da Silva—Spaniards in thrillers are always that, or Garcia). It's all perilously near what used (until the *Nova* revolution) to be called 'women's magazine' style—West End, rustic high life, able young asses who teach the police their job, loads of money, and butlers, butlers, butlers (yes, even a Shot Butler). In one book the characters in order of appearance bear the names Amberley, Brown, Collins, Dawson, Fountain, Gubbins, Harper, Jenkins, Ludlow, Matthews. Some better historian will surely tell me that that's been done before; all I can say is that this is where I first noticed it. And yet Georgette Heyer has a quite remarkable gift for reproducing the brittle and ironic conversation of the upper middle class Englishwoman of that age (immediately before 1940). I am bound to say that Vicky Fanshawe in *No Wind of Blame* (1939) is very nearly the funniest fictional female I have ever met—and it needs exquisite judgement to create a convincingly comical young woman in any kind of novel.

In this section of the procession there is quite a bunch of gifted women writers, who will get little more than a glance because they are, as it were, now walking three or four deep. Among the older school Mary Fitt is very much to be recommended for a reflective kind of character-detection (*Requiem for Robert*, 1942: *Clues to Cristabel*, 1944). Patricia Wentworth and Elizabeth Ferrars were more prolific and more conventional—sound practitioners in a post-Christie manner, with less tension of plot and more sensitiveness of style. Mary Stewart, the well known Scottish novelist, usually writes thrillers with plenty of European travel in them, but occasionally she takes in some part of the detective country, and she never disappoints her reader. Mary Kelly is one of the most attractive and promising of the authors who first appeared in the sixties; in *The Spoilt Kill* (1961) and *Dead Corse* (1966) she shows a talent inherited direct from Dorothy Sayers for describing special environments: characteristically, her situations are in British industry, rather than in the more relaxed places Dorothy Sayers described. Being taken round a factory by her is fascinating.

The rapprochement between the thriller (in which a live enemy is outwitted) and the detective story (in which truth is discovered) is to be seen increasingly in the years after 1945. Winston Graham's very fine stories, some of the best since Buchan in the line of travel and adventure, but much more sensitive to the pathos of character, often bring in a detective interest (so for that matter did Buchan), and, when they do, it is done with great judgement. Macdonald Hastings's amusing books about Mr Cork, the London insurance tycoon, with pleasing titles like *Cork in Bottle* (1953) and *Cork on the Water* (1951), are urbane examples of the thriller of improbable adventure rather than detective stories of the normal kind. They follow the fairly well-worn convention of placing an *a priori* unadventurous character in dangerous situations and showing his mastery of them. It is, indeed, interesting to notice what kinds of people are regarded as good candidates for the 'improbable adventurer' role. I suppose the series may begin with Father Brown himself; but it goes on through the 'little men' figures of the twenties and thirties (Mr Satterthwaite from Agatha Christie, Mr Ambrose Chitterwick from Anthony Berkeley) towards the intellectuals (V. C. Clinton Baddeley's Dr Davie, for example, and some of Michael Innes's deracinated bookworms) and the stiff professionals, like Mr Pettigrew (Hare) and Mr Cork (Hastings). When the reader is sated with supermen with whom he can identify himself, he takes some pleasure in seeing his sort of person substituted for the superman and being given superhuman things to do—and doing them with success.

But when it is all said—and I think the same conclusion would be reached through an argument four times as long as this, with forty times as many citations—the detective novelist carries his point by mixing in the right proportions what the reader knows perfectly well with what is strange to him. The great advantage of specialised or strongly drawn local backgrounds is that they can be used either way. If the reader is strange to them, it's an adventure to be introduced to them (if the author knows his work). This is where it is interesting to compare, say, the typical 'Oxford' detective story (odd that there are far fewer 'Cambridge' ones—an Allingham and a Punshon, but few more, surely) with things like the horse-racing stories of Dick Francis. Oxford became fashionable after *Gaudy Night* (1935), but actually J. C. Masterman, then a don at Worcester and subsequently provost of that college, had written *An Oxford Tragedy* three years before, and that is a slightly more academic exercise than Dorothy Sayers's book. Its atmosphere is very faithful—worthy to be mentioned in the same sentence with *The Masters*. And Masterman as Provost followed it twenty years later with *The Problem of the Four Friends*. Yes; well, Oxford seemed to take on popularity both with those who had lived there and with those who had not. To many readers the use of real streets and even real people (Crispin) in an Oxford story evoked eloquent memories: to others it was just the romance of the unknown. Correspondingly, Dick Francis's recent horse-racing books do an excellent piece of work in using the racing scene as a discipline within which all the adventures move. These are (quite unusually in the literature) bound together by no characters, but only by all being more or less about racing. There is no other series of detective thrillers that is so closely confined within one area of interest. As a reader who knows nothing, and has to confess to caring less, about racing, I can testify to the way in which Dick Francis communicates and compels every time.

One real masterpiece came from Gollancz in 1956—Stanley Hyland's *Who Goes Hang?* Here is that 'specialised' technique carried as far as it will go—and with great distinction. Stanley Hyland was librarian of the House of Commons, and in his novel caused a body to be discovered in the 'Big Ben' tower during the extensive repair operations which were in progress there during the middle fifties. In the narrative Hyland was able to bring in just about as much real history, concerning the building of the Palace of Westminster, as Josephine Tey got into *Daughter of Time*, and the result was a real classical sexless cerebral detective story; perhaps the very last of the line.

Finally some examples of the 'east-windy' style reflecting the unease of our present age. I found in some stories of John Trench (a member of the famous family of Chenevix Trench), notably *What Rough Beast* and *Dishonoured Bones*, a streak of anger which I could not remember encountering since H. C. Bailey. *What Rough Beast* (1957) has a devastating picture of a corrupt suburban society destroying an ancient cathedral town: *Dishonoured Bones* (1955) has the best piece of symbolic description associated with modern technology that I have found in this kind of book—that description of the walking dragline in the opening chapter is absolutely haunting, the kind of thing that changes for good your view of opencast mining. I met, a few years ago, on Sheffield station waiting for the midnight train, a man who made walking draglines, and found with astonishment that he was human and without tail or horns. Detective fiction doesn't usually go in for this kind of direct protest, associating crime with the corruption of society: but it did in the Allingham *Tiger*, and Trench isn't a bit less fierce than that—perhaps more so.

Spy stories and double agent stories I decline to admit within the field of detection: my full reasons for that decision follow in the closing chapters. Inasmuch as Penguin publish Holly Roth and John le Carré in green covers, I am happy to mention them, and since both of them write admirably I would recommend them. They are not evidence for what I want to demonstrate here, but they are at the top of their class in suspense and character study. There is, however, a kind of international exception to the puritan rule about detective stories, which is both fascinating and disconcerting. I have in mind two authors primarily: and one of them clearly is Simenon. The amazing success of the Maigret books is a really astonishing phenomenon when one thinks how much fiction of this kind could have been internationally marketed in Europe. Simenon is almost always translated in a mannered and imperfectly idiomatic style, and I suppose that this has its own way of holding the reader's attention. He is, however, unlike anybody else, and his sensitive, courageous, whimsical Maigret has things to say which could only have been said by a Frenchman, and therefore fills many needs that are left open by English stylists. He cannot be central to this study because of his Frenchness: but a very respectful salute over the Channel is in order.

Nicolas Freeling is by way of showing the same picture from another angle; he is an expatriate Englishman who has lived in Holland and France, and has placed all his stories in one or other of these countries; his policeman is called Van der Valk and has a French wife. This is not the travel-agency style of Freeman Wills Crofts: it is the new Common Market style. Simenon sounds as French as Messiaen or Debussy; Freeling sounds Anglo-Saxon-Protestant and is appropriate to a setting which is often placed in the only non-English-speaking country with a genuine puritan tradition. Van der Valk is sent through some pretty demanding and harrowing adventures in his pursuit of justice; and the background of, for example, *Because of the Cats* (1963) is very well assimilated by people who don't happen to live in Holland but do know about the 'generation gap' in the Anglo-Saxon progressive states.

But despite Simenon and Freeling, detective story writing seems still to be a NATO operation rather than a Common Market enterprise, and one of the enigmas proposed by the immediate future is what may happen to the detective story when Britain really 'goes into Europe'? Will that which so easily settles in Australia, New Zealand, Canada, and South Africa find it more difficult to take root in Ghana or in Zurich? That is for discussion in a moment.

16

Certain Americans

WITHOUT MAKING THIS book twice as long as it has so far proved to be, there is no hope of our doing justice to the great variety of detective literature that has come from the various regions of America. In a sense it is a separate subject. In another sense America is at the very heart of the story.

Naturally: for where was Edgar Allan Poe born? Boston.

Poe. What a mysterious name! No country is so rich in improbable names as the United States, for nowhere, especially since 1945, do all the European cultures meet so completely. They meet, of course, in a common wrestling with the English tongue. Monosyllables like Moe and Boe are met with among the Norwegian stock of Minnesota and Illinois. But Poe of Boston! In that one association lies a whole essay in cultural confrontation.

It was in the confused romantic mind of Poe that the modern detective story was born. He was in his youth brainy and bohemian—a good student, dismissed from the University of Virginia through contracting gambling debts; placed at the West Point Military Academy but dismissed for excessive drinking; literary prizewinner at the age of twenty-four; died after a drinking bout in Baltimore at forty. And the detective story (in 'The Purloined Letter', 'The Mystery of Marie Rogêt', and 'The Murders in the Rue Morgue', not to mention the archetypal cryptogram story, 'The Gold Bug') was born in that context. It came really of a violent encounter between the puritanism of Boston and the romanticism of Poe; it came from the mind that so vividly captured the spooky and the supernatural, the horrid and the bizarre. It came from an expatriate European who chose to set his detective scenes in Paris, and who wrote stories which combine suspense and logical surprise with pages and pages of the driest and most pedantic dialogue.

But see it from the right angle, and it is obvious that this is the key to the whole affair. For the puritan culture of insularity, success, industry and moral rigorism was never seen in a stronger solution than in New England—the New England of Hawthorne, and later of Emerson and Thoreau. Writers of that kind give us puritanism direct—logical, polite, efficient and much given to good conversation. A writer like Poe gives us the reaction—wild and rebellious. He represents the escape from the urbanities of puritanism. And yet within all that wildness comes his invention of the modern detective story. It is not at all surprising when one looks at the actual texture of his detective writing. It is pure diagram, pure logic—not moralistic in the least. There is no memorable character. Some of the people are represented by initial letters. This is the freethinker's logic, the rationalist's logic, not puritan logic at all. In a sense there was no future for detection as Poe wrote it, for as Poe wrote it it isn't literature. There is nothing here in the mannered style of Doyle; there is nothing commanding, nothing imaginative. It is two-dimensional stuff: it merely indicates that the thing can be done and, for a few occasions, done without positive failure. It is an extraordinary demonstration that a man with the imagination of Poe could produce such fleshless narrative. It was, frankly, an experiment.

So far as American detection was concerned, it was a false start, and it is perhaps sufficient to say that until the twentieth century was well advanced American society did not produce anything in this line that was not strictly derivative from English models. The great days of American detective writing were from about 1930 onwards. Not but what John Dickson Carr was partly American, and set several of his stories in the U.S.A., including the very early *Poison in Jest.* But quite naturally America had to wait for the federal America to come to life before it could put flesh on the bones of its native literature in this field. One feels that something less refined and more contrapuntal than the undiluted rectitude of New England was needed. The subsequent story confirms this.

Nowadays the whole business seems to gather round one

extraordinary and mysterious name—that of a certain Ellery Queen. Now in history 'Ellery Queen' is two cousins, Frederic Dannay and Manfred B. Lee, who were both born in 1906 (Lee died in April 1971), and who jointly wrote *The Roman Hat Mystery* in 1929. They made a resounding success of it. In fiction, Ellery Queen is a New Yorker, born about 1903, living in an apartment with his father who is Inspector Richard Queen of the New York Crime Squad based on the 87th Street precinct. So the central character of many (not all) of the stories written by 'Ellery Queen' is Ellery Queen: and he is by profession a novelist who writes detective stories. In *The French Powder Mystery* (1930, op 2) he is described as looking thirty but being actually younger. In the foreword to a later edition of that book it is said that later he married and had a son. As it turned out, it was unwise of his creators to provide this information.

For 'Ellery Queen' turned detective story writing into an industry. In founding *Ellery Queen's Mystery Magazine* in 1943, and publishing a series of short detective stories thereafter, and offering substantial awards for winners of competitions, 'Queen' aroused the talent of new writers all over the world, and drew on the gifts of the already-tried writers as well as finding occasion to include many new stories of 'his' own. And although our intellectual friend Ellery was still going strong in the 1960s, and, what is more remarkable, his father was still serving in the New York police, there is no record of the original biographical foreword being admitted to be a forgery. Quite clearly Queen started something which 'Queen' did not envisage.

This is a delightfully characteristic thing to happen in America. What had become a respectable sideline in the English writing trade became, under the guidance of those two geniuses, very big business indeed. The two authors managed to find time to write, as well as many 'Queen' stories, several other lines of fiction under at least one other name, and using other sets of characters. But what is also characteristic of some, though not all, American enterprise is the way in which the Queen output defeats every possible attempt to label it cheap, stylised, or narrow in its range. There is surprisingly little repetitiveness in the plots, and a remarkable faculty for coming up with something quite fresh. This perhaps is the advantage of having two minds operating on one another: it is just the reverse of what happened to that thriller-machine Edgar Wallace.

Indeed, what Ellery Queen excels in is sheer, indefatigable observation. 'He' has noticed everything, and has managed to get inside all manner of different imaginative situations. Look at a sample of his plots (we'll stick to the singular). There was *The Siamese Twin Mystery* (1933)—a very typical closed-in situation in a forest fire on the mountains, but with the slightly Poe-like addition of a pair of Siamese twins in the very centre of the picture, twins of about eighteen years old. There was *Cat of Many Tails* (1949), a study of the reduction of a great city to panic by a single desperate criminal. There was *The King is Dead* (1952), set on an Atlantic island which was owned and ruled by a power-crazy tycoon. There was, above all (by far my own favourite), *The Glass Village* (1954), set in a closed-up little New England village community and centred on a village church. There was *The Finishing Stroke* (1958), whose climax turns on an ability to read and understand the Hebrew alphabet (and in which, by the way, Ellery says 'In 1930 I was very young . . .'). There was *The Player on the Other Side* (1963), which is a variation on *The Finishing Stroke*, and uses the august motif of the Hebrew 'tetragrammaton' in the development of its plot. And for good measure there was *And on the Eighth Day* (1963, dramatic date 1943), set in a completely isolated desert community which had had no contact with the outside world for seventy years.

And so on. Sometimes the story turns on a detail of observation (there is a short story which is solved by Ellery's observation that American telephones don't have the letter Q on their dials). Sometimes there is an historical emphasis (as in another where Ellery finds a treasure buried enigmatically by George Washington himself in a roadside farmstead). Several stories move out of New York to the typical up-state township of Wrightsville, where Ellery was born [for example, *Calamity Town* (1942), *The Murderer is a Fox* (1945), and *Double Double* (1950)]. But whatever 'Queen' picks up he treasures carefully and describes accurately.

He is not a violent type at all—he is an eastern seaboard intellectual. His affection for his father is most endearing; and he sets (I think) the style which Perry Mason followed of annexing a very pleasant and devoted secretary who is, so far as the reader is concerned, everything but his wife. Nikki Porter is not quite so irreplaceable as Della Street, and a little more believable.

There is breadth, but there is also a genuine depth, in the 'Queen' outlook. It is impossible not to be fascinated by his occasional excursions into the religious field—and this again is very characteristically American, and indeed Eastern American. One very often notices in American detection the unself-conscious way in which clergy and churches are mentioned. This hardly ever happens in English detective fiction—just occasionally an author manages it, but almost all the time that side of things is left out, flatly denied by a central character, or introduced with laughable clumsiness. We remember the benign, scholarly, absent-minded vicar and E. C. Bentley's Congregationalist corpse and an awful Methodist aunt in G. D. H. Cole; Alleyn's scepticism, Holmes's sentimental anti-religion, Roger Price's ninth-hand Bradlaughism. But in the U.S.A., religion, in the detective story era, is part of the legitimate scenery, and it is the most natural thing in the world for 'Queen' to invent *The Glass Village*, and to get as much atmosphere out of a meeting of the elders of a puritan church as he does out of a case of amnesia in Wrightsville. But more than this: those Phoenician characters and Hebrew mysteries fascinate him, and Ellery treats a knowledge of such things as being all part of an educated man's equipment. More yet: the whole form and dramatic movement of *And On the Eighth Day* is curiously scriptural: and I mean 'curiously' in the precise sense. For the action takes place over eight days, April 2 to April 9, 1944: and the climactic death is a death of atonement on April 7th; on April 8th there is no action, described in a chapter of six words. And on April 9th a new character is introduced who comes parachuting down from a burning aircraft (a 'chariot of fire') and is last seen going into the strange community of the valley to give it new life. Now it has been computed by some investigators (the computation is, of course, challenged on many scholarly grounds, and there is nothing verifiable about it) that the events leading to what Christians know as the Crucifixion and the Resurrection did in fact take place on days identifiable as April 7th and 9th with a day of mysterious inaction between.

All this is external and of no importance whatever except as evidence of the tendency in the 'Queen' mind to try to reach out beyond triviality: to treat with respect things that in the human tradition of the West have been regarded as important, and to be quite without affectation or awkwardness in doing so. This says nothing about the 'Queen' belief, which anyhow is irrelevant to this field of investigation: nor does it say anything about their work as literature, although in fact on other grounds it can be shown to be very good literature indeed—remarkably free from cliché and verbal adiposity, in a style very well adapted to the conveying of character. The police tradition is obviously one of extreme rectitude, if a little more rugged than the English. Sergeant Velie is believable and just manages to be likeable, although he isn't at all on the Sergeant Dixon pattern.

I think I know of only one black sheep in the Queen fold. *A Study in Terror* (1966) is a story in which Ellery Queen finds an unpublished manuscript of Dr Watson's about a Holmes exploit, from which he deduces the identity of Jack the Ripper. (It really is not quite clear whether the deduction is Holmes's or Queen's). Apart from its being an uneasy association of fiction with history, this is how its narrative opens:

> It was a crisp morning in the fall of the year 1888.

All the reader can expect after that is that the manuscript will turn out to be a forgery. It must be! Watson could never have written 'fall'. Nor could he have written all the other Americanisms in this document. Still less could he have attributed such expressions to Holmes himself. This is entirely surprising in an author-partnership whose longest suit has always been minute observation of details, and whose stories actually contain plots based on the difference between English and American idiom. A staggering lapse, this. Perhaps the whole book is a forgery.

But that apart, the Queen empire is not without culture and the gentler virtues.

One goes on from there in one direction to the Perry Mason saga: and here we are on very different ground. The Erle Stanley Gardner enterprise is less like a corporation, more like a highly successful one-man industry. Gardner (1889–1970) wrote under several pseudonyms and in several styles, but it is only the Perry Mason and 'D.A.' series that can be called detection. He was a lawyer, and his strong suit is naturally the law. He turned out his stories with relentless efficiency. He rarely moved away from the exordium in the office and the climax in the courtroom, with inevitable defeat for the Establishment, but quite often at the end of one case we have an intimation of the next, with the next client actually at the door. The stories have nothing like the individuality of the Queen stories, yet any of them taken singly is a good craftsman's job. Mason can be more violent than Queen, and he usually provides the reader with a good 'vindication' scene—there is always a happy ending, and confusion to the fraudulent client or to whoever is representing the District Attorney's office. The very titles are stylised; for a time they were alliterative (*The Case of the Perjured Parrot, The Case of the Shoplifter's Shoe*), but this is sometimes varied by a touch of oxymoron, as in *The Case of the Runaway Corpse*, and *The Case of the Stuttering Bishop*. Not infrequently a story is prefaced with a tribute to some distinguished jurist or forensic physician known to the author, and here and there one gets interesting bonuses of curious information, as one does concerning the making of artificial eyes in *The Case of the Counterfeit Eye*. (I omit dates for all these titles deliberately: there is absolutely no sign of any change of style from the early books to the late ones.)

Mason is strictly a mythological character: neither he nor Della Street ages over the years. Miss Street is always 'crisp and efficient' and twenty-seven. She often nearly marries the boss but never quite does so. The locale is Los Angeles—the 'second city' so far as American detective fiction is concerned (it must be obvious why hardly anything comes from Chicago). The picture of Los Angeles you get in the stories is several shades brighter than you get if you visit the place. Indeed, it is all strictly artificial and nobody is taken in for an instant. Yet it is this unvarying rhythm and this sense of ultimate security that makes Perry Mason sell. You're dead safe, however high the precipice you're looking over. Heaven knows this appeals to Englishmen, so what must it be as a sedative for the citizens of Los Angeles?

In America there is a good deal of straight novel-writing in

G

detection: and one of the more attractive American novelists is Patrick Quentin (alias Q. Patrick), who is particularly skilful at extracting the psychology of a crime situation; with him, in the same *genre*, one would put Helen McCloy, with her sensible, orthodox Basil Willing, psychiatric and forensic medicine-man. The more romantic and old-fashioned weird superman is found in Rex Stout's Nero Wolfe, and a vigorous line in feminism is followed in M. G. Eberhart's Susan Dare stories and in the older yarns by Stacy Aumonier featuring Madame Rosika Storey. (There are one or two ways in which women's emancipation has made headway in the U.S.A. beyond what the English are accustomed to: detective heroines are one, and high-grade church organists another.)

One of the most cheering appearances in American detection in more recent years has been Francis Kemelman's 'Rabbi'. Here again, if any English author tried to set a story of this sort in a Jewish community he would fall over his feet trying to make it credible to gentiles. In the U.S.A., not at all. The Rabbi has made an excellent start with *Friday the Rabbi Slept Late* (1966) and two sequels featuring *Saturday* and *Sunday*. One hopes there will be room for more than a total of seven. The Rabbi doesn't have to extinguish his religion or turn aside from it; it is indeed his religion that provides many of the connections between the clues he is given. He is America's answer to Father Brown, and an entirely capable and graceful job he makes of it.

In the U.S.A., then, the detective industry is going well: and for that we have to thank partly Ellery Queen and partly the fact that up to now social change in America has followed social change in Britain a generation later—until, that is, the racial issue came back on the scene. Until very recently America was a much more churchgoing nation than ours has been since 1918; social attitudes which we recognise as typical of those who were adults in the 1920s are still very much to be found in the urban American from coast to coast. Almost certainly the gap will close, and when it does the detective story in the U.S.A. will feel the east wind. But at present one can always look out for Raymond Chandler, Howard Browne (*Thin Air*, 1955, is very much to be recommended), Stephen Ransome (*Night Drop*, 1955), Emma Lathen, with her John Putnam Thatcher novels of business life, and especially the current 'Vic Varallo' Los Angeles saga of Lesley Egan.

Varallo—there's a minor but significant point. If you actually go to the U.S.A. and move in circles where people are thinking and composing and inventing, one of the first things to strike you is that unpredictable cosmopolitanism of their names, of which 'Poe' was an example. Americans are very punctilious about introducing one another and acknowledging the introduction, and well they may be when to the insular British ear the names are often so foreign that one wants to say (but etiquette forbids it) 'How's that spelt?' In any gathering you are liable to meet a Norwegian name, or a German or Spanish or Italian or Czech one: or an anglicisation of one of these. I have good friends in the U.S.A. called Huffstutler, Pfautsch, Dietterich and Krapf; I have books on my shelves bearing the names of Tillich, Pellikan, Dittmanson and Fischer. And how many foreign-based names do you find in the 'good' characters in Erle Stanley Gardener? Or even in 'Queen'? The detective story belongs to the insular puritan culture transplanted to the U.S.A. rather than to the cosmopolitan society which in the last two generations has grown up in America. The assumptions are that law and order are preserved by the first families of Massachusetts; Cape Cod corresponds naturally enough to the Agatha Christie country house, a puritan-style minister to the country vicar.

Two things can be said about American detective fiction. One—which may seem hazardous but which I still think is true is that it is less stiff, less dominated by cliché of character or situation, and less confined in social leading-strings than English literature of the same kind and the same era. On the surface that may seem to be instantly refutable by reference to the actual literary style in which the American detective story is written and the dialogue transcribed. But most of that impression is due to the very slight foreignness of the way in which Americans use words, the salty and spirited idiom which has become a common heritage of English and Americans but which the fastidious still call American. Even the quite familiar spelling of 'traveling' and 'labor' makes the old-fashioned English reader sensitive to a style and liable to call it excessively mannered. That is not what I mean here by cliché. I mean that complex of social assumptions which English detective writers mostly don't question. The greater freedom of movement in American society, the absence of an hereditary aristocracy, the whole 'democratic' assumption, graceless though it appears from one point of view, does deliver from vexatious mental habits authors who are always in danger, because of the nature of their material, of falling into them. I suppose that if any American writer of standing can be compared with Agatha Christie in his tendency to tell stories in hunks rather than in elements, it must be Erle Stanley Gardner. His plots are splendid, yet each one is like the others, and having read a string of his books you still can't tell, looking at the titles on their spines, which was which. There is Perry Mason pacing the floor of his office, head hunched forward, thumbs in the armholes of his vest—he's on record as having travelled many miles like that; there is Della Street's crisp efficiency: there is always a doting moment when she doesn't get proposed to after all. All that side of Gardner is pure corn—and the same goes for the non-Mason stories, which were nearly as successful and precisely as conventional. Gardner saved himself simply by being a courtroom novelist. There in the courtroom you have a ritual, a liturgy—'Irrelevant, incompetent, immaterial and not the best evidence': 'Overruled': 'Sustained'—and within the predictable liturgy things happen predictably. Nobody minds that. It's only when the judge looks thoughtfully over his desk and allows a risky move by Mason with a twinkle in his eye that the reader says, in whatever language, 'Uh-uh'.

But there is in American detection, as in American essay-writing and poetry, and indeed in any major product of the American culture, a pretty wide and spacious high-level table-land of good stuff. There are more American writers who would get sixty per cent at Cambridge or Beta double plus at Oxford than there are English ones. There are more English Alphas or seventies than American. That I would concede. But I would also say that the effect of American writing on English detection has been not inconsiderable, and certainly salutary. One of the special services which Americans seem appointed to do for England at present is to provide a stiffening of professional and disciplined craftsmanship to support the failing energies of what used to be England's inspired amateurism. This is just what happened when the half-American John Dickson Carr began operations in the English market. It was very like what Henry Ford did for motor-manufacture. 'This is what you really meant to do.'

The fact that American 'free-range' society made a world safe for gangsters is only another example, in a different mode, of that ease of movement which distinguishes Americans from the English. You couldn't have Al Capone in a society which hadn't bred real social confidence. Every quality has its underside, and gangsterism and lawlessness, which flourish on so large a scale in the U.S.A. that the smug English continue to think of them as American inventions, provide copy for detective writers in America: so, naturally, does violence. What the Ellery Queen consortium calls 'Black Mask'—realistic narration of adventures that combine, and for the sociologist significantly relate, sex and violence—is characteristically American only inasmuch as it was in that wide country that behaviour of this sort occurred in places where it would get written about and among people who had memory and self-consciousness enough to exploit it. Sex and violence aren't American inventions. John Wesley could have told us that.

[illegible] from the [illegible]
[illegible] German supremacy [illegible] which makes [illegible]

happens when the tall American John DeLorean [illegible] operations in the [illegible] Ford did not manufacture [illegible] [illegible]

[illegible] American [illegible] [illegible] in a [illegible] of [illegible] Britain [illegible] the [illegible] [illegible] the U.S.A. that the [illegible] American [illegible] [illegible] [illegible] which [illegible] [illegible] [illegible] of this sort [illegible] [illegible] [illegible] [illegible] DeLorean [illegible].

IV

EXCELLENCES AND LIMITATIONS

17

The Case against the Detective Story

THERE ARE MANY kinds of people who have no use for detective stories, and there are several routes by which one can argue towards the conclusion that they, and the people who read them, are trivial. I am prepared here to examine three lines of argument—a moral line, a social line, and a philosophical line. And I get the moral line from an opinion expressed not long ago by the well known novelist L. P. Hartley.

In *The Novelist's Responsibility* (1967)—that is the title both of the book and the first essay in it, from which I am here quoting—Hartley is, towards the end of an argument against irresponsible and nihilistic novel-writing, led into a discussion of the disappearance of a sense of justice from common life. Compassion, he notes, has come to mean something very different from what it used to mean, and the change of significance he finds sinister.

> Compassion is the order of the day. The highest praise that a reviewer can give a novelist is to say that he writes with compassion. I had a letter from a stranger the other day in which he said he was sure my books came from an unusually compassionate heart. Well, I have nothing against compassion, far from it: if one considered only a millionth of the sufferings of mankind, not to mention one's own, one's tears would never be dry. But the reviewers mean another sort of compassion, compassion for men's misdeeds, and with that I'm not sure I am altogether in sympathy. What becomes of justice? Is it to be completely drowned in compassion?[1]

[1] L. P. Hartley. *The Novelist's Responsibility* (Hamish Hamilton, 1967), pp. 15–16.

So far the argument is very clear. Compassion without justice becomes sentimentality, and sentimentality becomes cruelty: so compassion defeats itself if it is not subordinate to justice, which says that a crime must be punished, not that compassion may condone it. He goes on to give a specific example of the moral error he is exposing.

> A little while ago there was a case of a young woman who was telephoning from a public call-box . . . and two youths who had possessed themselves of some firearms and were crawling about on the roofs nearby, shot her. I don't know how seriously she was injured, but some of the comments, I was told, ran like this: 'Why did she choose that moment to be telephoning, when two high-spirited lads were crawling about the roofs, armed with guns? What more natural than that they should shoot her? It was a provocative act on her part. . . .' In their eyes the boys were to be pitied much more than the girl. There are a great many people, and some very good people, who are more shocked by punishment than by crime.

Now between the statement about the corruption of justice and that narrative, so placed that it forms a direct link between them and completes a continuous paragraph, there is this sentence:

> Detective stories have helped to bring this about, and the convention that the murderee is always an unpleasant person, better out of the way.

Detective stories have helped to produce a society in which justice abdicates and compassion goes sour: that society has produced incidents like the story of the girl in the telephone box.

I find that fascinating. It is, on the face of it (and was fastened on by certain reviewers as being), an argument from moral premises against detective stories. It is a little less crude than the argument that detective fiction causes people to accept violence without protest: but it is of much the same kind. It is an argument one often hears.

My question is, what does Mr Hartley think a detective story is? At least, that's my first question, but I have others. The notion that what he calls the 'murderee' (if that's all right for a good novelist it should be all right for me, but I still find it a bit gritty) is an unpleasant person who is rightly got out of the way is a very unsafe induction from the various fields of detective fiction. One of the Sherlock Holmes short stories could be described in that way—'Charles Augustus Milverton'. I suppose it was E. C. Bentley who made the 'justifiable homicide' aspect of the detective story fashionable: but we recall that his historic contribution was by way of being a detective story to end all detective stories.

It is indeed very strange that people should so often say that the detective story is immoral. It is necessarily proper to distinguish between detective stories that are authentic and those that are in one way or another degenerate. Not only is it proper so to distinguish: it is affected and stupid to pretend that the distinction isn't perfectly easy to draw. And the detective story which conforms to the basic design of the form is the most moral kind of literature there is. It precisely doesn't commend a society in which crime gets more compassion than suffering. Indeed, it can't live in such a society as that—and it is dying before our eyes in a society which Mr Hartley quite rightly describes as sick of that disease. Its whole assumption is that of 'law and order', and if law and order is a moral notion, then detective fiction is a very soundly moral form of fiction.

The fact is that Mr Hartley is hanging a respectable argument on the wrong peg and supporting it with a very tendentious illustration. It was naughty of him to produce so emotive a story with so little collateral evidence. Who says that the story is true? It is so vague as to be unverifiable. We don't know even whether the guns were popguns or twelve-bores, whether the girl was frightened or killed, whether the police were involved and the culprits apprehended; above all, we don't know who said those unsurprising things about the incident. We can guess; we can guess so easily that it's tempting to believe that Mr Hartley simply made them up and attributed them to public opinion in general in the style of a Greek chorus or a speech in Thucydides. Indeed, the whole thing has an oddly Greek flavour—it reminds me of the epigram in the Greek Anthology about a character who was so polite that when somebody stepped on his toe he invariably apologised for putting his toe in the way of the other man's foot. I needn't believe Mr Hartley's story, and the fact that he's so ready to produce it without any facilities for the reader's verifying it tends to indicate that the point he is making is an emotionally loaded one. It is indeed: the previous paragraphs prove that. He is one of those people upon whom the fashionable asperities of society are bearing very heavily; like any traditional western artist he is an individual who is worried about the increasing difficulty of being an individual in a crowded society. Fair enough. Anything that looks like contributing to that difficulty will be condemned. So he has a side-swipe at the detective story. But the proposition is derived from the wrong premises.

The moral argument that will stand up is this: that the detective story is the product and the weapon of a middle class puritan society whose morality makes claims that have no foundation. The point to attack is that at which the detective story makes the criminal (not the 'murderee') the undesirable person. It encourages us to be too sure who is wicked, and too little hesitant about who is disposable. It throws too much weight into the scale-pan marked 'justice', too little into 'compassion'.

That is the direction the argument ought to take. It can, I think, be refuted by repeating the distinction between true detective stories and imitation ones which fail to show understanding of what the form is really for. It is all the bastards and hybrids that do the damage, or at least make it possible for the analysts to represent them as falsifying morality.

The person who should attack the morals of detective fiction is not the tory first-culture novelist but the situation-ethics avant-garde philosopher. Where morality is re-stated in terms of situation instead of in terms of prevenient dogma, then the detective story is bound to suffer revision. The situation-ethics man will not want any novel to reinforce *a priori* assumptions about morals ('This is always and everywhere wrong'); he will only want it to uncover truth. He will be prepared to assume that deceit is wrong—for the condoning of deceit and lies will make communication impossible. He is less interested in advertising the opinion that murder, or theft, or fraud are always and everywhere wrong. In practice he will never defend a blackmailer, not often a forger, fairly often a thief, and very often indeed a murderer. But he will never consider defending a writer who himself falsifies evidence, and he will be content with a detective story that simply detects.

Now the argument against dogmatic morals will succeed provided it really admits that it is a social argument—an argument against social attitudes disguised as moralities. It is no argument against a detective story to say that it accepts basic *a priori* moralities, because in a totally amoral society there is no chance for its survival at all: indeed there is no chance for the survival of anybody who is weaker than anybody else. And in practice it will be found (we have already cited sufficient examples not to have to go over them again) that decent detective writing preserves a nice balance between moral dogmatism and the compassion which Mr Hartley wants. It was inevitable that in the end detective writing should become detection of character; and where a novelist really knows how to depict character, the very last thing he or she will allow is the forcing of character into a preconceived moral mould. The good novelist doesn't even tell the reader what a character is: he leaves it to the reader to gather that, paying the reader the compliment, by what is left unsaid, of assuming his capacity for receiving the message, and making sure, by what he does say, that the reader is in no danger of being misled.

It is this overstatement and oversimplification of background assumptions that the detective novelist has to guard against. Incautious technique at this point leads to the kind of error that makes the modern sociologist and anthropologist react at once. But for all that there has to be a minimal background assumption that what is metaphysically or morally self-contradictory is wrong and inadmissible. Loosen that assurance, and no kind of pattern can be built up at all.

There is a social argument against the detective story which would be closely allied to what we have just been representing as the moral argument. This would be to say that detective stories perpetuate and celebrate a set of social assumptions which are undesirable and ought to be discouraged. To put it less precisely, detective stories are reactionary. They rely on the acceptance of assumptions about law and order, about the rights of property, about the sanctity of human life, and about the propriety of the punishment of wrongdoers, which should be allowed to change, or perhaps should at once be changed.

That is, anyhow, the argument. And naturally it comes from those who do not regard an established social order as self-evidently beneficial. The question is how far detective fiction does rely on an unchangeable social order, and it can at once be seen that any who would defend the detective story against the charge of incorrigible political illiteracy will have to take a long journey round some forbidding obstacles.

The exceptions are sufficiently rare to prove the general rule that the detective story is socially smug. We are not now speaking of morals: I should contend that in assuming that murder is wrong a detective writer is within his rights. The more awkward question is whether the social assumptions are healthy. In building up the case against the detective story, the prosecutor would be likely to mention the preoccupation of detective writers with the affluent and the literate, and their assumption that what happens to such people is interesting, whereas what happens to people in the lower ranges of society would not be worth writing about. If it be answered that the detective writers only took over where the Victorian novelists left off, and that it certainly was the assumption of Trollope and Wilkie Collins and many other popular Victorians that affluence made a better story than poverty, the prosecutor can then reply that the detective writers kept the fantasies of affluence and heroism going much longer than other novelists did.

One thing one notices in detective stories that indicates how far a detective writer seems to have to limit his social apprehensions is in the manner in which children are treated in them. The obvious assumption is that children have no place in these incidents at all. What on earth (saving only the Baker Street Irregulars) have children to do with the Sherlock Holmes world? Or that of Thorndyke? Or of Father Brown? We have already seen how difficult detective writers find children when they are writing straight detective novels, and although there were some conspicuous exceptions—one or two pleasant and intelligent children, one or two terrible ones—and although Mr Fortune had that peculiar horror of cruelty to children which appears in a number of his adventures, the detective world is obviously a world in which children count for no more than they counted for with Trollope. Since so many novels of middle class life from 1940 onwards handled children very well and calmly, it is clear that here again the detective story was socially laggard. But the reason is that the detective story is not really a middle class story in its essence—which is why it made such clamorous appeal to the middle classes. Those things which are especially middle class have become material for novelists only since life became difficult for the middle classes, and since the middle class became the object of scorn and hatred. In the world in which Holmes moved, as in that in which Poirot was at home, children were about somewhere but simply didn't bother adults. When that world disappeared and even tolerably affluent professional fathers were taking quite a new attitude to the kitchen and the nursery, the novelists seized on it and made a meal of it; but not the detective writers, because unless they were very careful the introduction of all this would bring a disturbing element into the story which they did not want.

That is it: the detective story has to maintain a nice poise or it will collapse. It simply won't do what it is designed to do. It will gather to itself a seriousness, a message, a mission, and in the end a conscience; and the result of all that will be that no problem will be solved at all.

What we have just said has really introduced our third point, which I call a philosophical one, although it is really made most often by men of letters.

I here bring in evidence two passages from the recent work of literary critics: the first is from Frank Kermode's *The Sense of an Ending* (New York, Oxford University Press, 1967), who quotes Sartre.

> Novels, says Sartre, are not life, but they owe their power upon us, as upon himself as an infant, to the fact that they are somehow like life. In life, he once remarked, 'all ways are barred and nevertheless we must act. So we try to change the world: that is, to live as if the relations between things and their potentialities were governed not by deterministic processes but by magic'. The *as if* of a novel consists in a similar negation of determinism, the establishment of an accepted freedom by magic. [p. 135]

Sartre, that pervasive pessimist, reveals the 'make-believe' of all fiction. To him all life, all human existence, is to some extent fiction. Kermode is content to apply his pessimism to the novel.

Later (p. 140) he says, 'The novel has to lie. Words, thought, patterns of words and thought, are enemies of truth.' The whole chapter (indeed the whole book) deserves careful attention on the part of anyone who would investigate the truth content in literature. But the reader will by now have grasped the point that is relevant here. It is that if any novel is artificial, a detective novel is more artificial than the rest: more subject to imposed pattern. Holmes must not only work a minor miracle in reading Watson's thoughts: he must be right. His rightness strains the reader's credulity. A more subtle and sophisticated detective story may by-pass the reader's critical faculties and therefore arouse no anxiety. But what about the anxiety he would have felt had he been wide-awake, or not taken in by the author's dexterity? There can be no planning of a plot without contrivance and artificiality and an assumption that the reader will leave certain questions unasked. The chief question he may not ask is, 'Who are you, the author, to say that? By what right did you make your character like that?' Kermode, in the passage quoted above, mentions a remark of Sartre's about his own inventive processes. 'Sartre,' he summarises, 'determines . . . that Lola shall possess the money Mathieu needs for Marcelle's abortion.' So does Dorothy Sayers determine that Wimsey shall have independent means, and Doyle that Holmes shall be free to build up as well as pursue a practice, and Bailey that Mr Fortune shall not have too busy a consultancy, and Ngaio Marsh that Roderick Alleyn shall be physically compelling. Exactly. It depends where the particular reader is sensitive; but in one way or another he says 'Hey! By what right did you do that?' It isn't precisely the clay asking the potter by what right he made that jug or that basin (as in Paul's argument in Romans 9), but it is the tourist visiting the pottery at Barnstaple and asking what he shouldn't ask of the patient potter, who would be happy to tell him anything about his craft but that. It is a matter of evaluating the conflict between the author's and the reader's right to take decisions; and the detective form of literature seems to move within a set of conventions that admits the author's right to take a number of decisions concerning the plot—rather more than the normal number: and rather less than the normal number of decisions about morality.

The decision that lies furthest away from the author's choice, however, is that there shall be a solution, a revelation, a restoration of a broken pattern. The object of detection is to detect, not to document failure. This brings the detective author into conflict with those who hold that the greatest of all literature is tragic. On this subject an essay by D. D. Raphael entitled *The Paradox of Tragedy* (Allen & Unwin, 1960) makes an important and disturbing point concerning tragedy and religion. To summarise a fascinating argument, Mr Raphael shows us the difference between the values of tragedy and the values of orthodox Christianity. Every statement about human destiny in the Scriptures, he shows, presupposes some kind of 'happy ending': the redress at last of injustice, the special certainty of the faithful that God will, however improbable human experience makes it appear, bring things in the end to a righteous solution. Job, he says, after a great spiritual struggle, submits: that is a happy ending. The Psalmist's agnosticism about human perfectibility is absorbed in his faith in the power of God to overrule human misfortune and injustice for good purposes. All the way from there to the Resurrection, 'the religion of the Bible is inimical to tragedy'. And of all tragedians he goes on to show, Shakespeare is the most ruthless. He contrasts the story of *Lear* or of *Romeo and Juliet* with the Biblical stories of Jephthah and Samson (referring explicitly to Milton's retelling of that second story and to the well-known parallel, and contrast, between Jephthah and Iphigenia), showing that whereas a Shakespeare tragedy brings grief and death upon its central figures, with no thought of justice and very little suggestion that the consummation of this evil or sorrowful episode left the way clear for a good or happy chapter to open (a touch of it in *Romeo*; none in *Lear*), the Biblical stories always lead directly to either a vindication of the moral law or the demonstration of a good which the tragedy made possible (in the Old Testament, usually another step in the preservation and maturing of the people of Israel).

We cannot here pass judgement on the dispute whether tragedy is incomplete religion, or whether religion, lacking tragedy, is illiterate. But any religion, as Raphael points out, is an escape from tragedy, and certain religions, notably that of Christians, are a denial that tragedy has the last word. Tragedy, says the Christian religion, is that which brings people to repentance, which reminds us of the overwhelming weight of evil, error and nonsense in the world that we know: tragedy is a General Confession which is answered by an Absolution. The Absolution is not in the tragedy—tragedy can't provide it, doesn't seek to provide it, doesn't even need to admit its possibility.

That could be a philosophical point against the detective novel, which cannot ever allow the open-ended style that many novels nowadays affect. Once again it's a Victorian novel that hasn't grown up, or moved with the times. Trollope must provide some sort of tying-up of loose ends in his last chapter even when the actual crisis of his story (as in *The Eustace Diamonds* or *Orley Farm*) is strictly tragic. The worst of his characters is never wholly condemned—not even Sir Felix Carbury, to whom in the end the worst Trollope can do is send him to Germany with a hired clergyman as mentor. In more protesting and dissenting fiction than that—much of Dickens, of course—the tragedy in the foreground is set against a background of comedy in which righteousness (though not the righteous people in the book) does by implication triumph. A nihilistic novel was unthinkable in the age when detection entered fiction, even though a tragic novel wasn't. So it could be said, and indeed often is said, that about the detective novel there is necessarily something immature.

It could also be said that the detective novel could not have emerged otherwise than from an age which was to a quite unusual extent explicitly religious. To that point I shall return later.

I think, however, that these three charges, the moral, the social and the philosophical, can be quite successfully made against the detective story. There are few enough such stories which offer any serious attempt at refutation. *The Tiger in the Smoke* is inevitably one: it comes as near tragedy as such a story possibly can. I can recall in a few others being left with that sense of something profoundly unsolved lying just behind the foreground solution of that particular crime. And that makes me feel that the way to put the Raphael point about tragedy and religion is really this: that tragedy and religion (anyhow, Christianity) are fundamentally opposed: religion does talk of a victory. But it is vitally important to insist that before the solution, or absolution, or resurrection can be understood and appropriated, before anyone has any shadow of right to claim that he can answer tragedy, tragedy must be allowed to run its full course. The 'strange and dreadful strife' of Martin Luther's Easter song is a strife which in anybody's life must be allowed to build up, not suffocate by false optimism. All the virtuosi of religious experience have agreed on that. It is a question of 'Out of the deep'. Therefore literature which is true 'tragedy' is never to be regarded as 'opposed to' religion in the sense that religion has a right to suppress it. No true religion shuns controversy; no true religion suppresses dissent. A religion that really embraces the universe is a function not of harmony but of counterpoint, not of dogma but of conversation, not of law alone but also of covenant, not of fantasy but of tragedy. It is only in the end, the farthest end, the remote and assumed but hardly ever experienced perfection (called heaven), that the final chord is sounded: up till then—dialogue, or duel, or war in heaven.

The case against the detective story, then, would not rest so much on its being impervious to tragedy: it doesn't have to be although it often is. The case rests most firmly on the extent to which detective stories can trivialise the conflict. They can be like a false religion in which everything comes right at cut rate. They can appeal to people who are in that sense trivial-minded, and encourage and nourish trivial-mindedness. That, anyhow, is a serious charge.

18

On Being Serious-minded

'The puritan spirit lies heavy within us, like gas on a troubled stomach'

—Judge Lewis Shinn, in *The Glass Village* by Ellery Queen, ch. 1

WHY THEN DO serious people read detective stories? Researchers whose purposes are far different from mine have admitted that the reading of detective stories can be something more significant than a mere aberration or self-indulgence. The reader of these pages will have gathered already what kind of explanation I propose in the end to offer, but I must first comment on two explanations which I don't personally believe to be primary.

The first is the very obvious critical comment, very frequently made and treated as almost axiomatic, that it is the puzzle that attracts the reader. Clearly this can't be denied, simply because so many people believe it that it can't be entirely untrue. But I am equally convinced that it is not more than a part of the truth. To speak personally, I have never myself been particularly held by a story whose only attribute is that it is a good puzzle. I should feel short-changed if the author didn't in the end tell me whodunit; but that would be a resentment comparable with which I should hear a piece of music—or, come to that, a piece of prose—which didn't make sense. I certainly don't want the author to leave that undone; but if that is all he does, he leaves much else undone which I most certainly do want done.

There are many people who would state their experience differently. It is almost certainly true that some readers find the same satisfaction in detection that they find in doing a demanding crossword puzzle, or in answering those depressing questions and brain-teasers in the Sunday newspapers. This is an intellectual satisfaction and altogether without emotional associations. You are competing with an adversary who cannot possibly cheat you, and need never outwit you, because his statement is frozen on the paper and he cannot, as he would in, say, a game of chess, adjust his strategy to yours. If you know enough, or have noticed enough, or are alert enough or retentive enough of memory, you can beat him. This naturally gives great satisfaction. It's good for the ego.

Moreover, it is undeniable that many crossword puzzle addicts and successful answers of general knowledge quizzes are also hospitable to detective stories of the classical kind. Stories about special genius in puzzle-solving, or puzzle-setting, are told about the same kinds of people, among whom the more eminent clergy are conspicuous (Ronald Knox being the patron of them all).

But quite apart from my own personal testimony that I read detective stories for the people rather than the plot, and that I go back to those whose people interest me even when I know the answer to the 'puzzle' perfectly well, I find a more public and convincing proof of the inadequacy of the mere intellectual puzzle argument in the extraordinary literature that has grown up around the Sherlock Holmes tales. Not only is this literature of interest to those who know the plots perfectly well; it specialises in people and situations and para-history, and says very little (and then indulgently) about the intellectual content of the puzzles. In these pages I have indicated that the intellectual content of the Holmes stories is well below what one who placed a high value on 'puzzle content' would be bound to regard as a normal level.

And once you have arrived at the detective novel proper, why, the 'puzzle' aspect is never more important than it is in any other novel. *The Tiger in the Smoke* isn't a 'puzzle' novel at all, but it's a great novel. In my own view, when a detective story or novel springs a surprise at the end the writer's purpose is much less to evoke in the reader admiration for the cleverness of the plot than to produce a moment of self-criticism in which the reader says 'Now, I ought to have seen that'. This 'ought' may have only the lightest moral content—or, as in late Allingham, in Fortune and in Father Brown, it may have a quite weighty moral content.

I should distinguish, anyhow, between those detective novels which detect moral truth as well as the specific truth about the murder or theft or suicide from those which are primarily designed to puzzle the reader. And I should further assert that whatever the 'puzzle' content, whatever the moral weight, the reader's satisfaction in what he calls a good detective story has much more to do with his need for moral and psychological security than with his superficial pleasure in solving puzzles. Moreover, I suspect that the later Allingham has a better chance of surviving the permissive blizzard which is engulfing so much detective fiction at present than, say, the more stilted and contrived puzzles of John Dickson Carr. The 'puzzle' is part of something larger and deeper.

This is usefully confirmed in the following passage from a detective story published in 1935 by G. D. H. and Margaret Cole. The Coles were in their time the most celebrated husband-and-wife pair in the detective field, and they were also pioneers in 'academic' detective writing. They record the following conversation between two of their characters:

> 'You do like detecting?' she returned to the question she had put before.
>
> 'Why, I'm not sure,' Everard said with some hesitation. 'I suppose I do.'
>
> 'The chase? The exciting hunting? To catch your criminal hot, and hang his brush round your neck?' Felice suggested.
>
> 'No! It's not that at all. I am not in the least anxious to "catch anybody hot", as you put it,' Everard said. 'Or to hang scalps round my neck. I don't think I desire anybody's death, for which reason I should probably make a very bad policeman—not that I mind particularly when criminals are hanged. I think most of them probably deserve it, and I've no strong feelings about the sacredness of human life; most human lives seem to be extraordinarily expensive and tiresome to keep going, and on any showing not worth the trouble. But if I eat meat, that doesn't make me want to be a head-hunting member of the Worshipful Guild of Butchers.'
>
> 'Then it is the puzzle, the chess, you like? You like to pursue

the clue to its last lurking-place and say, "There, I have you! This smut, that fell sideways on Allister Quentin's nose, is tied to a long, long, winding string and it leads me through thousands of calculations to the criminal at the other end." '

'It's not quite that, either, though I suppose it must be partly that. At least when I find a mystery, even a small one, I do want to know what the answer to it is, and I do, of course, sometimes mess around with what one would call chess. But what interests me more is looking at what people are like, what they do and why they do it, and it always seems to me that when there are crimes about, the working of people's minds gets much more easy to trace. They seem to become undressed, to come out into the open, if you see what I mean. And you can see much more how they can become thieves and murderers, even if they don't.'[1]

Note there how the romantic style denies vengeance and discovery as motives for detection and concentrates on mastery of another person's psychology; note also a puritan detachment from the notions of 'the sanctity of human life' when they collide with the claims of justice. What Everard Blatchington there claims for himself may well be attributed to many readers of such stories.

But secondly I venture to introduce and comment on a psychological assessment of detective reading which, first uttered in 1956, was made current in a recent book. It will strike some readers as being just about as esoteric as the 'puzzle theory' is ubiquitous. In Dr Charles Rycroft's *Imagination and Reality*[2] there is an essay entitled 'Analysis of a Detective Story', and its opening sentences are these:

Of the various psycho-analysts who have discussed the psychology of the detective story only one, Geraldine Pedersen-Krag, has put forward a specific hypothesis to account for their popularity. In her article 'Detective Stories and the Primal Scene' (1949) she suggests that it arises from their ability to reawaken the interest and curiosity originally aroused by the primal scene. According to her the murder is a symbolic representation of parental intercourse, and

[1] *Scandal at School* by G. D. H. and M. Cole, 1935 (paperback ed., Collins), pp. 198–9.

[2] Hogarth Press, International Psychoanalytical Library, no. 75 (1968).

> 'the victim is the parent for whom the reader (the child) has negative oedipal feelings. The clues in the story, disconnected, inexplicable and trifling, represent the child's growing awareness of details it had never understood, such as the family sleeping arrangements, nocturnal sounds. . . . The reader addicted to mystery stories tries actively to relive and master traumatic infantile experiences he once had to endure passively. Becoming the detective, he gratifies his infantile curiosity with impunity, redressing completely the helpless inadequacy and anxious guilt unconsciously remembered from childhood.' [p. 114]

Thus far Rycroft takes over the argument set in motion by Pedersen-Krag; but the rest of his essay is devoted to a confirmation, or illustration, of this analysis by reference to Wilkie Collins's story *The Moonstone*.

This story is exposed by the Pedersen-Krag line of argument as 'an unconscious representation of the sexual act'. Very briefly, the symbolic correspondences by which Rycroftt illustrates this suggestion are these:

1. the theft of the Moonstone is a defiance of the prohibited intercourse between Franklin Blake and Rachel Verinder;
2. the Moonstone itself, with its central flaw and lunar changes in lustre, is a female symbol;
3. the theft is also the dream of a man in sexual conflict, and therefore it is significant that the theft is found to have taken place during a sleep-walk;
4. the hiddenness of the Moonstone, its unavailability, is the traditional convention that upper middle class women in 1850 knew nothing at all about sex;
5. Rachel's denial that the stone has been stolen at all is her conventional ignorance of sex: that insincerity of the denial symbolises the hollowness of the convention;
6. Rosanna Spearman, in love with Franklin Blake, is Rachel's suppressed sexuality: Godfrey Ablewhite, betrothed to Rachel but not in love with her, is Blake's repressed sexuality.

Many smaller details fit in with this system of interpretation. And while from some points of view the whole structure of the argument looks bizarre, it is, to put it at its lowest, a possible interpretation of what one finds in the text of *The Moonstone*.

Dr Rycroft brings in evidence one other story by the same author, a far less famous one called *Basil*; and after showing many points of resemblance between the two stories he reminds the reader that while *Basil* was published in 1852 as a contemporary tale, *The Moonstone* was published in 1868 but gives its narrated events the date 1850. *Basil* is found to be a cruder and less convincing performance than the later book: and indeed it is. Is not the later book, then, argues Dr Rycroft, to be related to the earlier as Rachel to Rosanna, or Blake to Ablewhite?

Collins, anyhow, is shown to have a peculiar obsession with 'the primal scene'. Now I have no means of knowing how much of Wilkie Collins Dr Rycroft read in preparing his paper. It happens that many years ago I had, and took, the opportunity of reading more than half his novels in a very old edition (and in eerie circumstances which I must not pause here to recount), and I formed the impression that Collins was indeed an obsessed author; but I saw it at that time not in terms of sex but more naïvely in terms of [a] mental abnormality or imbecility and [b] his violent hatred of the Roman Catholic Church. The atmosphere of Trollope's *The Way We Live Now* repeats itself often when Collins mentions the Catholics, and there are few of his stories which don't make some sort of play either with idiocy or with an attempt to derange the mind of another. I am quite ready to be told that there is a sexual association with what to Collins is the exotic and baneful power of the Church of Rome. This was the period immediately after Emancipation and leading up to the Establishment of the Hierarchy (1850). The encounter with Catholicism—an encounter from which since 1688 puritan Englishmen had been able to regard themselves as immune—aroused all sorts of strange rumours and evoked many irrational fears. That is all quite understandable, especially when Collins's own puritan background is remembered. And the puritan's approach to the spooky and sinister would most naturally be through the corruption (accidental or deliberate) of the intellectual faculties of people—for to a puritan those were his most precious possession and their corruption the greatest grief.

What I should say by way of criticising the Rycroft approach to detective stories is that what he brings in evidence does not by any means justify his statement, which he makes at the beginning of his article, that 'the detective story writer connives with the reader's need to deny his guilt by providing him with ready-made fantasies in which the compulsive question "who-dunit" is always answered by a self-exonerating, "Not I".'

For, in the first place, it was unwise to take *The Moonstone*, as it would have been unwise to take any work of Collins, as evidence for propositions about detective fiction: and in the second, the 'It wasn't I, anyhow' reaction to detective fiction needs much more delicate handling than it gets at the hands of the psychologists; it's the beginning, not the end, of an argument.

It was unwise to base the argument on *The Moonstone* precisely because that is such a sensational and romantic story. When Eliot gave it that accolade which has become so famous he did it no service and confused the whole issue. *The Moonstone* isn't a detective story: it is a love-story. (By the same token *The Woman in White* isn't a detective story but a romantic thriller.) The police interest is negligible. The whole point of the story is that the police retire baffled. Later the central crime is found not to have been committed at all; the guilt which the reader hoped to see fixed on an identifiable individual was not there. The whole business was accident, not crime, and the criminal intentions and devices are confined to the sub-plot. It's a story about the relations between Franklin Blake and Rachel Verinder, with just about the same detective content (and in both the detective content is perfectly sound and agreeable provided it is not asked to carry any weight) as you find in Trollope's *John Caldigate*. If *The Moonstone* is 'the first, the longest and the best detective story in the English language', then *Bleak House* is a detective story, and so are *Is He Popenjoy?* and *Orley Farm*.

So that won't do as evidence for saying that when you read a detective story you are looking on the criminal with what Alexandre Dumas called 'egotistical pity', and saying 'Thank God I am not as other men'. Or perhaps more precisely: 'That's one thing I can be certain not to be blamed for'.

This argument is both too solemn and too unsoundly based to be appropriate. It is true that the curious sense of 'release' that reading a good detective story gives to a certain kind of reader is worth explaining, but it may be doubted whether such majestic machinery is needed for the explanation. As handled by Dr Pedersen-Krag it looks as if at any moment it may behave like the dragline in John Trench's *Dishonoured Bones* and fall through the supporting ground. It is the insistence on 'guilt' that is the doubtful part of the ground.

The argument would stand up better, and have the advantage of somewhat lighter construction, if for 'guilt' we read 'anxiety'. The reader of detective stories probably does read them partly because of the curious property they have of providing relaxation from anxiety. If the reader identifies himself with the successful detective, and to some extent with the forces of law and order, he gets some satisfaction from seeing crime brought home to the right culprit, honesty vindicated, and the law protecting society, including himself, from the consequences that would come if the crime were allowed to run free. He gets satisfaction from this precisely because he is worried by the extent to which, in real life, crime does run free.

Yes: but until that statement is modified it goes far beyond the evidence. Two things must be said at once. The first is that the typical detective story reader is not a person who is in fact involved in the situations that free-running crime produces; and the other, associated with that proposition, is that the amount of anxiety which the detective story can allay is very narrowly limited.

Nobody will turn to a detective story if he is really in deep trouble. I can't believe that detective stories are read in concentration camps, or in countries subject to natural disasters just after earthquakes or volcanic eruptions, or in times of violent political revolution. Nor do I believe that they are primarily read by people who are governed by violent passions (whether benevolently or antisocially directed). They are not the characteristic relaxation, I believe, of social reformers, and I should be surprised to learn that they formed any considerable part of the luggage of a pioneering missionary.

The suggestions of Dr Rycroft were subjected to a penetrating comment in a review of this chapter of his book by Dr John Wren-Lewis.[3] This review expresses dissent from Dr Rycroft's

[3] 'Adam, Eve, and Agatha Christie' by J. Wren-Lewis, in *New Christian*, 16 April 1970, pp. 9–10.

analysis, but goes on to make a much more damaging point in the case against the detective story. Dr Wren-Lewis wants to associate detective stories not with the 'primal scene' but with a psychological interpretation of the Fall itself: in other words, with something that has gone wrong, and always tends to go wrong, with human nature. The Fall (the story in Genesis 3 about Adam and Eve and the Serpent) he takes to be a distortion of man's view of the nature and role of goodness in the world. Near the end of the argument he writes as follows:

> The Adam and Eve story unmasks the least likely character as the real cause of all the trouble. Adam and Eve's basic alienation of themselves from each other and from the creative power which operates in their relationship is induced by *eating of the tree of the knowledge of good and evil*—in other words by moralising. Just as it is the policeman in *The Mousetrap* who is really the murderer all along, so it is the activity which normally represents itself as the only hope of rescuing human life *from* inhumanity which turns out, in the final analysis, to be the root cause of man's inability to pull himself out of inhumanity.

And the concluding words are these:

> The world's deepest need is precisely for a new morality—a morality in which people respond to God in creativity and love but recognise that the tendency to try to be as gods themselves, judging good and evil, is the fundamental perversion of human freedom against itself.

I think that Dr Wren-Lewis is saying, in the first of the above quotations, that the real villain of the Fall story is God himself as there represented. Theologically this is, I believe, quite right. But the point about moralising is the point to concentrate on here. If the detective story really did come of age at two cardinal points where it transcended itself—in Father Brown and in *The Tiger in the Smoke*—then Dr Wren-Lewis is abundantly vindicated: for, as I have tried to show, both these moments were moments when a detective-story author found it possible to show awareness of the futility of moralising. Father Brown does not moralise, although his statements are unequivocally moral. The Jack Havoc situation is shown to be far beyond moralising.

This is the right ground on which to build the case against the detective story. There is a real danger that readers of detective stories, if they become addicts, will be persuaded that moralism—judging right and wrong in others with no doubts about one's own rightness—is a legitimate and sufficient way of life. It may well be possible to show that addiction to detective stories nourishes mental philistinism. If it is possible to show that (we'd need to call in the statisticians, I suppose, to prove it), then we have yet another point of meeting between detective literature and the puritan tradition: for it is the occupational disease of puritanism to become facilely and blindly moralistic.

I believe that the ideal client of the detective story writer is the man or woman who is near enough to the moral workshop of society to know what the problems and necessities are, but is not actually either so close to a position of ultimate command as to be able to take radical decisions, nor profoundly concerned with repairing, replacing or updating the machinery. The detective writer will sell nothing to a reader below a certain level of intellectual attainment who cannot attend to a rational plot; but neither will he have any success with a person who lives very close to that moral machinery, for such a person will repudiate the fantasy of detection as an insulting comment on the problems he is handling.

No: just as the most anxious people in the Second World War in Britain were neither the air-raid wardens nor the dwellers in Lewisham, Bermondsey and Clydeside, but the people who lived in Oxford, to whom nothing had happened but who were persuaded that at any moment it might, so the level of anxiety in a reader to which a detective writer can respond (on which, if you insist on being unkind, he can cash in) is that which is reached in a person who has intellect enough to see the need for a stable society, just enough property to wish to keep that society stable, and the capacity to see what things would be like if that stability disappeared.

This is enough to explain the popularity of detective stories among the clergy of a generation and two generations ago. I should expect that popularity to be much less among modern clergy. The clergy in the stable society of yesterday spent their lives in an area in which there was very little talk about either justice or reason, and a great deal of talk about the problems of a developing society. In their world any amount of wickedness went unpunished and even received honour, and often they knew more about this than anyone else. Let a clergyman suffer a certain pressure of conscience which really causes him to be troubled by the irrationality and injustice which are permitted to prevail *in his own world* (I don't at all mean the secular world: that is the point—it's his own world in which people were beginning to become most disobedient and sentimental and unamenable to the demands of either reason or justice), and the sound predictable rhythm of Agatha Christie is just about what is needed to keep him sane.

I doubt if this is over-speculative. It is demonstrable that the age in which the detective story held its highest place was the age in which gradually the notions of authority and stability in society were questioned and began to be radically changed. So long as it did not seem too seriously probable that the foundations of society were going to be attacked, the detective story served people whose anxieties were at that optimum level. In the age which has succeeded that one, in which it is perfectly clear that very few of the values familiar and precious to people who were born between 1830 and 1930 have the least chance of survival, detective fiction withers. There is now too much anxiety altogether: the bombs are falling. Neither are writers inspired to write them nor readers prepared to read them any more. It is quite likely that the readership of detective stories will be forced further and further out towards the fringes of society.

If that happens it will be because one of the values which is being turned upside-down and will probably be completely revolutionised in the seventies is that of amusement. The sixties certainly saw a deep and irreversible change in the ethos of entertainment. Now, in the world of entertainment, detective fiction occupies a position right at one far end, as it were, of the territory; it is an extreme form of private entertainment, distinguished very clearly from sociable or mass entertainment. The spectrum used to be familiar enough: at one end, mass entertainment in which large numbers of people were influenced and pleased by gifted soloists: in the middle, sociable entertainment which included all forms of games from the point of view of the participants, from the muscular to the intellectual: and at the other end the man in the corner curled up with a book, reading it for pleasure (not for study). It is now as if that whole plateau had suddenly lurched downwards at one end, so that immense emphasis is placed on public and mass entertainment at the expense of that which is sociable and at the very heavy expense of that which is private. And so we are left with the sociological fact that in our kind of culture that which is private will suddenly become far more expensive than it was in the recent past (more like its condition in the remoter past), while that which is dispensed on the large and indiscriminate scale will get the rewards and the approval of those whose voices form public opinion. Trend is not now set by the private person but by the demagogue of entertainment.

I think, then, that detective stories are strictly literature for amusement, accidentally swerving now and again towards more serious fields, and perhaps accidentally slipping on other occasions towards the underworld. But they served an age in which increasing numbers of literate people were becoming conscious of the need for honouring the notion of moral and social stability. These things were no longer to be counted on as human rights; but people were secure enough to look steadily and unshockably at the crimes which brought into play the genius of the detective and the strength of the law. To many they provided release from a nagging feeling of helplessness, and a confirmation of their faith in the rightness of orderly and peaceable societies. Had they been confused by such clamorous feelings of guilt as the psychologists attribute to them, would the posture of guilt in the very conventional fashion of the ordinary detective story have helped them? Had they been looking for a release from those oedipal complexes which link sex and violence, would the discipline which the best detective fiction observes concerning violence have provided a better response than the Gothic thriller that they had had for two or three generations?

The detective story reader is not a lover of violence but a lover of order. I do not say that a lover of order must needs be more moral than a lover of violence: obviously a fascist can approve violence for the sake of keeping what he takes to be order. I only say that the detective story reader, who is often (I should say always, if he is a real *aficionado*) left cold or repelled by thrillers, spy-stories and science fiction, does not love violence, and is not even primarily interested in what is bizarre. He can take 'The Speckled Band', but it isn't the snake that makes it a great story for him but 'dummy bell-ropes and ventilators which do not ventilate'. What he gets from Dr Priestley, Reginald Fortune, Roderick Alleyn at their best is entirely different from what he gets from the deliverance of the hero, tied to the railway line, from the oncoming express with seconds to spare. It's not a matter of fear or guilt, but of assurance: it's not being held over hell and drawn back at the last moment, but being allowed for a space to go in out of the draught of doubt—that's what the detective story reader thanks his author for.

And this feeling of surprising comfort is achieved not merely by the drawing of a satisfying rational diagram (though this in itself gave some pleasure when the draughtsman was Austin Freeman), but most of all by the disciplined dance of character which detection calls for and makes possible. Time and again we have said that detective stories often deal in pale and unconvincing characters. When they do they fall short. There are enough stories in this form which introduce really credible and dynamic characters without trivialising their intellectual content to show not only that the counterpoint between reason and emotion can be achieved, but also how pleasant and satisfying it is when it is achieved.

* * *

By way of epilogue I must now return to that point which I have intermittently made, and with the deliberate intention of tantalising the reader, in the course of this essay. I must now say what I mean by my suggestion that detective literature is a puritan form of fiction.

By this stage my reader and I should be on fairly friendly terms, so I will shamelessly say that I am about to summarise a thesis which I fully intend later to expound at length. But first I can remind the reader that I have mentioned the English puritan tradition six times (more, possibly, but these are the ones that count) in the foregoing pages. I have associated it with [1] commerce and the values of the city (chapter 5), [2] rationalism and a suspicion of the supernatural (chapter 7), [3] the assumption that work is a virtue and idleness a vice (chapter 11), [4] the cult of masculinity (also chapter 11), [5] the relegation of sex to a subordinate place in the scheme of human values, exemplified not least in the commendation of late marriage for men (chapter 13) and [6] a special love of good conversation (chapter 16).

These points emerged naturally from the story I was telling: they were not, and are not now, arranged as they would be had this been a book about puritanism—or as they will be when that intended book is written. But every one of these descriptions of puritanism will be found to have a place in the total picture you would be drawing after a close study of its origins and character. Among certain other attributes of puritanism, which we have more cursorily mentioned in this account, are xenophobia, Englishness, a suspicion of artists, and a profound fear of the young. All these are qualities which appear strongly enough in all English literature in the period under review, but which are brought together in a unique combination in detective literature. Detective literature, we have shown, accepts these values and retains them long after other literature, reflecting movements of social thought, has reacted against them.

In two particulars we find this thesis confirmed. Two subjects on which you will always get a positive reaction from the puritan tradition are sex and money. Sex in detective literature is handled on strictly puritan lines. The novelist may be somebody who would be horrified to be called a puritan—but if we were right about the effect of mixing the detective up with sexual tensions, then there are enough examples to demonstrate that detective writers have in the end been thankful to rely on the puritan pattern that makes sex secondary to intellect and muscle and work. Nobody but a fool pretends sex doesn't exist, but we don't have to talk about it and there are other things to write novels about—that is, broadly speaking, the Doyle maxim. As for money, its lack is a stock situation that produces anxiety and greed; but for the rest, everybody on the 'right' side is pretty comfortable. The police take the advice of John the Baptist in not complaining about their wages (and it was my guess that Lomas and Alleyn don't live on them either). Even the artists, if they aren't actually in dubious situations, are tolerably pecunious in Innes. Debt is a major vice in the puritan culture, but the puritan never exalts poverty.

Detective fiction, then, I repeat, is entertainment for puritans. It cannot withstand the assaults of 'respectable' critics nowadays simply because it does not attempt, in the style of serious novels, to react to life. Here again it is conservative—so conservative, say its detractors, as to be infantile. Here on the one hand is D. H. Lawrence pouring out his soul concerning the monstrous and loathsome evangelical culture of those sordid little South Derbyshire industrial towns—and there is Agatha Christie posturing in drawing rooms at places where bodies are found in libraries by butlers. Very well. On the assumption that literature must react to life, detection stands no chance. Neither does Trollope, nor do most novelists before Dickens. You can defend the detective story only if you admit sabbaticals for the serious-minded. And you are bound to admit that detective fiction can do harm to people who abuse it and treat all life as a sabbatical. They can be used to give assurance and respectability to trivial and irresponsible attitudes. Or I suppose they can, though if pressed I'd have to admit that I never actually saw one doing it.

The puritan association of detective literature is, obviously, confirmed by what has happened in America. The true home of detection there is New England. Savour again that marvellous improbability, 'Mr Poe of Boston'. The puritan belief in the perfectibility of human society (entertainingly at odds with the calvinist belief in the depravity of man, which was also in their tradition) produced that New England out of which American detective fiction sprang. It is the New England environment that remains the most characteristic milieu for detective writing. It went naturally from there to New York and from New York to Los Angeles, the home of Perry Mason and Vic Varallo; and from there to San Francisco, Chief Ironside's manor. Not, interestingly, to Chicago. But the explanation is obvious in the light of what we said a page or two back: Chicago was always too close to the raw heart of crime. Chicago has been for two or three generations—well, since the time of Mr Abe Slaney and Killer Evans—a symbolic centre of crime and racketeering. The nowadays even more emphatic association of New York and Los Angeles with extreme urban problems is a very recent growth, and one wonders how soon it will stifle the appeal of Nero Wolfe, Ellery Queen and Lesley Egan's salty characters. Anyhow, if the western seaboard cultures seem to be unpuritan because unprotestant, the answer is that the culture that imposed itself on them and produced a milieu for detective fiction was the puritan culture of work and urbanism, and the values which prevail at the level from which detection comes and to which it makes its appeal are indistinguishable from those which prevail in Boston, whatever the ethnic background of either may suggest to the contrary.

To such large generalisations many exceptions will come to the reader's mind. This is not the place in which I should attempt to tie down the contention about puritanism with any pretence of completeness. I would rather leave it as a point of speculation and discussion. However, somebody will certainly have asked already, 'If you think this way about puritanism and the detective story, why have you attached so much importance to Father Brown instead of regarding him as a papistical deviation?' The answer is that puritan values are by no means denied consistently by all high church anglicans or Roman Catholics in England and America. On the contrary, the puritan style is something which Roman Catholicism has spent a hundred years coming to terms with, and which has at the present time (1970) received some very large tributes from the Catholic tradition (such as the immense enthusiasm with which the concessions of Vatican II were accepted in England, and immediately interpreted with a much greater liberality than the Curia originally looked for, and the remarkable energy with which in the Netherlands—the one non-English-speaking country as we have seen, that can be said to have a puritan tradition—revisionist courses are being pursued by eminent Catholics).

To me Father Brown is Chesterton's commendation of the Catholic Church as a possible proposition for educated Englishmen (that is, for puritan-background Englishmen). Himself the son of a nonconformist father, he exemplified in his own person the ex-puritan convert. Father Brown exposes many puritan errors but uses the puritan language of reason and the puritan values of plainness and simplicity in the process of that exposure.

No: what seems to be quite clear is that the puritan culture is vulnerable, and that the detective story is vulnerable, for exactly the same reasons. I mean both that they can be faulted, and that in our time they are under extreme and possibly fatal pressure. I do not know whether they can survive it. It is unquestionable that those who read for amusement—themselves an ageing and diminishing number—are turning more to science fiction and spy stories and thrillers than to detective stories for what they need. Too much of what the detective story counted on has been, in the eyes of most people, discredited. Detective stories don't go with permissiveness; they go with convention and style and dogma and assurance; they go with such assumptions as that a society in which authority is accepted, and correction by wiser people of the unwise or the young is permitted, is a good society. For the time being we are all suffering still from the shock of Auschwitz, from the withdrawal of moral landmarks; to the point of moral hypochondria we are paralysed by the vision we have had of humanity's possibilities for evil and for nonsense. For this it has become, at present, fashionable to blame any system which admits the authority of anybody, and naturally there are many things in common life which simply are not trustworthy any more. People as insecure as we have become find detective stories perhaps a mockery of our condition. There's nobody in the detective story with whom we can identify ourselves because life has gone too far in the direction of unreason and unpredictability. The healing of that condition (if the assumption that it's pathological is correct) is too great a task merely for the puritan culture to handle. Something larger will need to tackle it.

In a perfect world there will be no need for detective stories: but then there will be nothing to detect. Their disappearance at this moment, however, will not bring the world any nearer to perfection. The high-minded would say that the removal of this form of relaxation would free the energies of the literate for the contemplation of real mysteries and the overcoming of real evils. I see no reason to count on that. If we are constantly told that there is no morality, no justice, no trustworthiness, and therefore no human society at all: if we are taught with unrelieved assiduity that there is no distinction of character to be admired, no integrity of personality to be corrected by, I see no reason why we should be more likely than we were thirty years ago to exercise such admiration, submit to such correction, and pursue such ideals in real life. What is more, I am quite clear that men who are too serious ever to appreciate any art provided for amusement or even to admit their need of relaxation are neither men whose advice I would cross the road to get nor men by whom I wish to be governed.

Indeed, I don't mind too much if I am wrong about my modestly serious deductions concerning the social standing of the detective story. What means much more to me is to be able to say that without it I should have found the world a less agreeable place. I would rather be ruled by contented men than by discontented men, and I am not sorry to be surrounded by examples of credible goodness. What harm did they ever do? I think that one admirable phrase from a contemporary critic sums up with complete justice and precision what I believe about these things. Writing of detective fiction, with its admixture of science and morals, with its touch of occasional passion and anger, with its modest openings towards greater issues which greater prophets are left to explore, Colin Wilson says that detective stories are 'imaginings with a certain authority'.[4]

[4] Colin Wilson, *The Strength to Dream* (Gollancz, 1962), p. 108.

V

APPENDICES

APPENDIX I

For the Tidy-minded

An Analysis of the Holmes Stories

Key to symbols:

Column 3: 'Problem'	1. Murder
	2. Theft
	3. Inheritance or Fraud
	4. Political
	5. Blackmail
	6. Social scandal
	7. Matrimonial
	8. Abduction
	9. Coining
Column 4: 'Result'	1. Arrest of criminal
	2. Death or suicide of criminal in (not after) the story
	3. Escape of criminal
	4. Release of criminal
	5. Vindication of accused person
	6. No result or failure
	7. No crime
	8. Earlier crime uncovered.
Column 7: 'Style'	1. Watson's narrative
	2. Holmes's narrative within Watson's
	3. Holmes's narrative
	4. Third Person
Column 10 'Social Milieu'	A: Aristocracy
	Ac: Academic
	F: Foreign
	LM: Lower middle
	M: Middle
	UM: Upper Middle

Chart of Holmes's Cases

1.	2.	3.	4.	5.	6.	7.	8.	9.	10.
No.	*Title*	*Problem*	*Result*	*Locality*	*Secondary Locality*	*Style*	*Weather*	*Police Officer*	*Social Milieu*
1.	Bohemia	6	6	London		1	Wind	——	A
2.	Redhead	2	1	London		1		Lestrade	LM
3.	Identity	7	4	London		1	Sun		LM
4.	Boscombe	1	4/5	Hereford	Australia	1	Thunder	Lestrade	M
5.	Orange Pips	1	6	London	India	1	Storm		M
6.	Twisted Lip	7	7	Kent		1		Bradstreet	M
7.	Carbuncle	2	4	Wallington		1	Dry	Bradstreet	LM
8.	Speckled Band	3/1	2	Leatherhead	India	1			M
9.	Thumb	9	6	Reading		1		Bradstreet	
10.	Bachelor	6/7	7	London	U.S.A.	1	Storm	Lestrade	A
11.	Beryl	2	3/5	Streatham		1	Snow	Baynes	UM
12.	Beeches	3	2	Winchester		1	Dry		M
	**********								
13.	Silver Blaze	2	2	Dartmoor	Winchester	1		Gregory	UM
14.	Yellow Face	7	7	Norbury		1	Thunder		M
15.	Stockbroker	2	2	Birmingham		1			M
16.	Gloria Scott	5	8	Norfolk	Australia	2	Dry		UM
17.	Musgrave	2	2	Sussex		2			UM
18.	Squires	2	1	Reigate		1		Forrester	UM
19.	Crooked Man	6/1	8	Aldershot	India	1	Thunder		M
20.	Resident	1	1	London		1	Rain	Lanner	M
21.	Interpreter	8	3	London	Athens	1	Thunder	Gregson	F
22.	Naval Treaty	4	4/5	Woking	London	1	Rain		M
23.	Final Problem	—	—	Switzerland	London	1			
	**********								

24. Empty House	1	1	London		1	Thunder	Lestrade	M
25. Norwood	1	1/5	Norwood		1		Lestrade	M
26. Dancing Men	1	1	Norfolk	U.S.A.	1		Martin	UM
27. Cyclist	8	1	Farnham	U.S.A.				M
28. Priory	8 + 1	4 + 1	Derbyshire		1			A
29. Black Peter	1	1	Forest Row	Dundee	1		Hopkins	M
30. Milverton	5 + 1	2 + 4	London		1		Lestrade	M
31. Napoleons	2	2	London	Italy	1		Lestrade	LM
32. Students	2	4	?Oxford		1			Ac
33. Pince-Nez	1	2	Chatham	Russia	1	Storm	Hopkins	UM
34. Threequarter	6	7	Cambridge		1	Sun	Hopkins	Ac
35. Abbey Grange	1	4/8	Chiselhurst	Australia	1	Fog	Hopkins	UM
36. Second Stain	4 + 1	4	London		1		Lestrade & McPherson	A
37. Wistaria	1	2	Esher	S. America	1			M
38. Cardboard Box	1	1	Croydon		1	Hail	Lestrade	LM
39. Red Circle	1	4	London	Italy, U.S.A.	1		Lesouter (U.S.A.)	F
40. Partington	4 + 1	1/5	London		1	Fog	Gregson	M
41. Dying Detective	3 + 1	1	London	Asia	1		Morton	M
42. Carfax	8	1	France/London	Australia	1		Lestrade	A
43. Devil's Foot	1	4/8	Poldhu	Africa	1			M
44. Last Bow	4	1	Sussex	U.S.A.	4	Hail		UM
45. Illustrious	6	2	Harrow	Austria	1			A
**********								
46. Soldier	6	7	Bedford	Africa	3			M
47. Mazarin	2	1	London		4	Fine	Youghal	A
48. Gables	6(5)	4	Harrow	U.S.A., Italy	1			UM
49. Vampire	7	7	Sussex	S. America	1			M
50. Garridebs	3	1	London	U.S.A.	1			M

1.	2.	3.	4.	5.	6.	7.	8.	9.	10.
51.	Thor Bridge	1*	2/5	Winchester	Brazil, U.S.A.	1	Wind	Coventry	UM
52.	Creeping Man	6	7	Cambridge	Germany	1			Ac
53.	Lion's Mane	–	7	Sussex		3	Fine	Anderson	M
54.	Veiled	1	8	London	Berkshire	1			M
55.	Shoscombe	3	7	Berkshire		1	Thunder		A
56.	Colourman	1	1	Lewisham		1			LM
	**********								
I.	Scarlet	1	2	London	U.S.A.	1		Lestrade:Gregson	M
II.	Four	1	1	London	India	1		Jones	M
III.	Baskervilles	1	2	Dartmoor		1			UM
IV.	Valley of Fear	1	3	Sussex	U.S.A.	1		Macdonald	UM

Column 3: [1] Murders: 22 (in stories 1–23: 5): [2] Thefts: 9 (6) [3] Inheritance 5: [4] Political 4 [5] Blackmail 3 [6] Society scandal 6 [7] Matrimonial 4 [8] Abduction 3 [9] Coining 1

Column 4: [1] arrest: 16 (3) [2] death or suicide: 12 [3] escape: 3 [4] release: 11 [5] vindication of accused: 6 [6] No result or failure: 3 (3) [7] No crime: 9 (3) [8] Earlier crime: 5

* Suicide

A Selection from Dr Thorndyke

Title	Crime Alleged	Result	Place	Local Details	Technical Details
1. The Case of Oscar Brodsky	1	suicide	Essex	railway	spectacles: boots
2. A Case of Premeditation	1	escape	Kent	railway	dogs (85. 87)
3. Echo of a Mutiny	1	manslaughter	Kent	lighthouse	pipe
4. Wastrel's Romance	2	no crime	——		dust
5. The Missing Mortgagee	1	accident	Kent	insurance	
6. Percival Bland's Proxy	3	detected	London	insurance: fire	bones
7. The Old Lag	1	hanged	London		Blood analysis
8. The Stranger's Latchkey	8	arrest	(country)		dust, hair
9. Anthropologist at large*	2	recovered	London		skull measurement: dust
10. The Blue Sequin	1	accident	Kent	railway	animal pathology
11. The Moabite Cipher	2	recovered	London	Hebrew script	invisible ink
12. The Aluminium Dagger	1	suicide	London		dagger from rifle
13. The Magic Casket	2	recovered	London		Japanese language
14. A Mare's Nest	3	arrest	London	cremation	bones
15. The Stalking-Horse	1	suicide	Kent	railway	secret writing
16. The Naturalist at Law	suicide	murder	Bucks/Essex	railway	duckweed
17. Mr Ponting's Alibi	1	hanged	London		phonograph
18. Pandora's Box	1	hanged	Kent		tattooing
19. The Trail of Behemoth	1	no crime	London		elephant hair: dust
20. Pathologist to the Rescue	1	suicide	'Southaven'		blood groups
21. Gleanings from the Wreckage	1	arrest	London	fire	filiarisis
22. The Puzzle Lock	2	arrest	London	strongroom	cipher
23. The Green Check Jacket	1	arrest?	Kent		chalk
24. The Seal of Nebuchadnezzar	1	death	London	(cf. 'The Six Napoleons')	footprints
25. Phyllis Annesley's Peril	1	no crime	London		binocular vision

26. The Sower of Pestilence	4	suicide	London		Asiatic fleas
27. Rex *v.* Burnaby*	1 (att.)	doubtful	London		allergy
28. A Mystery of the Sandhills†	1	escape	Kent		sand: dust
29. Apparition of Burling Court	conspiracy	escape	Kent		optics
30. The Mysterious Visitor	1	fraud	?Kent		observation
31. The White Footprints	1	arrest	Kent		medical (ainhum)
32. The Blue Scarab	–	hidden treasure	?		cipher
33. The New Jersey Sphinx	1	arrest	London		reconstruction
34. The Touchstone	1	accident	(country)	railway	dust
35. A Fisher of Men	2	arrest	London	river	hair
36. The Stolen Ingots	2	arrest	Kent	docks: railway	metallurgy
37. The Funeral Pyre	1	suicide	Kent	fire	

* Features both Anstey and Jervis. † Related by Anstey.

FATHER BROWN

Title	*Locale*	*Problem*	*Milieu*	*Moral*	*Clues*
Innocence:					
1. The Blue Cross	London	2	M	——	(22) Hartlepool
2. The Secret Garden	Paris	1	A	Anti-clericalism (38)	(26) 'younger'
3. The Queer Feet	London	2	UM	Social insensitiveness (53)	
4. The Flying Stars	——	2	A	The Meanness of Crime (64)	
5. The Invisible Man	London	1	M	Social insensitiveness (77)	
6. The Honour of Israel Gow	Scotland	no crime	A	Presbyterian literalism (88)	
7. The Wrong Shape	London Suburbs	1	M	Humanist morality (103)	
8. The Sins of Prince Saradine	Norfolk	1	A	Dangers of assuming the worst (117)	
9. The Hammer of God	(Country)	1	A	Pride (130)	
10. The Eye of Apollo	London	1	M	Cruelty of bogus religions (142)	(131) Camberwell
11. The Sign of the Broken Sword	?Brazil	1	A	The puritan error (152–3)	
12. The Three Tools of Death	London suburbs	suicide	M	Suicidal cheerfulness	
Wisdom:					
1. The Absence of Mr Glass	Scarborough	no crime	M	——	(173) Scarborough
2. The Paradise of Thieves	Italy	2	M	Delusiveness of romance (195)	
3. The Duel of Dr Hirsch	Paris	no crime	M	Logic (206)	
4. The Man in the Passage	London	1	M	'Seeing yourself'	
5. The Mistake of the Machine	U.S.A.	no crime	A	Sentimentality of Scientists (231)	(221) Chicago
6. The Head of Caesar	London	5	A	The greed of collectors	(233) Cobhole
7. The Purple Wig	Devon	no crime	A	Hatred of truth (254)	
8. The Perishing of the Pendragons	Cornwall	at/1	UM	Misdirection (269)	
9. The God of the Gongs	Essex	1	Inter-racial	Colour	(270) Cobhole

10. The Salad of Colonel Cray	London	prevented murder	Army	Superstition and colour (291)
11. The Crime of John Boulnois	Oxford	suicide	Ac	Could not tell a lie (302–4)
12. The Fairy Tale of Father Brown	Heiligwaldstein	1	Army	—— (end)
Incredulity:				
1. The Resurrection of Father Brown	S. America	sacrilege	Foreign	Anti-clericalism (320)
2. The Arrow of Heaven	U.S.A.	1	U.S.A.	Justice (351)
3. The Oracle of the Dog	Yorkshire	1	M	Animal-superstition (364)
4. The Miracle of Moon Crescent	U.S.A.	1	U.S.A.	Justice (386)
5. The Curse of the Golden Cross	Sussex	1	M	Superstition about history (401)
6. The Dagger with Wings	West Country	1	UM	Superstition about oriental philosophy (423–4)
7. The Doom of the Darnaways	Sea coast	1	A	Special knowledge (443)
8. The Ghost of Gideon Wise	?London	1	——	Monopolies (457)
Secret:				
1. The Mirror of the Magistrate	?London	1	Ac	Sociology (477)
2. The Man with Two Beards	London suburbs	1	M	The brutality of contempt (496)
3. The Song of the Flying Fish	(village)	2	M	Misdirection (510)
4. The Actor and the Alibi	London	1	M	Special knowledge (525)
5. The Vanishing of Vaudrey	(village)	1	A	Hatred (540)
6. The Worst Crime in the World	Yorkshire	1	A	Misdirection (553)
7. The Red Moon of Meru	(country)	2	A	Stolen credit (565–6)
8. The Chief Mourner of Marne	(country)	1	A	Charity (583)

Max Carrados

Title	Subject	Place	Details
Max Carrados			
1. The Coin of Dionysus	Forgery: no arrest	London	Introduction of M.C.
2. Knight's Cross Signal	Multiple manslaughter. Escape	London	Railway
3. Tragedy of Brookbend Cottage	Att. Murder. Suicide of victim	suburbs	Trams
4. The Clever Mrs Straithwaite	Fraud. No case	London	Expensive society
5. Harry the Actor	Theft.	London	Satire on wealth
6. Tilling Shaw Mystery	Murder, blackmail, suicide	'North'	Handless watch
7. The Comedy at Fountain Cottage	No crime	London	Treasure in garden
8. The Game played in the Dark	Theft: arrest	London	Advantages of the dark
The Eyes of Max Carrados			
1. The 'Virginiola' Fraud	Fraud: solution after 2 years	London	Bibliography
2. Disappearance of Marie Severe	Kidnapping? No crime	suburbs	Christian Science
3. Secret of Dunstan's Tower	No crime	'Nether Hempsfield'	Madness
4. The Poisoned Dish of Mushrooms	Murder? Accident	suburbs and midlands	Chemistry
5. The Ghost at Massingham Mansions	Nuisance	London	Automatic gas lighter
6. The Missing Actress	Impersonation: blackmail: suicide	London	Royal intrigue
7. Ingenious Mr Spinola	Fraud. Exposed	London	Gambling machine
8. Kingsmouth Spy Case	Espionage	S. Coast	Numismatics
9. Eastern Mystery	No crime	London	Mystical
Max Carrados Mysteries			
1. The Secret of Headlam Height	Espionage	S. Coast	August 1914
2. The Vanished Petition Crown	Theft. Recovered	London	Numismatics
3. The Holloway Flat Tragedy	Murder? Suicide	London	
4. The Two Left Shoes	No crime	suburbs	Matrimonial trouble
5. The . . . Mind of Rigby Lacksome	No crime (attempted)	Stratford	Suffragettes
6. The House in Culver Street	Fraud. Arrest	London	
7. The Case of Roger Bycourt	?Att. murder. No crime	'Overbury'	Historical spookery thriller
8. The Missing Witness	Abduction & Conspiracy: foiled	London	

APPENDIX II

For the Faithful

As, in other contexts, 'Apart from the Bible and Shakespeare', so, in this, 'Apart from Holmes and Father Brown'—

A GRATEFUL BUT IDIOSYNCRATIC BIBLIOGRAPHY

Dorothy Sayers, *The Nine Tailors*
Michael Innes, *Lament for a Maker*
H. C. Bailey, *Black Land, White Land*
Ngaio Marsh, *Surfeit of Lampreys*
Christianna Brand, *Green for Danger*
G. V. Galwey, *Murder on Leave*
Ellery Queen, *The Glass Village*
John Dickson Carr, *Bride of Newgate*
Margery Allingham, *The Tiger in the Smoke*
Stanley Hyland, *Who Goes Hang?*
Agatha Christie, *The Pale Horse*
Josephine Tey, *Daughter of Time*

INDEX

INDEX

References to stories and books are grouped under their authors, full-length books or collections in *italic*, short stories between quotes. Except for Doyle and Chesterton, references to books will be found within the space indicated by the page-reference against the author's name in heavy type; where references are to be found elsewhere also, the page number outside that space is given. Names of characters are in small capitals, e.g. ALLEYN.

Ages of characters, 138–9
Allen, H. Warner, 122
ALLEYN, R., 125, 138, 147–9, 165, 191, 224
Allingham, Marjorie, 130, 137–9, 146, **149–56**, 172, 177, 184, 185
Beckoning Lady, *Cargo of Eagles*, *China Governess*, *Coroner's Pidgin*, *Death of a Ghost*, *Fashion in Shrouds*, 176, *Flowers for the Judge*, 125, *Hide my Eyes*, *Mind Readers*, *More Work for the Undertaker*, *Mystery Mile*, *Police at the Funeral*, *Tiger in the Smoke*, 185, 210, 213, 220, 243
AMBO, MR, 177
Americans
with Sherlock Holmes, 38–9; in 'Father Brown', 104–6; detective authors, 187–97; names in detective stories, 195
APPLEBY, J., 158–61, 165
Armstrong, Anthony, 128
Aumonier, Stacy, 194

Bailey, H. C., **81–8**, 148, 185
Bishop's Crime, *Black Land, White Land*, 'Children's Home', *Dead Man's Effects*, 'Key of the Door', *Mr Fortune Finds a Pig*, *Slippery Ann*, 'Yellow Cloth'
BARLOW, C., 168
BATHGATE, N., 147
Bell, Josephine, 172, 173
Belloc, H., 100
Bentley, E. C., **119–24**, 137, 191, 203
'Clever Cockatoo', *Those Days*, *Trent Intervenes*, *Trent's Last Case*, *Trent's Own Case*
Berkeley, A., 169–71
Jumping Jenny, *Mr Priestley's Problem*, *Murder in the Basement*, *Poisoned Chocolates Case* (= 'The Avenging Chance'), *Second Shot*, *Trial and Error*

Bingham, J., 164, **166–8**
Fragment of Fear, *Marion*, *Murder Plan Six*
Blake, Nicolas, 179–80
Malice in Wonderland, *Question of Proof*, *There's Trouble Brewing*, *Thou Shell of Death*, *Worm of Death*
Birmingham, G., 128
BOYCE, P., 144
BRADLEY, DAME B., 175–6
Bramah, E., 73–80
'Brookbend Cottage', 'Coin of Dionysius', 'Cyril Bycourt', 'Eastern Mystery', 'Fountain Cottage', 'Game Played in the Dark', 'Headlam Height', 'Holloway Flat', 'Knight's Cross Signal', 'Marie Severe', 'Massingham Mansions', 'Rigby Lacksome', 'Tilling Shaw'
Brand, Christianna, 176–7
Death in High Heels, *Death of Jezebel*, *Green for Danger*, 243, *Heads You Lose*
BRAUNKOPF, 158
BROWN, FATHER, 34, 81–2, **89–116**, 138, 144, 194, 206, 210, 227
Browne, Howard, 194
Thin Air
Buchan, J., 51
Bush, C., 109
Bush, G., 164
BUNTER, M., 140, 149

CAMPION, A., 138, 149–56
Cannan, J., 164–6
Long Shadows
Carr, J. Dickson, 13, 63n, 93, 139, 188, **172–4**, 176, 197, 214
Bride of Newgate, 243, *Devil in Velvet*, 'Highgate Miracle', 63, *It Walks by Night*, *Judas Window*, *Life of Sir A. Conan Doyle*, 17, *Nine Wrong Answers*, *Poison in Jest*, 188, *Problem of the Wire Cage*
Carr, Glyn, 177
CARRADOS, MAX, 73–80, 113
Carter, P. Youngman, 149
Chandler, R., 194
Chesterton, G. K., **89–116**, 144, 227
Father Brown Stories: 'Absence', 90; 'Actor', 111; 'Apollo', 90, 98; 'Beards', 106; 'Blue Cross', 90; 'Boulnois', 90, 111; 'Broken Sword', 93, 100; 'Caesar', 90, 105; *The Club of Queer Trades*, 116; 'Colonel Cray', 98; 'Dog', 90, 96; 'Darnaways', 111; 'Fairy Tale', 90, 93; 'Flying Fish', 111; *The Flying Inn*, 110; 'Flying Stars', 104; 'Garden', 99; 'Golden Cross', 104; 'Gongs', 90, 97; 'Gow', 90, 101–2; 'Hammer', 98; 'Hirsch', 111; 'Invisible Man', 93–4; 'Machine', 90, 95, 127; *The Man who was Thursday*, 110; 'Moon Crescent', 90, 105–6, 109–10; 'Mourner of Marne', 106–8, 113; 'Paradise of Thieves', 90; *The Paradoxes of Mr Pond*, 116; 'Passage', 97; 'Pendragons', 90, 111; 'Prince Saradine', 90; 'Queer Feet', 94; 'Resurrection', 90, 99; 'Secret', 90, 112; 'Three Tools', 93, 102–3; 'Vaudrey', 105; 'Wig', 90; 'Worst Crime', 111
CHITTERWICK, A., 171, 183
Christie, Agatha, **129–37**, 139,

Christie, Agatha—*cont.*
146, 156–61, 169, 172, 182, 183, 195–6, 222, 226
After the Funeral, Death Comes as the End, Endless Night, 4.50 from Paddington, Murder at the Vicarage, Murder of Roger Ackroyd, Murder on the Orient Express, Mysterious Affair at Styles, 123, *Pale Horse,* 243, *Sad Cypress, Ten Little Niggers*
Clark, Gordon, 179
CLIMPSON, K., 141
Clinton-Baddeley, V. C., 183
CLUNK, J., 85–6, 125
COCKRILL, INSP., 176
Cole, G. H. D. and M., 191, 214
Collins, Wilkie, 119, 216
The Moonstone: The Woman in White: Basil, all at 216–18
Coward, Noël, 126, 140, 171
Cox, A. B., 169
Creasey, J., 124
Crispin, E., **162–4**, 169, 184
'Baker Dies', *Buried for Pleasure, Case of the Gilded Fly, Frequent Hearses, Holy Disorders, Long Divorce, Love Lies Bleeding, Swan Song*
Crofts, F. W., 89, **124–7**, 186
Cheyne Mystery, The Cask, Death of a Train, Inspector French's Greatest Case, Starvel Tragedy
Crompton, R., 36
CROOK, A., 125, 178

Dannay, F., 189
DARE, SUSAN, 194
DAVIE, DR, 183
Daviot, Gordon, 180
Dickens, C., 37, 43, 56–7, 210
Dickson, Carter (*see* Carr, J. D.), 173
DIXON, G. ('of Dock Green'), 168
Doyle, Conan, 17–59, 138, 188, 225 and *passim*
Sherlock Holmes Stories: 'Abbey Grange', 40, 48, 50; 'Beryl Coronet', 46; 'Black Peter', 41, 45; 'Blue Carbuncle', 54; 'Boscome Valley', 40; 'Bruce-Partington', 41, 46, 51; 'Cardboard Box', 46, 47, 53; 'Case of Identity', 33, 50; 'Charles A. Milverton', 50, 203; 'Copper Beeches', 32, 33; 'Crooked Man', 38; 'Dancing Men', 39, 51; 'Devil's Feet', 31, 40, 44, 49; 'Disappearance of Lady F. Carfax', 40, 53; 'Dying Detective', 45, 49; 'Engineer's Thumb', 30; 'Final Problem', 31, 35; 'Five Orange Pips', 30, 38, 45, 46, 48; 'Gloria Scott', 40; 'Golden Pince-Nez', 41, 46; 'Greek Interpreter', 41; 'His Last Bow', 35, 75; *Hound of the Baskervilles,* 119; 'Lion's Mane', 45; 'Man with the Twisted Lip', 41; 'Mazarin Stone', 45, 71; 'Missing Three-Quarter', 28; 'Naval Treaty', 32, 46; 'Noble Bachelor', 38, 48; 'Norwood Builder', 51; 'Priory School', 41; 'Red Circle', 33, 41; 'Red Headed League', 29; 'Reigate Squires', 44; 'Retired Colourman', 35; 'Scandal in Bohemia', 30; *Sign of Four,* 30, 38, 44; 'Six Napoleons', 31, 41, 51, 68; 'Solitary Cyclist', 33, 53; 'Speckled Band', 38, 224; *A Study in Scarlet,* 18, 29, 39; 'Sussex Vampire; 40; 'Three Gables', 32, 39; 'Three Garridebs', 37, 41; 'Three

Doyle, Conan—*cont.*
Students', 38; 'Thor Bridge', 39, 40; *Valley of Fear*, 31, 39, 45; 'Wistaria Lodge', 35, 37, 40; 'Yellow Face', 28, 30, 37
Other stories: 'Lost Special', 54; 'Man with the Watches', 54; *White Company*, 42
Dunbar, W., 159
DUPIN, A., 19, 52, 113

Eberhart, M. G., 194
Egan, L., 195, 227
Eliot, T. S., 19, 218
Ervine, St J., 171
Eustace, R., 142
Evil, problem of, 153–6
Exploits of Sherlock Holmes, 63n

FELL, DR GIDEON, 139, 173
FEN, GERVASE, 163–4
Ferguson, J., 128
Fitt, Mary, 182
Clues to Christabel, *Requiem for Robert*
FITTON, AMANDA, 149
FLAMBEAU, 35
Forsyte Saga, The, 36
FORTUNE, REGINALD, 34, 81–8, 144
FOX, EDWARD (Insp.), 147
Francis, Dick, 184
Freeling, N., 186
Because of the Cats
Freeman, Austin, **63–72**, 224
'Anthropologist at Large', 'Case of Premeditation', 'Contents of a Mare's Nest', 'Case of the White Footprints', 'Echo of a Mutiny', 'Fisher of Men', 'Gleanings from the Wreckage', 'Magic Casket', 'Missing Mortgagee', 'Mr Ponting's Alibi', 'Mysterious Visitor', 'Mystery of the Sandhills', 'Naturalist at Law', 'New Jersey Sphinx', 'Pathologist to the Rescue', 'Phyllis Annesley's Peril', 'Seal of Nebuchadnezzar', 'Sower of Pestilence', 'Touchstone', 'Wastrel's Romance'

Galsworthy, J., 56
Galwey, G. V., 177, 243
Murder on Leave
Gardner, Erle S., **192–3**, 195, 196
Counterfeit Eye, *Perjured Parrot*, *Runaway Corpse*, *Shoplifter's Shoe*, *Stuttering Bishop*
Garve, Andrew, 178–9
Cuckoo Line Affair, *Death and the Sky Above*, *End of the Track*, *Galloway Case*, *Golden Deed*, *Hole in the Ground*, *Narrow Search*, *Prisoner's Friend*, *Sea Monks*, *Very Quiet Place*
Gilbert, Anthony, 178
Golding, Louis, 36
Golding, William, 98
Gollancz, Victor, 157, 164, 167, 169, 184
GOYLES, G., 144
Graham, Winston, 183
GRANT, A., 187

Hannay, J. O., 128
Hare, Cyril, 179, 183
'Markhampton Miracle', *Tragedy at Law*, *When the Wind Blows*, *With a Bare Bodkin*
Hartley, L. P., 201–5
HASTINGS, CAPT., 133
Hastings, Macdonald, 183
Cork in Bottle, *Cork on the Water*
HAVOC, JACK, 153–6

Haycraft, H., 163
Heyer, Georgette, 181–2
No Wind of Blame
HOLMES, MYCROFT, 41
HOLMES, SHERLOCK, 17–59 and *passim*
Character, 27–9; and music, 29; and sex, 29–30; and friendship, 31–2; and women, 31–2; age of, 35, 138; and foreigners, 37–40; and science, 43–5; and travel, 44–5; humbug in his style, 53–5; and Thorndyke, 64ff; and Fortune, 82–3, 87; and Carrados, 72–3; and Father Brown, 89, 113; caricatured, 109; in error, 172; religion, 191; speech, 192; the superman, 208; S. H. Society, 213
Huddleston, Bishop T., 148
Hyland, S., **184**, 243
Who Goes Hang?

Iles, Francis, 171 (*see* Berkeley)
IRONSIDE, CHIEF INSP., 226
Innes, Michael, 130, 133, 139, **157–61**, 164, 172, 180
Appleby on Ararat, *Appleby's End*, *Connoisseur's Case*, *Daffodil Affair*, *Death at the President's Lodging*, *Hamlet, Revenge!*, *Hare Sitting Up*, *Journeying Boy*, *Lament for a Maker*, 243, *Old Hall, New Hall*, *Operation Pax*, *Weight of the Evidence*, *What Happened at Hazelwood*

JEEVES, 132, 140
JERVIS, C., 65

KAPLAN, HYMAN, 158
Kelly, Mary, 183
The Spoilt Kill, *Dead Corse*
Kemelman, H., 194
Kermode, F., 207–8
Knox, Ronald, 53, 89, 91, 100, 115–16, 174, 179, 213

Lathen, Emma, 194
Lawrence, D. H., 226
Le Carré, J., 185
Lee, Manfred B., 189
Left Book Club, 157
LESTRADE, G., 31, 124, 165
Lewis, C. Day, 179
Lewis, C. S., 47–50, 144, 162
LUGG, M., 149
LUKE, C., 151–3
Luther, M., 211

McCloy, Helen, 194
Mackenzie, Compton, 36
MAIGRET, 185
MARPLE, MISS, 131–2
Marsh, Ngaio, 124, 133, 137–8, **146–9**, 156, 169, 172
A Man Lay Dead, *Artists in Crime*, *Clutch of Constables*, *Death at the Dolphin*, *Death and the Dancing Footman*, *Death in a White Tie*, *Death in Ecstasy*, *Enter a Murderer*, *False Scent*, *Final Curtain*, *Hand in Glove*, *Off with his Head*, *Opening Night*, *Singing in the Shrouds*, *Spinsters in Jeopardy*, *Surfeit of Lampreys*, 243, *Vintage Murder*
MASON, PERRY, 191, 226
Masterman, J., 184
Oxford Tragedy, *Problem of Four Friends*
MERRIVALE, SIR H., 139, 173
Milton, J., 209
Mitchell, Gladys, 175–6
Death at the Opera, *Devil at Saxon Wall*, *Laurels are Poison*, *Spotted Hemlock*, *Watson's Choice*
Montgomery, Bruce, 162

Neill, A. S., 175

OATES, STANISLAUS, 152
OLIVER, ARIADNE, 133, 134ff

PARKER, CHARLES, 141
Patrick, Q., 194
Pedersen-Krag, G., 215–19
Peel, Sir R., 20
PETTIGREW, M., 179, 183
PHELPS, MARJORIE, 141
Poe, E. A. 19, 42, 51, **187–8**, 226
'Gold Bug', 'Murders in the Rue Morgue', 'Mystery of Marie Roget', 'Purloined Letter' [51, 187]
POIROT, H., 109, 131ff, 138
Police, English, 20–1 (history), 51, 124–5 (fictional), 167–8 (corrupt)
PORTER, NIKKI, 191
PRICE, RONALD, 86, 165–6, 175
PRIESTLEY, DR, 127, 224
Psychology, 132, 175
Public School (English), 171
Punshon, E. R., 184
Puritan values
the City, 55; suspicion of the supernatural, 79ff, 92; Chesterton's view, 100; humourlessness, 102; moral assurance, 123; the virtue of work, 124; enterprise and moral rigour, 125–6; insularity, 185; good conversation, 188; puritan values in detective literature, 225–9
'Puzzle' element in detective literature, 213–14

Queen, Ellery, **189–92**, 193–5, 212, 227
And on the Eighth Day, *Calamity Town*, *Cat of Many Tails*, *Double Double*, *French Powder Mystery*, *Glass Village*, 212, 243, *Finishing Stroke*, *King is Dead*, *Murderer is a Fox*, *Player on the Other Side*, *Siamese Twin Mystery*, *Study in Terror*
QUEEN, RICHARD, 189ff
Quentin, Patrick, 194
QUIN, HARLEY, 133

Railways, 125–6
Ransome, Stephen, 194
Night Drop
Raphael, D. D., 209
Rhode, John, 127
Rosten, Leo, 158
Roth, Holly, 185
Rycroft, C., 215–20

Sartre, J.-P., 207–8
SATTERTHWAITE, MR, 183
Sayers, Dorothy L., 19, 130, 134, **137–45**, 146, 156, 157, 162, 172, 183
'Bone of Contention', *Busman's Honeymoon*, 'Cave of Ali Baba', 35, *Clouds of Witness*, *Documents in the Case*, *Five Red Herrings*, *Gaudy Night*, *Hangman's Holiday*, *Have His Carcase*, *In the Teeth of the Evidence*, 'Incredible Elopement', *Lord Peter Views the Body*, *Murder Must Advertise*, *Nine Tailors*, 243, 'Stolen Stomach', *Strong Poison*, 'Uncle Meleager's Will', *Unnatural Death*, *Unpleasantness at the Bellona Club*, *Whose Body?*
Other works: *The Man Born to be King*, *Unpopular Opinions*, 34
SCOTTER, 177–8

Sex, 22–3, 30, 225–6
Shakespeare, 209
SHERINGHAM, R., 171
Simenon, G., 185–6
Snow, C. P., 43, 160, 179
Stewart, J. I. M., 161 (*see* Innes)
STOREY, MADAME ROSIKA, 194
Stout, Rex, 194
STRANGEWAYS, NIGEL, 180
Street, C. J. C., 127 (*see* Rhode)
STREET, DELLA, 191, 193

Tennyson, A., 180
Tey, Josephine, **180–1**, 185, 243
Brat Farrar, *Daughter of Time*, 243, *Franchise Affair*, *Man in the Queue*, *Miss Pym Disposes*, *Shilling for Candles*, *Singing Sands*, *To Love and be Wise*
THATCHER, J. PUTNAM, 194
THORNDYKE, DR JOHN, 34, 62–72, 113, 206
TOFT, *Archdeacon*, 177
Train Robbery, 126
Trench, John, **185**, 219
Dishonoured Bones, *What Rough Beast*
TRENT, PHILIP, 119–23
Trollope, A., 43, 56, 206, 210, 217–18, 226
TROY, AGATHA, 147

VARALLO, VIC, 195, 226
VELIE, SERGEANT, 192
VENABLES, THE REV., 141, 145
Violence, 113–14

Warner, Jack, 168
Warrack, Guy, 29n
Warriner, Thurman, 135, 177
WATT, JOHN (Sgt), 168
Wesley, C., 85n
Wesley, J., 197
Wells, H. G., 43
Williams, Charles, 144, 151
Williamson, H., 36
WILLING, BASIL, 194
Willis, Lord, 168
Wilson, Colin, 229
WIMSEY, LORD PETER, 34, 35, 109, 138–45, 147, 149
Winterton, Paul, 179 (*see* Garve)
WINTRINGHAM, DAVID, 173
Wodehouse, P. G., 39, 56, 132, 140, 174
WOLFE, NERO, 194, 227
World War I and II, 123–4
Wren Lewis, J., 219–20

Yates, Dornford, 140

'Z-Cars', 168